Strand of Pearls

One Woman's Journey to Light and Peace

DEBORAH LIVINGSTON

BALBOA
PRESS

A DIVISION OF HAY HOUSE

Note From The Author

Some of the names of individuals in this book have been either changed and or last names left out to protect their privacy.

Balboa Press books may be ordered through booksellers or by contacting:

Balboa Press
A Division of Hay House
1663 Liberty Drive
Bloomington, IN 47403
www.balboapress.com
1-(877) 407-4847

Because of the dynamic nature of the Internet, any web addresses or links contained in this book may have changed since publication and may no longer be valid. The views expressed in this work are solely those of the author and do not necessarily reflect the views of the publisher, and the publisher hereby disclaims any responsibility for them.

The author of this book does not dispense medical advice or prescribe the use of any technique as a form of treatment for physical, emotional, or medical problems without the advice of a physician, either directly or indirectly. The intent of the author is only to offer information of a general nature to help you in your quest for emotional and spiritual well-being. In the event you use any of the information in this book for yourself, which is your constitutional right, the author and the publisher assume no responsibility for your actions.

Any people depicted in stock imagery provided by Thinkstock are models, and such images are being used for illustrative purposes only. Certain stock imagery © Thinkstock.

ISBN: 978-1-4525-4436-6 (sc)
ISBN: 978-1-4525-4437-3 (e)
ISBN: 978-1-4525-4438-0 (dj)

Library of Congress Control Number: 2011963385

Printed in the United States of America

Balboa Press rev. date: 1/18/2012

Strand Of Pearls

From My Heart and Soul to Yours

"In these pages lies a true testament of the power of healing through spiritual unfoldment—even when we are consciously unaware that this very process is taking place. In this story of the life to date of Deborah Adams Livingston, she identifies the problem, the history and pre-history, the at-times torturous recovery, and her emergence into a life of acceptance. The spark of divinity, which is in all of us, shines through the healing process that has become the life of Deb."

—Reverend Ronald P. Monroe
Spiritualist Minister
Commissioned Healer
Certified Medium
Facilitator of Spiritual Unfoldment

"Strand of Pearls is the kind of book that will keep you up all night because you just can't stop reading. This compelling tale of a woman's journey through soul-crushing life experiences is presented with sincerity, sensitivity, and fearless candor. ... This is truly a book of hope, redemption, and the potential for renewal that lies within each of us. Reading it may forever change the way you view the world."

—Sandra Corbitt-Sears, MS, counselor and consultant

"If you are looking for hope, healing, inspiration, and transformation, Deborah Livingston's new book, Strand of Pearls, is ... one you will not be able to put down. Her story is compelling, heart-wrenching, and fearlessly honest. In her journey to find herself and her soul, she almost loses everything that was important to her including her family and friends. ... Today, she is a spark of light and love and helping others to change from the inside out. Her life story is truly miraculous and one you will not forget."

—Pat Hastings, MS, CPC, inspirational speaker and author of Simply a Woman of Faith

Table of Contents

If you are looking for inspiration and guidance, you have come to the right book! If you have extreme difficulties in your life that you would like to transcend, you have come to the right book! And for some who have already transcended many difficulties, you will cry tears of joy as you read Strand of Pearls, as the story of Deborah Livingston will speak to the heartfelt experiences you have been through.

Deborah is a survivor of the highest order. The very young Deborah survived living with a father, who could be charming and irresistible, yet was abusive to his wife and children. As her story unfolds, we come to understand that for Deborah, pearls became symbolic jewels of wisdom, and as she collected each pearl, she was transported, pearl by pearl, out of a destructive life towards a new life of joy and transformation. Unlike Deborah, her mother was not able to find pearls of wisdom. During Deborah's childhood, however deeply she loved her daughter, she was not able to protect her. Her spiritually gifted child was fortunate enough to collect the pearls that would create the full strand of wisdom Deborah is able to share with us today.

Deborah's life is whole now and she shares her wisdom, not only with us, but with her mother, who is now in the process of finding peace in life. Deborah's gift to each one of us is her book "Strand of Pearls."

Deborah writes:

> "We are all on our own path, and we need to find our own way. However, if I can show one person that happiness and joy can come from surviving the difficult times, then my purpose in writing this book will have been fulfilled. All anyone has to do is allow and believe."

Survival is not easy and if we wallow in our sorrow we will not survive. Deborah Livingston gives us her support and her love. She alerts us to the fact that if we are open and willing, we will see those beams of light that bind together to create a spiritual life raft.

Deborah encourages each one of us to have the strength to see the light of survival that comes to us, *in whatever forms it may be.* Deborah may see pearls and I may see heart shaped stones on the beaches of Maui. Perhaps the Divine speaks to each of us through our own unique metaphors. *How does the Divine show its light to you? Do you allow your soul to grasp these Divine messages so that you are able to survive whatever challenges life has presented to you?*

In this book you will receive the spiritual tools for survival in the form of a powerful story that will motivate you and ignite your personal power. You will move ahead on your own journey to a more successful life. What each one of us needs is the *desire* to move ahead, to learn, to become better people so that we can help others and ourselves. In order to find that deep desire within, we need to let go of the past and move on into the future. We need to know that change for the better *is* possible.

Deborah writes:

"If I have learned anything from my awakening to peace, it is that nothing is permanent. Impermanence enables evolution on every level, which makes each day an opportunity for transformation. The only requirement is desire."

Not everyone survives a difficult childhood. Some live out their lives in desperation. The path to spiritual freedom, which loomed ahead, was not easy for Deborah to find or to walk. She could have made the choice to turn back She might have stayed in the energetic vibrations of her horrible experiences, allowing herself to sink into and settle into her abusive childhood. ***But she made another choice:*** the spirit within this young girl called out to her and let her know that there was a light inside her, if hard to see at the moment, would ultimately lead her out of this cave of emotional despair.

This very young child could only see a mere drop a light: a glistening pearl.

We all know many people who grew up in abusive homes who went on to collect abusive friends and even marry abusive people: addicts of one kind or another: slaves to liquor, drugs, smoking, food or abusive emotional relationships. A lot of us joined these large ranks of addicted people.

Do you count yourself as one of the "many people" who were submerged in dysfunctional environments? Why is it that some of the people or I should say "some of us" who are submerged, survive and transform while others are stuck in lives of desperation and unhappiness? Why is it that some of us, like Deborah, are able to grasp the pearls of wisdom and transformation that are shown to us along the way, and come out of these experiences enlightened and spiritually uplifted?

What was it about Deborah that made survival possible?

As I read her story, I experience Deborah as she awakens and begins to see with her spiritual eyes. When in trouble, she is able to see the one flowering branch, blooming in an otherwise yucky pond of mud and quicksand. While another person in this pond might sink into the quicksand, Deborah has the spiritual instinct to grab onto that branch and clutch it for dear life, knowing that as it grows taller, it will lift her up and she will climb out of the muddy pond.

What makes it possible for Deborah to survive is her *courage*, her *strength*, and her *deep desire* to live a better life. She knows what she wants, and even in the hardest of times, if there is any light around to grab, she grabs it. Little by little, step-by-step, and year-by-year she transforms her life.

"Strand of Pearls" is a flowering branch that each one of us can grab onto if we are stuck at the moment and want to be free. As you read your eyes will be opened and you will find the wisdom within yourself.

Deborah writes:

"Through my extremely difficult yet awakening experience, I could barely see with my eyes. Now I am able to view the world and all its offerings though the windows of the soul."

On a personal note: I know Deborah Livingston. I have the honor of having her sit in one of the spiritual circles I facilitate. She is a joy to work with and is as beautiful a soul as she is a person to behold. With an eye for beauty, she is always dressed in a way that would inspire anyone to want to clean out their entire house, their closet, and begin again. She has excellent taste. (In fact my husband gets nervous when I see Deborah, as he knows I will be inspired to go shopping!!) I mention her eye for beauty because you will find the same beauty in her writing that I find in her personality and her appearance. She leads us to understand that beauty in life IS there if we will simply trust and allow the Divine to guide us.

It is my belief that the Divine is there for all of us. Perhaps you prefer another name: God, Great Spirit, the Beloved. My hope is that you and I find the God of our understanding within our hearts.

Strand of Pearls is part of me now. I loved this book and I do not want to hold your attention for one more second. I am eager for you to jump right into Deborah's story.

I wish you well on the spiritual journey you are about to take. I will be looking over your shoulder reading along with you.

Carole Lynne
www.carolelynne.com

Carole Lynne is the author of four books:

Heart and Sound

How to Get a Good Reading from a Psychic Medium

Consult Your Inner Psychic

Cosmic Connection

Acknowledgements

As a new author, I feel blessed and grateful for the many gifts and treasures life has offered during the process of writing and publishing this book. I must first acknowledge God, spirit, and the universe and extend my eternal love, light, and gratitude for guiding me into self-realization and peace. I am infinitely blessed by the treasured gifts of this life, especially my family and friends who continue to provide loving support and encouragement.

Thank you to my husband Joel and my daughter Cassandra. I appreciate the endless love, support, and beauty you bring to me every day in your own special ways. I love you both with all my heart. Thank you to my mom, Wendy, for being my biggest fan and believing in me no matter what during my writing. To the rest of my family, thank you for inspiring and encouraging me and for accepting me for who I am. I love and cherish you all.

Thank you to all of my spiritual groups and friends that have sustained and inspired me throughout this journey, including the Swampscott Church of Spiritualism and all of its members. I offer a special thank you to Mike and Donna, facilitators of Spirit Walk Circle, for providing a safe place to come together and connect with spirit for the purposes of healing and growing. To Empower Yoga Studio, its teachers and attending yogis, thank you for your poetic words of wisdom and your grounding, harmonizing flow. The lovely studio has enabled me to keep my body, mind, and soul whole and free from blockages, which is welcoming after slouching over a computer for months.

To all of my teachers, thank you for your guidance and wisdom. I am deeply grateful to Barbara of the retired Acupressure Therapy Institute for educating me in Traditional Chinese Medicine and for the life-changing educational trip to China. To my spiritual teachers, Reverend Ron Monroe and Reverend Carole Lynne, thank you for your guidance in my spiritual unfoldment and for providing a safe place for the practice of psychic/mediumship. Light and love to you. To my tutors at the Arthur Findlay College in the UK, Minister Brenda Lawrence, Libby Clark, and Sheila French, thank you for the many gifts of spirit we shared and for the lifelong friends I made there.

To all of those who made this memoir possible, thank you from the bottom of my heart. I extend my gratitude to the Balboa Press publishing team for their hard work, expertise, advice, and wisdom. I offer my appreciation to those who became dear friends along this journey while coaching, guiding, taking beautiful photos, and editing. Thank you, Bruce McAllister, for guiding me into writing to the best of my ability and having faith in me. Thank you, Sandi Corbitt-Sears, for your exquisite work on editing and your lovely friendship along the way. To Lisa Tulk, who is gifted with beautiful windows of the soul and who captures her vision of the world for everyone else to enjoy, thank you for the gorgeous photo you provided for the cover art design. A special thank you to my yogi friend and talented photographer, Amanda Edwards, for capturing a beautiful bio picture. You have all touched my soul on a deep level. This has been a life-changing journey, and I thank you all for your support and love.

Introduction

A pearl begins as a small grain of sand and gradually transforms into an object of tremendous value and beauty. Pearls symbolize feminine wisdom, which also takes a long time to develop and is of great value. For some Eastern cultures, pearls symbolize purity, love, and spiritual transformation. Those who wear them are said to walk with dignity. Pearls offer the healing effect of wisdom by allowing us to receive spiritual guidance, realize self-acceptance, and promote peacefulness. They help us appreciate the simple, honest things in life.

My transformation has taken a lifetime and is not yet complete. It has led me from fear, sadness, depression, inferiority, abandonment, and constant turmoil to acceptance, forgiveness, love, compassion, truth, peace, and a great feminine wisdom that continues to unfold.

It is my belief that the title of this book was not only predestined, but it also formed the foundation for my utmost challenges, growths, and transformations. As we are born, the slate is wiped clean, and we start as innocents once again. For me, that innocence ended quickly. While still in diapers, I was playing with a strand of pearls and accidently broke them. I couldn't know then that the experience would come to represent my purpose in this life. Metaphorically, I was the broken strand. The pearls were—and continue to be—my lessons. My destiny was to repair the *Strand of Pearls*.

As a forty-six-year-old woman, I am extremely grateful for the gifts of transcendence and transformation for my mind, body, and soul. Before my extremely difficult yet awakening experience, I could barely see with my eyes. Now I am able to view the world and all its offerings through the windows of my soul.

My biggest lesson was learning to accept everything and everyone for what and who they are. I trust that we are all exactly where we are meant to be. I am still learning and will continue to learn, as we all do. However, I can now accept what the universe has to offer me, because I am ready to receive. I want to share the challenges and lessons I have been so very fortunate to receive thus far, and I want to send a message to anyone who is ready to accept it.

I can only have faith and trust that my message will be received by other souls on the deepest level, a level where they may have buried their gifts and treasures. Your treasures can be revealed if you approach your deepest fears and painful feelings with an open mind and heart and a willingness to experience the pain and fear truthfully.

By allowing yourself to feel, you can peel away layer after layer, revealing your bright, golden treasures. This is achieved by discovering your lesson within each life challenge. My experiences in this lifetime taught me to feel pain and emotions and accept them as my friends. Fear is my enemy, and I have learned to let go of it.

In the past, burying my emotions and carrying fear led to physical manifestations such as illness and unexplained pain. I now welcome, feel, embrace, and accept pain. Then I say goodbye to it. Letting go creates space for the energies of love, light, and learning.

There are many women and men who have provided great inspiration and have served as superior role models for me. The two women who have most inspired me to share my truths have made a tremendous difference in many lives and have contributed to wonderful outcomes. Those women are Oprah Winfrey and Barbara Walters. They both demonstrate feminine wisdom with grace, a quality many of us seek to attain.

On December 9, 2010, I watched as Barbara interviewed Oprah. At one point, Oprah said, "Every life is a story!" I knew in that moment that it was time to document my experiences and, hopefully, to touch someone as these women have touched me during my growth.

Every life is, indeed, a story, and I hope mine can be instrumental in making a difference in someone else's. Oprah and Barbara both possess the grace of truth that has inspired me to reveal the truths that have unlocked my treasure chest and opened my heart to give, receive, and give back.

One of the many gifts in my treasure chest is wisdom. Wisdom is a knowledge acquired only when one is ready. It is not something that happens in an instant. It requires patience and work. When I first discovered my soul, I wanted to shout it from the rooftop! I wanted everyone to live at peace and in harmony with their surroundings as I had learned to do. After experiencing many disappointments, I came to understand that it doesn't work that way. We are all on our own individual paths, and we need to find our own way. However, if I can show one person that happiness and joy can come from surviving difficult times, then my purpose in writing this book will have been fulfilled. All anyone has to do is allow and believe.

This book is about setting your spirit free from self-bondage and reclaiming your zest for life. Give yourself the gift of being present during every moment. Gain the faith that gives you clarity to see how limitless life can be.

If you have doubts that it is possible to live without limitation, I understand. Had someone suggested five years ago that I could completely rediscover myself, I would have told them they were full of what makes the grass grow green. If this transformation can happen to a Leo with the attitude I had, it can happen to anyone!

Chapter One

Two Worlds Collide

Love looks not with the eyes, but with the mind.
And therefore is wing'd Cupid painted blind.

~ Shakespeare ~

I was running down the dark, quiet street, whimpering from fear. Something wet, warm and sticky covered my body. I remember wondering if it was blood. I couldn't see anything in front of me, but there was a faint blinking behind me. I had to get away. I wasn't sure what I was getting away from, but I couldn't look back, because I knew whatever was back there was bad.

What I really needed was a luminous light to guide me onto a path of self-realization, but I wasn't ready for that kind of healing. The only healing I wanted that night came from a purely physical need. I wanted someone—anyone—to wash me up and put me to bed so I could wake up in the morning and be relieved that it was only a dream.

An endless path of darkness loomed ahead as I ran down the pitch black road. With every sprint, my purse bounced off my side, causing pain as sharp as a knife. Each time I went from walking to running, cold air penetrated my body and sliced through my lungs.

My blood roared through my body. It was like the rapids of a river reacting to my fright, flight, fight response from whatever I'd left behind me. I could feel my heartbeat pulsating in every vein and pounding in my ears, but I couldn't understand why. I did understand that I needed help, and I needed it right away. I felt alone, hurt, very cold, and confused.

I knew it was late because no lights were on in any of the homes I passed. I finally saw the flickering light of a TV in a window, and a sense of relief flooded through me. I ran to the house and frantically banged on the door. When the outside light flashed on, I squinted against the sudden brightness. I was confused when I realized that the woman who answered the door was the mother of a friend of mine named Rob.

As she rushed to help me up the front steps, she gasped and said, "Oh, my God! Debbie, is that you? What happened to you?"

I couldn't answer. She sat me down and asked me again what had happened. In the light, I could see that I was definitely covered in blood. I began to shake. I'd seen that type of injury on TV, but I never thought anything like it would happen to me.

"I don't know," I finally said as tears rolled down my face.

"I'm calling the police," she said.

Suddenly, I remembered that I had been with Rob. "Rob and I were going to get cigarettes," I sobbed. "Where is he?"

Her eyes grew wide as she realized that her son might have been in whatever accident had left me bleeding and injured. "You were with Rob?"

As she ran to the phone, I screamed, "Yes! Where is he? Where is he? I think he's hurt! Oh, my goodness. I think we were in a car accident! Why is this happening?" My heart raced with fear for Rob's safety. "We need help! Get help! Where is he? Is he hurt?"

That night, I could not have imagined that something as simple as my willingness to accept pain and suffering would one day enable me to discover the granular seed of my soul. The strand of peace, which now holds the pearls of my lessons, helps my soul continue to grow. When acceptance, forgiveness, and love are present in your heart, the gifts of life's treasures are infinite.

The strand of pearls that symbolizes my soul's awakening and defines my being was my father's gift to my mother when they married. Although they were given as a symbol of love, those pearls came to represent my mother's transition from a happy young woman to a victim of struggle and weakness. Eventually, they became a symbol of my weakened spirit, as well.

Pearls are a traditional wedding gift that celebrates the union of two worlds and the creation of a new one. The coming together of my parent's worlds wasn't a union. It was a collision. The minute those pearls were purchased, the strand began to weaken, and my mother moved toward the fate that would sweep me along with her.

It makes sense that the pearls came from my dad, because his spirit was broken first. He hid it from everyone, including himself. When life's events fed his weakness and ego, he could no longer hide his broken spirit. Out of control, he would strike like a rattlesnake, injecting his venom into my mom's spirit and, later, into mine. While everyone's strand grows weak at times, it breaks only if we allow ourselves to continue to suffer.

My parents met in 1962. My mother, Gwendolyn (Wendy) Hart, and her brother spent summers at the family's retreat in Nova Scotia, Canada. Situated in a remote seaside setting in beautiful North East Harbour, the house overlooks the vast, ice blue ocean. At sunrise each morning, the fishing and lobster boats can be seen as they head to sea.

The sun appears at breathtakingly different angles in the early morning and late afternoon. It's the perfect spot to capture the beauty of the coast on canvas. My grandmother created several oil paintings of the ocean and the house. It was her way of relaxing. Every summer, she captured the views from her perspective and took them back home to Massachusetts.

I remember the smell of clean, salty ocean air mixing with the sweet scent of Grandmother's honeysuckle, wild roses, and colorful lupines when the wind was just right. Those scents still remind me of her and make me smile. I associate those aromas with the simple blossoming energy of her love. My grandmother lived with an open heart.

My mother was the middle child of three. She was a shy, skinny, porcelain-skinned girl with dark hair and green eyes. Her hometown of Nahant, Massachusetts, is on a little island attached to the mainland by a causeway. Nahant is a great summer beach town, and it's close to Boston.

In the summer of 1962, Mom was on break from her secretarial major at the Chandler College for women. She had no desire to leave her home in Nahant and travel to boring Nova Scotia. She would be leaving her friends Ginger and Deborah and her almost-fiancé David behind. The thought saddened her, but she had no choice. My grandfather, Fred Hart, Sr., had insisted that the family meet at their summer house because it might be one of the last opportunities for the whole family to get together.

My mother was only 18 years old, the same age that my daughter Cassie is now. My daughter's aspiration to become a successful worldwide entrepreneur is crystal clear for her, and I couldn't be more proud. My mother didn't seem to give much thought to her future when she was 18. Does the nature of our connections to our parents guide us to our paths, or is it something bigger than that? Only the universe knows.

As I view the strand of my past and the connections or lack thereof with my parents, I'm positive they guided me onto my spiritual path of healing. Heartaches and disappointments can be cultivated into pearls of wisdom. I'm also convinced that circumstances often happen for very good reasons. For example, if my mom had stayed home that summer, I wouldn't exist!

After school ended in June, my mom helped her parents pack the car. Then they headed for the ferry that would take them to Nova Scotia for the summer.

I loved that trip across the ocean as a child. It was exhilarating to feel the salty ocean air blowing on my face and through my hair as the water crashed against the ferry. It gave me a sense of freedom and allowed my soul a chance to breathe. The freedom of prana, aliveness, is a gift.

My mother's parents, Dorothea and Fred Hart, Sr., worked hard. My grandfather was a salesman for his own company, Macomber Looms, and that kept him on the road. Grandmother was sick a lot of the time due to severe asthma. When she wasn't ill, she was very busy. Grandmother modeled, owned a restaurant, and served as president of the local garden club. She lived life with passion and love. Grateful for the healthy interludes, she made good use of every moment and didn't allow illness to conceal her spirit.

The outdoors and nature were my grandmother's passions. She loved to garden, growing both vegetables and flowers. She adored birds, knew their songs, and fed them from her hands. Grandmother's love for me was complete and unconditional. She was a deeply caring and nurturing woman, and I loved her so very much.

As a child, I was jealous of my mother because she had the good fortune to grow up in the warmth of my grandmother's love. My mother didn't share that kind of love with me. What I had perceived as a child wasn't completely true. Although I viewed my grandparents as the perfect parents that I always yearned for, I now know that they weren't available to my mom as much as she needed them to be. My dad was an invitation to change her life, and she accepted.

My father was named Clyde Allen Adams. He was the fifth of six children and the youngest boy in the family. In the summer of 1962, he was a tough ladies man with blonde hair, blue eyes, and a warm summer tan. He was born on October 8, 1928, which made him fifteen years older than my mother. His parents, Mary Elizabeth and Lemuell, were separated, which was frowned upon in those days. Although Dad was 34 the summer he met Mom, he still lived with his mother in Upper Port Latour, Nova Scotia. His father led a promiscuous lifestyle, and the apple didn't fall far from the tree. Dad was a party animal who frequently romanced his conquests in the home he shared with his mother. What a guy!

My Nan put up with it until she could no longer expose herself or her other children to such behavior. She was a religious woman who didn't drink, swear, or cheat on her husband. She possessed spiritual gifts and was considered an intuitive by the locals. Nan accepted life's gifts without question. The pearls of courage and strength on her strand allowed her to stand up for herself and her children.

Nan was a tiny bit of a woman, but she was as tough as nails. After she left her husband, she built her own house and dug a well with her bare hands. Elizabeth Adams was an extraordinary woman way ahead of her time. I am proud to be her granddaughter.

Unfortunately, she tried to make up for their father's absence by spoiling her kids. Although she didn't have much money and they didn't have the finer things in life, she did everything for them. She even ironed my father's underwear.

Maybe it was the imbalance between his father's distance and his mother's spoiling that broke my dad's strand. Perhaps it was the lack of a loving connection between his parents. I don't know and probably never will, but this is the kind of question we all live with in our journeys, isn't it?

✑

Dad's formal education halted at the seventh grade because he had to help support his family. Although he was quite intelligent, he worked in whatever trade was hiring, becoming a fisherman, lobsterman, and mechanic. My father called himself a "self-made and self-educated man." Perhaps it was his way of coping with a bruised ego. The label helped hide his sense of inadequacy. In today's world, he might have been the inventor of some spectacular piece of technology. He could build and rebuild anything, both mechanically and structurally. When my dad took something apart and put it back together again, it would work better than the original design. His mind was sound, but his spirit was bruised, and he was never able to assemble *that* back into working order.

In his spare time, Dad liked to drag race, and he loved country music. I suppose those were the sparks that kept his pilot light lit. He also loved to watch the good ole boys in Western movies. He was John Wayne's number-one fan.

Dad's favorite pastime was singing duets with his younger sister Faye while he strummed the guitar. I can hear them now, belting out the words in perfect harmony to "In the Sweet Bye and Bye, We Will Meet at the Beautiful Shore." His loftiest dream was to sing a duet with Faye at the Grand Ole Opry. According to my dad, falling in love, getting married, and becoming a father squashed that dream. While Dad and Faye never performed in public, they sang duets whenever they got together. Those were the only moments when he felt comfortable enough to open his heart. They were also his happiest moments.

My dad's job during the summer of 1962 was driving a truck to deliver fill for a road crew. On a warm July day, he was delivering to the road right in front of my grandparents' house. Mom was resting on the front lawn that day because she was recovering from surgery to remove a benign tumor from her knee. In those days there were no simple laparoscopic procedures, so it was a rather serious surgery. She had been watching the trucks come and go for three days, and one particular driver stood out from all the others. He noticed her, too, and that day he pulled his dump truck into the driveway during his break and walked up to my mother's lawn chair.

She looked up at him, squinting from the sunlight shining in her eyes. He adjusted his position so that his body would block the sun for her. When she got a good look at him, her heart fluttered. She was sure her prince had come to rescue her at last. Butterflies danced in her stomach, and her heart began to race. All she could do was stare at the handsome man before her. *Wow*, she thought, *he looks like Alan Ladd.*

"Hi, there. Gorgeous day today, hey?" Pushing his blonde mane back, he reached for her hand. "My name is Clyde. I couldn't help but notice how beautiful you look, lying there in the sun. What's your name?"

My mother had no idea that her prince charming was 15 years older than she was. At 18, she had little experience with handsome men, and she was star struck. My father had plenty of experience with young women, and he had rehearsed his smooth, smart lines in advance. They had a charismatic effect on my mother, and memories of David faded into the background.

She eventually emerged from her mesmerized trance and reached up to shake his hand. "My name is Wendy. Wendy Hart. Your job looks hot. You must be parched. Would you like to stay and have a fresh, cold lemonade?"

Smiling back at her with his perfect set of white teeth, he said, "No, thank you. I'm in my dirty work clothes. I'll take you up on that another time, though."

My father's arsenal of protective mechanisms included acting shy in front of others. He was embarrassed by his appearance that day and what he did for a living. Why do we allow society's expectations to dictate how we reveal ourselves? The need for approval vanishes when we experience self-love.

The following Saturday afternoon a shiny Ford Galaxy with Corinthian white exterior and red interior pulled into the driveway of my grandparent's house. In the 1960s, that was considered a hot rod! Fancy cars made a big impression on my teenage mom, especially when the car was brand new and there was a guy who looked like a movie star climbing out of it. She was in awe.

My father was freshly shaved, he smelled of Old Spice, and he'd used just enough Brylcreem to convert the blond mane into a perfect, slicked-back wave. He wore a suit and carried two bouquets of roses. He handed the roses to Mom and Grandma, saying, "Lovely roses for lovely women."

They both giggled. "Ooh, roses—my favorite. Thank you. You're quite the gentleman," Grandma said as she winked at Mom.

My father made a great impression on both of my grandparents. He was well mannered, polite, intelligent, and good looking. He appeared to have money. It was the very image he hoped to project. My mother felt as if she were living in a fairy tale. *David who...?*

Mom had been swept off her innocent feet by a charming prince. What was missing from my mother's world that she would fall for such an illusion? They were both in search of something to fill a void. We are all in search of something. When we learn to accept who we are, we can stop searching and accept everyone and everything as they are.

A week later, my mother went to a local dinner and dance with her parents. My father had arranged to meet them there, and they all sat down to enjoy a ham and bean dinner together. Dad continued to impress. They all danced to the knee-slapping country music and had a wonderful time.

When my grandparents were ready to leave, Dad offered to take my mother home. It was the first time she had gotten to ride in his spiffy new car. She felt giddy, and the butterflies returned to her stomach.

Excitement and adrenaline flowed through her and put a smile on her face. That night marked the beginning of a summer-long relationship. She was glad her parents had insisted she go with them to Nova Scotia.

My dad went to my grandparents' summer house every night after work to see Mom. He was from a part of Canada that's always a decade behind the rest of the world. She was from an all-American rural family. Even though their worlds were completely different, they were captivated by each other. Mom was smitten by Dad's good looks and charm and the fact that he was so very different from anyone she had ever met. She didn't care that he was 15 years older. She admired the thrilling lifestyle he seemed to lead. In her eyes, he was her knight in shining armor. There was nothing that would change her young mind about that.

When we are young, we strive for what make us feel good inside no matter what it costs us. We seek happiness while wearing blinders, unable to see what will truly bring us joy.

One evening when Dad took my mother to a dance in Shelburne, Nova Scotia, they ran into a few of his friends. The group was having a great time reminiscing until Dad went to the bar for another round, and his friends approached Mom. They flirted with her at first. Then the mood changed. "Don't get too serious with him, Wendy," they said. "He has some troubles that you aren't going to like. He's just putting on a good face for you because you're new and he's trying to impress you."

She shrugged and said, "I don't know what you're talking about. He's fine when he's around me." My father returned from the bar before they could elaborate.

Today my mother knows just what they were talking about. She considers that conversation her first warning sign. But she was falling hard for the

Alan Ladd lookalike, not the real Clyde, because he kept his true self well hidden. She trusted the man he pretended to be.

August came fast. When it was time for my mom and her family to go back home to Nahant, she felt a lot of pressure. She was convinced that the fairytale was becoming a serious relationship, but were her feelings real or was it just fascination? She also had a boyfriend waiting for her back home. She was confused.

A couple of nights before Mom was to leave, my father came by to give her the news that he was moving to Hamilton, Ontario, where his sister Faye and her husband lived. He told her it was an opportunity for him to get a more consistent and reliable job. It was a chance for him to grow. He asked my mother if she would like him to stop by Nahant on his way to Hamilton. He told her he wanted them to get to know each other on another level because he intended to ask her to marry him.

Part of her was thrilled that he was thinking about marriage. However, she wasn't sure she was ready to take that step. Mom told my father that he was welcome to stop by, but she reminded him that she had a boyfriend back home and suggested they slow things down. It was not what Dad wanted to hear. As far as he was concerned, living in separate countries was slow enough. He would just have to turn up the charm.

That was my dad's opportunity to change his life inside as well as out. He ignored it. The challenges in our lives provide opportunities for transformation, and they are always available.

When Mom returned home, her confusion grew. She still liked David, but she didn't want to miss a chance to become engaged to her eccentric prince charming.

The child in me resents my mother for not appreciating what she had: two loving parents, a stable home, no fear, and a hopeful future. Why did she long to leap into a life of uncertainty? What was missing for her? Why would she distance herself from the very things my inner child searched for: a family connection and unconditional love? Today I acknowledge that something was clearly missing for Mom. Maybe what she sought was a lifetime spent strengthening her strand?

Every child deserves a safe, secure, and loving foundation in order to grow up healthy and whole in mind, body, and spirit. Without that foundation, the lessons are greater, which makes your strand longer and stronger.

My mother had been home only a couple of days when she made her decision. She called David and asked him out on a date. Even though she didn't know exactly where things were headed with my dad, she had to tell David. The burden of not being honest with him was weighing on her. By the time David drove her home from their date, my mother couldn't contain herself. As they sat in his car in her parent's driveway, she told him she had met another guy and that he was the one. David was devastated. He told my mother that she was the only one for him.

Hurting him was painful, but she had made up her mind. Mom never saw him again, but she knew he took it very hard. Friends told her he was never the same. She had broken his heart and weakened his strand.

Although Mom felt very sad for hurting David so deeply, she was happy to be free. She prayed that my father still wanted to marry her. It was very important to her because all of her friends were getting engaged, and she didn't want to be left out. Of course, none of them were marrying a movie star lookalike from another country.

Deep down, we all want the same things in life —love, family, happiness, and joy—but our competitive ego always insists on having and being the best. The best drifts our way when we dismiss our ego and live from the heart.

When a letter arrived from Nova Scotia, Mom ripped it open and scanned it quickly, looking for information about his travel plans. Dad wrote that he hoped to leave on December 1, 1962. He had enclosed a large sum of money and included an informal wedding proposal.

He asked Mom to go shopping and choose her own engagement ring, saying that he wanted her to have the ring of her dreams prior to his arrival.

A written proposal and mailed money is presumptuous and a little weird. True love isn't a piece of jewelry; it is the precious jewel of life. Mom thought buying her own ring was fabulous, but it was not a healthy, energetic flow of love. My mother willingly sacrificed one of the most cherished moments in a courtship. She allowed herself to be cheated out of the real meaning of receiving an engagement ring. Perhaps she was in a hurry to escape from her old self and jump into the hope of a real human connection.

We all make mistakes due to confusion when we try to feed our ego instead of surrendering. It's all part of the universe's plan to weaken the strand of pearls for the purpose of cultivating our souls. What adversity has the universe created for your growth?

Mom went ring shopping with one of her friends and came up empty. There was nothing she liked. A few days later, she drove to Boston and found the ring of her dreams in Longs Jewelers. She was so excited that she forgot where she had parked her father's car. When she finally found the beautiful red vehicle, it was being towed.

Oh, my goodness, she thought, *my father is going to kill me.* It was a traumatic event for a teenager embarking on adulthood. Running toward the tow truck, she screamed "Wait, wait! Please stop. I'm here. That's my father's car!"

The tow guy heard her shrieks of desperation and stopped. She explained that she had lost track of time in the store and was very sorry for forgetting to feed the meter. He grew tired of listening to her pleas and released the car to her. She felt extremely lucky and thankful that she had arrived in the nick of time to claim the car. If she'd had to call her father, the secret about why she went to Boston would have been revealed.

Was that the second warning to Mom from the universe about what was to come? The first had come from Clyde's friends, and it was blatant.

She never forgot the drama of that day. It was the first of many things in her life that would scare the daylights out of her.

My father arrived in December, as promised. Mom gave him the ring to keep for the special moment. She also explained that he needed to ask her father's permission and clarify his intentions toward her. He claimed he was too shy.

Dad wasn't willing to proclaim his love because that would mean opening his heart and stating his truths, and he was uncomfortable doing either. It had to be torturing him inside. He wasn't used to doing what people asked him to do. He'd always lived life on his terms.

Days went by and my mother kept begging Dad to have the talk with her father. She tried to be understanding. Mom told him she knew that his dad hadn't been around for his sisters and that it might not be the way engagements were approached in Nova Scotia. But in America a man was expected to ask a woman's father for her hand in marriage.

It took Dad about a week to work up the courage to have the talk with my grandpa. The smell of dinner permeated the house while the two of them, both men of few words, talked behind closed doors. They finally emerged with smiles on their faces.

Dad took the ring out of his pocket and asked, "Wendy, will you marry me?"

"Of course I will," she replied.

Dad hugged Mom, and they began to laugh and dance around the floor. They were officially engaged. As my grandmother watched the happy couple, she was pleased that the prince had succeeded in his courtship with his princess. My mother, too, thought she was beginning a lifelong fairytale.

Do middle children have the same connections to their parents as the first and last? Maybe they feel isolated in their central position. Was that the reason my mother felt compelled to change her life at such a fast pace? Why

15

do we act before thinking instead of accepting the pearls of wisdom and acknowledgement that will nourish our hearts?

My dad moved to Hamilton with the confidence that he and Mom would be married. She stayed in Nahant and continued her college studies. She missed him, but she felt sure of their love and couldn't wait to start a new life with him.

Mom was surprised to receive a letter from David as she waited for her wedding day. Inside the envelope was a charm with the Serenity Prayer printed on it: *God, grant me the serenity to accept the things I cannot change, the courage to change the things I can, and the wisdom to know the difference.*

She had no idea then why he'd sent her a charm, and she still wonders. She thinks he sent it to her because he loved her. Maybe so, but why did he choose that prayer? I understand it. It was another synchronistic event provided by the universe. It was the future. My mother still has the charm.

As she contemplated becoming Dad's wife, I doubt Mom looked at her future with messages from the universe in mind. She was yearning for the comfort of love, security, and a bright, strong destiny.

By Easter of 1963, Mom was missing my dad terribly. She had not seen him since before Christmas. Her parents were on their way to Nova Scotia to open the summer home for the season. Mom and her younger brother Rick stayed home. Also at home was her father's brand new Thunderbird. Mom and Rick decided it would be a clever idea to drive the car to Hamilton, Ontario, and visit her fiancé over the long Easter weekend.

They came up with the perfect plan and shared it with my dad. The only problem was putting so many miles on Grandpa's new car. Since my dad was a good mechanic, he knew how to disconnect the odometer for the ride home. He would show Rick how to hook it back up when they got back to Nahant.

Once the plan was in place, Mom took the dog next door for the weekend, made several sandwiches, and packed a few clothes for the 568-mile trip. When Mom and Rick arrived in Hamilton, they met Faye and Terrance Huskins and their two boys, Terry and Billy. Rick loved having two boys about his age to hang out with.

Faye and Terrance were excited about meeting Wendy and Rick, but they hadn't expected them, and they had made plans for the evening. My dad had agreed to watch his nephews, and Mom thought it would be a great opportunity to give all three boys the Easter baskets she had brought for them.

After playing and eating their treats, the boys went to bed. Mom and Dad snuggled on the sofa as they watched television. When Dad suggested that they experiment a little bit to see what it would be like when they were married, Mom became uncomfortable.

She was naïve and prudish and a little bit nervous. Mom had been raised in a very religious Protestant household, and it was the 60's. Having sex before marriage was not accepted behavior.

"I don't think that's such a good idea," she said. "We should wait until…"

He interrupted by putting a finger to her lips. "I'm in my 30's. I don't need permission from my parents or the church to fool around. It's perfectly okay to experiment."

"I still feel uncomfortable. I would like to wait." She was not interested in fooling around. She was afraid to even kiss Dad with three young boys in the other room.

Dad assured her the boys were fine. He had just checked in on them, and he insisted they were sound asleep.

Looking back on the situation later, Mom believed she was too vulnerable. She felt threatened by my father's unusually aggressive behavior. His charming self seemed to have been taken over by a controlling madman.

When she continued to object to his advances, Dad said, "If you can't have sex with me here and now, then you can leave and drive right back to your David in Nahant!"

That threat still lives with my mother today. If she can accept it now, it will empower her to let go. She allowed herself to be manipulated and used. She disobeyed her gut instinct and lost herself for the sake of pleasing my dad's animalistic cravings and lack of control. She later said, "I was forced into doing something that I didn't want to do, but I did it."

My father's insensitivity and need to control had been cleverly shielded until then, but my mother hadn't been willing to realize it or heed the warning. He had captured her mind and soul, which allowed him to let his shield down and begin revealing the tormented truth of himself. When he took her body, as well, my mother's wholeness—her oneness—ceased to exist.

Lead not with your ego and mind; lead with the heart.

Because my mother didn't want to be rejected, she gave in to his demands. But the event haunted her on the drive home. She wondered if she was doing the right thing by marrying him. Eventually, she pushed any negative thoughts aside and focused on the talk they had the night before. They had discussed a date for the wedding as if everything was perfect. They set the date for the weekend of her graduation and Rick's birthday. It would be a huge party for all three events.

It was a very unhealthy beginning for their marriage. For reasons I can only imagine, my father seemed in a hurry to get married. Did he think my mother could repair him? My mother went along with his manipulations because she was still very young and in love. Perhaps she was only in love with the idea of marriage. She had to have felt a sense of shame in allowing herself to be taken. It was a sign of powerlessness and disillusion. By pushing her feelings down instead of acknowledging them as pearls of wisdom, she left herself vulnerable.

When Dad arrived in Nahant on Memorial Day weekend, the whirlwind of festivities was ready to begin. Mom told him she was very unsettled about what had happened in Hamilton, and he smoothed things over by telling her they had to know if they would be compatible.

She allowed herself to be satisfied with his devious answer. It's possible my mother accepted his story as truth to avoid disrupting her rushed engagement and wedding. She was sacrificing the pearl of empowerment by resisting her truth. Two worlds were about to collide, fast and hard.

Mom's graduation almost seemed to get in the way of the couple's rush to marry, and it didn't get the attention such an accomplishment should receive. The next night, my mother's parents hosted a combination rehearsal dinner/birthday party/graduation celebration.

On June 2, 1963, my parents were married in the Big Stone Protestant Church in Nahant. Dad's mother was too ill to travel to the states, and Mom's sister wasn't there due to pregnancy complications. Mom was quite upset right before the ceremony because she had counted on her sister's supportive presence. However, Mom had borrowed her sister's wedding gown, and when she stepped into it, she felt closer to her.

Mom carried an all-white bouquet created from a variety of fragrant flowers. Her bridesmaids wore pastel green tea-length dresses and carried yellow and white daisies. My dad wore a white tuxedo jacket, black slacks, and a tie. He was very handsome, but in the wedding pictures, his face reveals confusion.

As I view the photographs taken that day, I see women dressed in a variety of patterned dresses with lovely hats. Most wore pearls and white gloves. The men were all in suits and ties. Back then it was important to dress for the occasion. Everyone looked elegant and classy; it was a scene right out of a movie. My grandmother was the most stunning. She wore a golden yellow dress with a wide-brimmed hat and a mink stole. Of course, she also wore her signature bright red lipstick.

What's missing from the weathered photos is a sense of the dedicated, lifelong love that couples promise to each other when they repeat their wedding vows. The pictures reveal forced smiles and an uncertain tension that have been frozen in time. Seeing those images while knowing what I now know is a bittersweet experience.

A catered reception was held in my grandmother's flower garden, where everyone could breathe and relax into the day. The numerous flowers that my grandma groomed with such care were in full bloom, displaying their bright colors and smelling wonderfully fragrant. The sweet little birds that Grandma fed were singing their songs to entertain the guests mingling below them.

Her wedding day should have been the day that my mother received the perfect nourishment to bloom into her future. Her wedding vows should have protected her from being profusely pricked by the thorns of life's struggles. Perhaps the songs the birds sang at the reception were warning calls, telling my mother of the dangers to come.

When my parents' auras joined that day, my fate began. They were escaping separate worlds of heartache, fear, and loneliness. They were unsure of who they were individually and more than a little frightened about who they would be together. Neither was able to accept life on life's terms or surrender to a higher power to learn the lessons of "theirs and mine." Seeing a photo of my parents cutting their wedding cake gives new meaning to the saying "You can't have your cake and eat it, too." Yet, for that moment, they appeared to be very happy.

Chapter Two

The Break of Innocence

The spirit of man can endure only so much;
when it is broken, only a miracle can mend it.

~ John Burroughs ~

Their two-week honeymoon started where they met, in Nova Scotia, Canada. After that, my dad wanted to visit Prince Edward Island. He had never been there, but he had heard how beautiful it was. Mom's idea of a honeymoon was traveling to somewhere warm, a place she had never been before. But her new mother-in-law was still feeling ill, and she knew my dad wanted to see his mother and the rest of his family.

They departed for their honeymoon in the late afternoon and landed in Maine to spend the night. They would board the ferry in the morning. It was their first night as husband and wife. Mom's concept of what took place between newlyweds on their wedding night involved the sharing of love. It should have been a memory cherished by two people, but theirs was a celebration for one. That was the night she really questioned what she had done and where her life was heading. The memory of her wedding night still haunts my mother.

It was not consensual sex. My father ripped off her clothes and forced himself on her like a wild animal. He exploited her trust, her emotions, and her body. While he physically forced his sexual power onto her, he looked into her eyes and said, "I am so glad we had our trial run on Easter." Seeing her blank stare, he said, "What's the matter? Don't you like this? You can still pack up and go back to your David if this isn't what you expected."

She looked away, feeling more alone than she had ever felt before.

The look on my mother's face as she told me about that night demonstrated that the pain remains raw, despite the years that have passed. Another slice of her soul had gone numb that night, and her strand was further weakened by fear and sadness.

For our souls to evolve, moments of weakness should be experienced in the present moment and then released. When we hold onto resentment, we give up the chance to face our truths.

Mom's dream of the perfect fairytale marriage was beyond her control, and it never became a reality. Her hope of a shared love had been shattered. Each time they had another one-sided sexual encounter, her soul shredded a little more. Layers of innocence, joy, and happiness were stripped away when the demons that tortured Dad awakened. She began to build defensive walls to hide the wounds deep within.

～◎

The next morning my dad was in a hurry to get on the road. "Get your things together and let's go!" he yelled.

They were on the highway shortly after dawn, traveling in silence. Mom retreated into herself as a reaction to Dad's overwhelming aggression the night before. She was intimidated by the new side of dad's personality.

It's hard to imagine how my mother must have been feeling. As a woman, my heart hurts for her. I feel sadness for my father, too, that he was so driven by despair that he lost himself.

Finally, Dad broke the silence by barking a question at my mother. "What are you so unhappy about, Wendy? We just got married. Smile!"

Mom cautiously replied, "It's because of the way you handled yourself last night. I didn't expect it to be like that."

"Well, if you don't think you love me, and you don't want to continue with this…" He reached behind her seat, pulled his wallet out of a bag, and threw a thousand dollars at her. "There's plenty of money. I'll drop you off at the bus station, and you can go back home to your mother and father!"

She looked at the money and started to cry. She felt vulnerable, uncomfortable, and alone. My mother had never experienced that type of behavior, and she didn't know what to say or do. Feeling confused and miserable, she just turned away. The tears in her eyes distorted the view that whizzed by outside her window.

She must have seen her future whizzing by, as well. She realized she had made a terrible mistake. It was the third time he had given her an ultimatum. Years later, she would say, "I don't know why I didn't take the money and run away from him as fast as possible. I should have, but I didn't." Mom's soul was becoming as veiled as Dad's.

Fifteen minutes went by as Mom looked out the window. Dad finally broke the ice again, saying, "So I guess this means that you're going to stay, aye?"

Her reply was simple, and it sealed her fate. "Yes, I am."

Dad's personality shifted as soon as he heard her response. He coddled her and told her how sorry he was. He was once more the man my mother had agreed to marry.

After the honeymoon, they drove back to Nahant to pick up their belongings and wedding gifts. Things seemed to be going well between them. Visits to my dad's roots always brought the best out in him. It took a couple of days for them to organize their belongings, and Dad rented a trailer to tow behind the car.

After they loaded up and said goodbye to Mom's parents, my dad moved my mom to another country, a place where she didn't know anyone. When they arrived at the border between the United States and Canada, they encountered a snag. Mom had to spend almost four hours filling out forms to allow her to live in Canada. Dad then announced that they would be living with his sister Faye until he found work and a place for them to live.

In August of 1963, they moved into their own place. The underground apartment horrified my mother. She couldn't see the light of any day unless she left the apartment. She had no friends to talk to or spend time with. Dad found a job working as a mechanic at a gas station in Hamilton. While he was at work, Mom was alone. She tried to keep busy by unpacking gifts and belongings and writing thank-you notes. She listened to the radio for the comfort of a human voice.

Every night, Mom had dinner on the table for Dad as soon as he arrived home from work. Her meals never met his expectations, and many of them landed on the floor. He had been too spoiled by his mother. Mom tried, but she couldn't please her new husband. He lacked the pearls of thankfulness and respect. Mom's soul was becoming as dark with despair as the dim hole in which she spent her days and nights.

The honeymoon and the move had burned through much of Dad's savings. He told Mom that they couldn't afford a house, but a mobile home would be within their budget. In December of 1963, they moved into a brand new mobile home in a trailer park. My mother was thrilled to become part of a community! There were plenty of people for her to meet, and she was no longer living in a dark hole.

There was a time in my life when I was embarrassed to say I lived in a trailer park. The reality I live in today allows me to view that trailer park as a piece of adversity that has helped polish my soul. It is one of the sacred gifts in the treasure chest of my heart and soul.

That Christmas, Grandma and Grandpa visited Mom and Dad for the holidays to see how the newlyweds were doing. Mom was happy to be in her first owned home as a wife, but she wasn't feeling well. She was afraid to tell my dad, so she told her mother instead. Grandma said she should be checked by a doctor.

In January, the doctor did a blood test and told my mother she was pregnant. She was terrified to tell my dad because he'd made it clear that he never wanted children. Because his in-laws were still there, Dad put on a happy face and pretended to be ecstatic over the news of Mom's pregnancy. But Mom knew the truth.

Dad had waited until they were already married to tell her there would never be children in their future. She tried to talk to him about his reasons, but he refused to tell her why. It was a subject he did not want to discuss, and he never did. It seems likely that he must have suffered some trauma as a child that left lifelong scars. When asked why she didn't push the issue with him, Mom said, "That's just the way it was back then." He ruled; she listened.

As her pregnancy progressed, tension in the house grew thick, and Mom got homesick. It should have been one of the happiest times of her life, but she felt more alone than ever. The longer she stayed in her new home, the more unhappy she became. She didn't feel well emotionally or physically, and she missed her parents terribly.

By April, she knew she had to get out of there. She didn't have a car, so she took a cab to the bus station and traveled by Greyhound to Boston. Her father picked her up and took her home to Nahant.

Mom spent weeks resting and absorbing all the comforts of home. Although she enjoyed being pampered by her parents, her sadness showed in her eyes, and Grandma asked her what was wrong. She said she was unhappy, but she didn't reveal just how unhappy she really was. She couldn't tell her mother the whole truth, because she was a married woman. She knew she had to go back, even though she wasn't sure she wanted to. Mom deprived herself of happiness by not following her truths.

Dad drove to Nahant to take Mom back to the home they shared. He said he didn't want her riding the bus in her condition. His mood and attitude had improved. He told Mom he had missed her. For a while, Mom's life with Dad seemed to be almost normal. He was attentive to her and her needs and never displayed anger about her condition.

He must have cared about Mom to drive so far to spare her a bus trip. And he must have worked very hard to convince himself to change, as it was clear that he had reached deep to find some compassion.

On a hot, humid day in August, Dad took Mom out in his speedboat to cool off after a picnic by the lake. She was due to give birth any day, and the ride was extremely rough. That evening, my mother started to get intense cramping pains in her abdomen that radiated to her back. She didn't know for sure what was happening to her.

My father got scared and drove her to the hospital. Mom had contractions all the way there. When they arrived, a nurse directed Dad to the maternity waiting room and whisked Mom away. Hospitals didn't allow fathers to be in the birthing rooms in 1964.

Mom was terrified. She was alone and in pain in a very dark room. She had no idea what to expect. The nurses checked on her periodically as the hours passed and the pain grew more intense. The last thing Mom remembers is lying on a hard table and hearing the doctor ask the anesthesiologist to put her under.

I was born in breach position, and the doctor delivered me with forceps, bottom first. I arrived at 7:00 a.m. on August 10, 1964, weighing seven pounds. The doctor told Mom that he should have performed a C-section, but there wasn't time. He reassured her everything was terrific and that her baby was just fine.

The doctor described my birth position to Mom, saying that my feet had been up over my head, and my right foot was turned all the way inward. My sense of being grounded was clearly off kilter the day I was born. He told Mom to buy corrective shoes and put them on my feet immediately. The doctor said that the shoes and special massages would turn my foot forward so it could point straight ahead. Fortunately, he was right.

My mother's stay in the hospital was miserable. She woke up in a room with four women who did not speak a lick of English. She felt so alone. She had just given birth to her first baby, there was no family around, and she couldn't communicate with her roommates.

Dad didn't show up until a day later. She didn't ask him where he had been. She knew he had gone to work and then gone drinking with his buddies. During Dad's brief visit, they easily came to an agreement about my name. My mother wanted to call me Deborah, for her best friend, and my father wanted my middle name to be Elizabeth, for his mother. So I was named Deborah Elizabeth Adams.

It's hard to believe that Dad left her there all by herself. It's even harder for me to realize that he didn't want to see me. Fatherhood was clearly not a priority for him.

He told Mom that day that he wished I had been a boy. That statement is one of the truest things he ever said. He reminded me of that truth often, telling me how disappointed he was that I was not his son. I would never succeed in life, because I was just a stupid girl.

He belittled me, and the lack of emotional nourishment ultimately stunted my growth. The necessary elements for my development—love, encouragement, joy, happiness, support, and peace—were denied me by my father. However, I recovered them all in time. I reversed his curse by honoring the spirit of my heart.

According to my mother, I had a great disposition and hardly ever cried. I slept through my first night home without waking up to eat or have my diaper changed, and I continued to sleep through every night after that. Because Mom was a first-time mother, she got up several times every night for months to make sure I was breathing.

Our mobile home didn't have air conditioning, and nights during the summer of '64 were very hot. Thunderstorms often developed over Lake Ontario and crashed over Hamilton. They came incredibly close, with loud rumbles of thunder and scary lightening strikes. The storms were so filled with energy that they lasted for hours, and they terrified my mother. She was amazed that I not only slept through the night but that I slept through every frighteningly loud storm.

Thunderstorms now remind me of my dad. It must have been unsettling to have random bursts of energy emerge from within him like unpredictable thunderstorms. It saddens me that he was never able to discover a spiritual path by facing and working through the emotional storms that held him captive throughout his life.

As a baby, I never cried unless it was time to feed me or change my diaper. Mom learned the differences between my cries and knew just what I was asking for. Mom and Dad took me everywhere, and I smiled at everyone. They took me with them when they went shopping, and they carried me to the lake and to restaurants. As long as I had the baby essentials, I was content no matter where I was or who was tending me.

My mother grabbed any opportunity to get out of the hot house when my father was at work. She walked me around the neighborhood in the Cadillac of carriages, a gift from my grandparents. The neighborhood women flocked to admire the most contented baby they had ever seen.

Mom and Dad began to make friends through the people Dad worked with at the service station. They spent a lot of time with a young couple who had three children, one the same age as me. Our life, at last, seemed normal. My parents had a new home, a new baby, and good friends. Mom was happy because they were socializing more. Dad was more content than he'd been for a long time, especially after visits with his older sister Daisy. Mom and Dad were getting along for the first time since they married. All was calm and serene during the first three years of my life.

In 1967, we were given the opportunity to move our mobile home from a street in the rear of the park to one in the front, closer to the main road. Mom was excited because it gave her a sense of moving up the social status ladder. She had hated being stuck in the back of the trailer park.

The move enabled Mom to meet Eileen and Lloyd, a couple with whom she would form a lifelong friendship. Mom fell in love with their friendly and welcoming attitude. The moment our home was moved to the front lot, Eileen became my mother's dearest friend. Eileen was a housewife with three children. She always knew exactly what Mom needed, whether it was a cup of coffee, a girlfriend chat, a good cry, or a back rub. Whatever my mother needed, Eileen was always there for her.

With Eileen, Mom was able to express herself on the level of a true relationship. She treasured Eileen's friendship. It enabled her to open up and be honest, knowing that her honesty would be returned. Their friendship would carry Mom through the storms to come.

Shortly after the move, my dad's weaknesses resurfaced. Each month, Dad gave Mom enough money to pay the rent. One day she needed groceries, and all she had was the rent money. She decided to use some of it to buy food, which left too little to pay that month's rent.

A week later, as Dad pulled into the trailer park after work, the manager waved him down. "Hey, Clyde, how's it going?" he asked. "I was wondering when I could collect this month's rent. It was due last week."

Dad was embarrassed, but he covered it with a chuckle. "I set that money on the table for Wendy to give to you. She must have forgotten. I'll get it to you tomorrow. Have a good night, buddy."

Dad did not like being caught off guard. His initial irritation blossomed into anger as he drove to our home. Thunder rumbled deep inside him.

He was silent, seething with anger, until Mom said, "Hi. How was work?" Then Dad exploded.

"What does it matter how work was? What the hell have you been doing with my hard-earned money? I gave you rent money, and you didn't use it for rent. God damn it, Wendy. The manager just stopped me and asked me for the rent. You're a stupid, good-for-nothing bitch."

"But, Clyde, you didn't give me enough for food or stuff for the baby, so I had to use some of the rent money."

"You're a fucking liar and a spoiled brat!" he roared. "Money doesn't grow on trees! This is Canada, not Nahant."

Mom got scared and quiet. She stopped defending herself.

Simple, everyday challenges were too much for Dad to handle. After that day, Dad often called Mom a liar and a thief, accusing her of stealing money from him. The name calling and accusations continued until they finally got divorced many years later.

Mom couldn't understand how her own husband could believe she would steal from him. She never understood how he could lose trust in her and treat her like a criminal. Perhaps the corruption he thought he saw in her was a character trait he really saw in himself.

Mom could have left him rather than staying with a man who considered her a lying thief. But time and time again, she made the decision to stay. She was living out the saying "I've made my bed and now I have to lie in it."

When we choose our journey, we choose our challenges. The keys to our challenges are the lessons we learn. The lessons make us stronger.

⤳

Unaware of the widening gulf between Mom and Dad, I was a happy little girl who felt secure in the love of her parents. I was also a very curious child who never wanted to miss out on anything. One particular morning as I climbed out of bed, my wet, heavy diaper felt gross. I pigeon-toed down the hallway in my pajamas to the living room where my toys were. When I plopped down on the floor, the smell of ammonia from my full diaper made my eyes water, but I didn't know where it was coming from. I forgot about the smell when I laid eyes on my rocking horse. "Giddy up, horsy!"

I clumsily ran over and climbed up on him. I loved my horsy and often talked to him. I rocked as hard and fast as I could. I laughed as I rocked, loving the way my head jerked backward just before I had the exhilarating sense of flying forward again. "Wheeeee!"

My rocking horse gave me the freedom to fly with an open heart, just as animals open my heart and sooth my soul today. My love for animals was strong even then.

Sometimes I would rock so fast and so long that the base would begin to move. When that happened, I eventually ended up on the other side of the room, and my parents would have to move my horse back for me. That morning when I hit the wall, something caught my eye.

I hopped off horsy to look at my mother's pearl necklace on the coffee table. That necklace was so inviting. When I picked it up to play with it, the pearls felt cold and smooth. The strand was hard to hang onto, and it kept slipping from my tiny hands.

I dropped it several times as I made my way to the other side of the living room to sit on the floor and stare at my pretty new toy. I loved the way the strand of pearls looked as it draped over my little fingers. I adored the noise the pearls made when I shifted them from palm to palm like a slinky. Each time I dropped the necklace on the vinyl floor, the pearls made a noise like the rain made on our tin roof.

With the light from the window reflecting off the pearls, they looked like little pieces of candy. I put them into my mouth…and gagged. They tasted the way my mother's hairspray smelled. It was icky.

I decided it would be better to wear them the way Mommy did. I'd seen her put them around her neck, so I knew the necklace came apart. I pulled, but nothing happened. So I tugged harder. When I remember what happened next, it's like watching a movie in slow motion.

Suddenly, the string broke. Pearls flew in every direction, and I heard them bounce off every surface. Several pearls bounced on the floor right in front of me. Slowly, they stopped bouncing and rolled in different directions until they came to a stop.

Throughout my life, those pearls have represented the sparkling stars that I would reach for after I had repaired the strand of my soul. My open heart keeps them on my strand today.

As I looked around, I saw my pretty, shiny pieces of fake candy scattered everywhere. Only a couple of them remained on the strand, which was weak and broken. Thoughts of the broken strand of pearls left my child's mind within seconds. Off I went to find another bright, shiny toy.

I hugged my doll house, which was as tall as I was, and began to move the furniture around. I heard voices in the other room and ran to greet my mother as she came down the hallway in her nightgown.

"Good morning, sunshine," she said, picking me up to give me a kiss.

"Sunshine" was a nickname given to me by my father. I know it came from his heart, the part of him that remained mostly closed. His heart was locked in chains. He wrestled with them, but he never found the key. Because he opened his heart long enough to give me that nickname, and because I am a Leo, worshipper of the sun, I will always treasure it.

Mom put me down and walked through the living room. She was about to step into the dining room when she gasped. Her head fell forward, and she began to make a funny noise. I didn't know what she was doing, because I'd never seen her cry. She didn't say a word. She just bent over and began collecting all the pearls, putting them into a square glass ashtray on the coffee table.

I went back to playing with my doll house.

My father entered the room, took one look at the pearls in the ashtray, and asked coldly, "How did you break those?"

"I didn't break them. The baby did. It's my own fault. I left them on the coffee table last night."

He spun around to look at me with eyes filled with rage. I had never seen him look that way before. "What did you do that for?" he yelled. "Stupid!!"

I didn't know what stupid meant, but the tone of his voice was so frightening that I knew stupid wasn't good. His face was bright red. He stomped over to where I stood and grabbed my tiny wrist. He yanked my arm so hard that I fell forward onto the floor. He was overcome by a dark force that I had never experienced, and I was completely helpless. My essence was literally in his hands.

Joy and trust drained out of me as he dragged my small body across the floor. Abruptly, he stopped. Yanking my arm again, he flung me onto my back. When he reached toward my hand, I thought it was to comfort me. Instead, he struck my hand so hard that my eyes blinked and my body jerked. I felt a burning pain in my hand and in my heart. As he pulled his hand back for a second strike, my body froze in shock and fear.

Tears filled my eyes as my father's love turned on me. His huge hand cut boo-boo's into my small one with every repeated strike. The loving hands that I had associated with tender hugs were stealing my innocence. I closed my eyes in terror and cried so hard that I hiccupped uncontrollably.

In between hiccups I whimpered, "Stop, Daddy. Daddy, please stop."

In those terrifying, incomprehensible moments, my strand broke. My father's punishments became commonplace throughout my childhood. His clouded intellect and unwillingness to address the root cause of his outbursts soon broke my heart.

I was just a baby. I had started life with a clean slate and a peaceful soul, character, and temperament. My father interrupted my growth by filling me with fear, hurt, nervousness, and a saddened spirit. With every abusive episode, another piece of my soul broke away and locked itself deep in my heart. My layers of unhealthy armor became thicker with each punishment. I wore the armor to protect myself. I didn't know that it was injuring me as much as his beatings.

The goodness of my essence would eventually be locked away in a dark dungeon, hidden from my conscious awareness. My character would have to be rebuilt slowly, one tiny sliver of light at a time.

That broken strand and the pearls that bounced and rolled away, scattering everywhere, are symbols of the many abusive incidents that corrupted and broke me. The necklace would be restrung, but it took years. Before that happened, the existing strand continued to wear thin until it became irreparable. I had to find the right strand of knowledge, patience, and trust on which to delicately string each pearl. I had to learn to trust that the new strand would be strong enough to hold the pearls as more and more were added. The strand of pearls symbolizes my life. The pearls were and are my lessons and challenges. The strand is me.

At one point while my father was beating me for the first time, I heard my mother scream, "Stop hitting her. You're hitting too hard. What are you doing? You're hurting her. Stop!"

Dad lunged toward her and yelled, "Mind your own business. I am disciplining her, so back off! I can handle this!"

Mom didn't speak again. She stood as still as a statue, watching in horror and disbelief.

I wondered in later years why my mother hadn't rescued me that day.

Why didn't she scoop me into her arms and carry me out of harm's way? I know now that she was as afraid of Dad as I was. She admits that she was a bit of a coward, so she did nothing. The event weakened my mother's strand, as well.

The sight of the broken strand of pearls triggered a violent outburst from my dad that set the tone for the rest of our relationship. He had never hit me before that day, and he had no idea that his beatings would cause emotional and mental scarring and stunt my spiritual growth.

That first beating was the beginning of a lifeless childhood. I wasn't allowed to walk, talk, or breathe without his permission. I lived in constant fear when I was in his presence. If I touched something, spoke when not spoken to, or just tried to be a happy kid, he would hit me. When he said my name in a certain tone, I knew what was coming next. If he yelled, "Damn it, leave that alone," and I didn't react instantly, he would take off his belt and whip my legs as if I were his slave.

Mom said I was fresh with him and that I liked to challenge him to see how far I could get. I don't remember doing that, but it explains why he whipped my legs so often. In the summertime, my bare legs made it easy for him. In the winter, he would order me to pull my pants down to my ankles.

I stood there shaking with fear, salty beads of sweat from my upper lip rolling into the corners of my mouth. I squeezed my eyes tightly shut and flexed my muscles from head to toe while he made me wait for the belt. The smell of beer and the smoke from his cigarette made me gag as he sat behind me, making a game out of my terror.

He would ask me over and over, "Do you know what you did? Do you know why I'm beating your ass?"

Every time he asked the question, he struck me with a leather belt. I usually didn't know what I'd done wrong. It was always something stupid. When that leather belt snapped across the back of my legs, it left lines of purple that eventually faded into a yellow green. Even if I managed to blurt out the correct reason, he forced me to stand in the corner until I stopped crying.

Dad made me cover my bruises by wearing tights. The neighbors had to know what was going on, at least in the summer. The trailer homes didn't have air conditioning, and they were only 20 feet apart. He screamed, yelled, and beat both me and my mother often.

We never knew if Dad would be in a bad mood, go for days without speaking, or come home drunk and happy. The silent treatment was the worst. We would walk on eggshells, waiting for his anger. Mom begged and pleaded with him to tell her what we had done wrong.

I suspect he just needed his moments. He struggled with himself just as I struggled before I discovered myself. My father's roller-coaster emotions were the only survival skills he knew. One minute he would be happy, acting like a normal, loving, kind, and giving husband and father. Moments later, he transformed into an angry, impatient, and abusive crazy person. I think the episodes of silence were an outward sign that he felt traumatized by his own actions.

Sometimes Dad sat and cried, apologizing for lashing out at us. I don't think my father truly knew how harmful his demons were. I don't think he was aware of the devastating effects his actions had on his wife and child.

My father had high standards for himself and those closest to him, so I imagine the severity of his actions touched his inner core. He must have felt shame, remorse, and guilt almost every time. His unhealthy emotional roller coaster had become a ride for three. He didn't know how to rectify the damage, and he was extremely embarrassed.

My mother put up with the abuse because, she said, "Back in those days, you stayed married. That's just the way it was. Divorce was frowned upon."

One day she realized she couldn't take any more, and she wouldn't let me take any more either. While Dad was at work, Mom packed a few clothes and grabbed a couple of toys to keep me occupied. We walked out to the main road and waited for the bus that traveled to Buffalo, New York. While we waited, Mom used a pay phone to call Grandma to tell her we were coming for a visit.

In Buffalo we boarded a smelly Greyhound bus bound for Boston. I remember the trip well. Mom bought me a darling little Greyhound suitcase. I loved it and pretended it was my purse. It kept me occupied for a very long time. I couldn't understand why the bus stopped in every city along the way. Every time the bus stopped, I thought we had reached Gamma's and Gampa's house.

It took only two days before Dad tracked us down in Nahant. He called and asked to speak to Grandpa.

"Hi, Fred, how are you?" he said. "I want to fix this, but I'm working my ass off, and Wendy is clueless when it comes to money. She is acting like a spoiled brat. When I gave her money to take care of the household responsibilities, she spent it on herself. She doesn't know how to pay the bills or how to budget for necessities. You wasted your money on college for that one. She's irresponsible, and I can't teach her anything."

Grandpa was at a loss. Mom had already told him her side, and he didn't really understand what Clyde was talking about. When Dad realized that Grandpa wasn't going to take his side, he got mad and said he would be coming to pick up his family.

Our escape was only temporary, because Mom agreed to go back with Dad. I was hopelessly trapped between them. Mom told me the ride home was unbearable, as Dad lectured her the entire way.

"Wendy, you don't know how to live responsibly. You were spoiled by your parents. Well, I'm just going to have to teach you myself. When we get home, I'm going to get a mailbox with a lock on it, and you will not get the key. Do you understand me? You will not be permitted to get our mail. You don't know how to handle money. You don't really know how to do anything. You will also be getting a job. If you aren't satisfied with the income I bring home, then you can start making money, too. This is for your own good. This will teach you."

Mom didn't respond. She just sat there. He was treating her as if she were hired help. He thought he was in charge and smarter because he was much older than she was. He told her she was stupid so often that she eventually started to believe it.

He brainwashed my mother and took control of her mind and free will. A healthy mind is an essential component for spiritual transformation.

Mom did as she was told and used her secretarial degree to get a job in a doctor's office. A lovely, elderly French couple watched me while Mom was at work. They reminded me of my grandma and grandpa, but they talked funny. The house always smelled like baking bread. I called them Meme and Pepe, and I cried when it was time to go home each day. They spoke to me in kind and caring voices, and they played games with me. They took me to the park so I could play on the swings. Best of all, they never yelled or spanked me. They loved me, and I loved them so very much.

Mom hadn't been working very long before Dad was offered the opportunity to take over a service station business as his own. An elderly man owned it, and he loved my dad. Dad must have shown him his hardworking, caring side. The old man was ill and needed to retire. He knew he could when he saw Dad's work ethic.

With a reliable income, family life became much smoother for Mom and Dad. Unfortunately, I continued to get into trouble with Dad over miniscule stuff due to his demand for perfection and need for control.

Chapter Three

And Then There Were Four

Grown men can learn from every little child, for the hearts of little children are pure. Therefore, the Great Spirit may show them many things which older people miss.

~ Black Elk ~

In the summer of 1968, Dad took Mom and me on vacation to his home in Nova Scotia. Aunt Faye and Uncle Terry had moved back there from Hamilton a few months before. Faye and my dad were the youngest of six, and they were very close.

There are several ways to travel from the mainland to Nova Scotia. The longest route requires driving, and it's a grueling trip. The preferred method is by ferry. In '68, three ferries were available, two from Maine and one from Saint John New Brunswick, Canada.

The ferry from New Brunswick to Digby, Nova Scotia, was a short ride, but after the ferry docked, there was still an hour-long drive to the small town of Clyde River where Aunt Faye lived. The Bluenose ferry took us on a six-hour ferry ride that arrived right in Yarmouth. The ferry from Portland, Maine, to Yarmouth took 10 hours.

We tried every route over the years, and I remember them all. My memories of those trips are so clear because they were joyous times for my dad. When Dad was happy, I was happy, too, because he lightened his usually tight control over me.

The joy of returning to his roots formed cracks in Dad's character, which allowed a hint of his authenticity to shine through. At those times, I knew he had a heart and soul. He just kept them locked away for protection.

During that first vacation to Nova Scotia, I got as sick as a sea dog. Dad had given me tapioca pudding to eat after lunch while he drank beer and smoked cigs in the lounge. The combination of smoke and a ferry that rocked with the ebb and flow of the ocean made me violently seasick. To this day, I avoid tapioca pudding.

The ocean is unpredictable, and the Gulf of Maine and the Bay of Fundy can be pretty rough. I always recovered quickly. When I resist the ebb and flow of life, my body, mind, and soul don't recover as quickly. I've learned to accept the fluctuations in the ocean of life.

By the time we arrived in Yarmouth, I was feeling perky again until I inhaled the smelly odor of dead fish on the docks. My queasiness subsided when a bunch of men wearing plaid skirts and knee socks caught my attention. They were playing strange instruments that created the sound of beauty. It was a harmonious choir of flutes and horns.

The music mesmerized me and created a peaceful feeling. Somehow, the sound was familiar. I was sure I had heard it before. I don't know where I would have heard Scottish bagpipes at such a young age. Perhaps the sound was a memory from a previous life.

After leaving the ferry, we drove through a countryside that was picturesque, scenic, and sometimes stunning. Of course, that wasn't what I was thinking as my four-year-old self gazed out the car window. Nevertheless, I was fascinated by the neverending quantities of blue water, fishing boats, and trees. There were lots and lots of trees!

"Nova Scotia is the ocean's playground in Canada," Dad said. I loved playgrounds, and I began to watch for the swing sets that were sure to appear. I hoped that Dad would stop the car so I could play.

I didn't know then that the playground he spoke of was a metaphor for those seeking the simple, peaceful sights and sounds in life. It's a shame that my father couldn't hold that beautiful concept in his troubled mind.

Nova Scotia is a peninsula surrounded on three sides by the ocean, so the ocean dictates the climate. One day the weather can be beautiful and sunny, with bright blue skies hovering over the rolling landscape. The next day can turn to pea soup, bringing a damp cold that seeps into you. It's so foggy that you can't see your own hand.

The area is filled with lakes, rocky coastlines, cliffs that spill into the ocean, coves, picturesque valleys, wooded hillsides, and mountains. The beauty of the land is breathtaking when it's not fogged in. The sudden change from bright, sunny skies to deep, murky fog always reminds me of my father.

After driving for a few miles, Dad asked Mom to drive so he could rest and drink a few beers.

"Why do you like beer so much?" I asked him. "Does it taste like pop?"

"It's good stuff! It'll put hair on your chest! Here, try a little sip," he said as he handed me the bottle.

I took a big gulp. It had the same bubbly texture as soda pop. Before I could swallow, the bubbles began to burn the inside of my mouth and my lips. It tasted terrible. I soon began to feel strange. My stomach got warm, and the sensation spread through my entire body until it reached my fingers and toes. I was a little dizzy and forgot all about looking for a playground. I liked the fuzzy, warm feeling.

That was the first of many times that Dad gave me a taste of his beer. The more I sipped, the better I liked it. But alcohol is not the type of spirit that heals.

I slept the rest of the way and woke to the sound of excited voices greeting us. As I looked around, I was confused. I thought we were going to Aunt Faye's and Uncle Terry's house, but we were parked at a gas pump, and my dad's family surrounded our car. Mom got out and gave my aunt a hug and a kiss.

"You Yankees finally made it!" my Uncle said, chuckling. "How was the boat ride over? You fellows must be tired."

"It was a smooth ride, Terry," Dad said as he gave his brother-in-law a hug. "How the hell are ya?"

"We're great. Just great. Come on in, and let's get a beer."

When Mom opened the car door to let me out, my aunt took one look and gasped. "What did you do to that poor child? She finally grew some hair, and you've cut it like a boy's. Shame on you. She's a little girl. Let that hair grow."

Dad was busy chatting with Uncle Terry and didn't answer. Dad treated me as if I were his son, so I guess he wanted me to look the part. It's no wonder I don't like short hair today.

When we walked inside the gas station, my uncle told me to pick whatever snack and drink I wanted. I was in heaven. The little store was filled with all kinds of chips, pop, ice cream, popsicles, gum, and candy. I chose an orange pop and the first bag of chips I saw.

As I licked what looked like red salt off my lips, I asked what kind they were. He told me they were called ketchup chips. I still love ketchup-flavored chips, but they are very hard to find in the mainland.

Uncle Terry picked me up and sat me on top of the ice cream cooler. I felt like a grownup because I could see the world from their vantage point. There were three doors leading from the room. One went outside, and another led to a garage where my uncle fixed cars. Through the third door, I could see a kitchen table and chairs. *That must be where they live*, I thought.

When a cat wandered through that door, I asked its name. Laughing, my aunt said, "Your cousins Billy and Terry named her 'Mom' because she was pregnant when she came to us, and it seemed appropriate. But now they have to call me Faye because I got tired of answering whenever they called the cat."

I felt free when we stayed with Aunt Faye and Uncle Terry. I was allowed to investigate, to touch stuff, and even to ask questions without getting yelled at. I could express my curiosity.

When he spent time with his sister, Dad's stone-hard layers temporarily peeled back so that his true self could shine through. His mood was consistently happy, and he had a smile plastered across his face most of the time.

My father had a beautiful, wide smile. His lips were perfect, and smiling revealed straight, pearly white teeth. When he was smiling, Dad was approachable, lovable, and full of funny things to say. At a very young age, I learned to sense my father's moods. I knew the moment his emotional state shifted, and I shifted mine accordingly. As a result,

I fluctuated between an almost normal existence and living like a robot.

Uncle Terry lifted me down from the cooler and led the way through the side door to their home. I thought my cousins were the luckiest kids alive to have a canteen filled with goodies just outside their front door.

The grownups entertained themselves by drinking beer and laughing and talking. Before long, Dad started playing the guitar and singing with Aunt Faye while she stood at the stove preparing her famous hot and spicy spaghetti sauce. I ate my "besgetti" with butter when I was four, but I came to love my Aunt Faye's sauce when I grew up.

Dad's heart opened as the four of them reminisced, told jokes, and teased each other. I so wish he could have found peace in his mind and held it long enough to connect with the Divine, but he just couldn't surrender.

Joy and laughter make the heart stay open. Love keeps it open and makes your strand infinitely strong and as long as life itself.

When they harmonized, Dad's and Faye's voices brought peace to everyone who listened. Together, they sang "Where is My Boy Tonight," "There Goes My Everything," "In the Sweet Bye and Bye," and "Amazing Grace." Their singing revealed the sounds of their souls. They adored each other, and it showed in their musical tones and tunes. That night they sang for hours, accompanied by the aroma of baking bread and the blend of garlic and spices in the sauce that bubbled on the stove. The singing, the familiar home-cooked food, and the closeness to his sister brought my dad out of the dark and into the light every time.

After dinner Uncle Terry took my father out to the garage. Curiosity got the best of me. I heard Dad swearing, but his voice didn't carry the scary tone it did at home. I pushed the door open a little and saw an orange dog behind a car, and I wanted to hug him. As I took a step toward the dog, the door shut behind me and made a creaking noise.

My dad and uncle turned when they heard the sound. When they saw me, I expected Dad to yell at me, because that's what would have happened at home. I froze in place.

Instead of yelling, my father said, "Well, there's my little pride and joy. Come on over here and see what your uncle has in the trunk."

I walked over to the trunk, excited to be included. When I looked inside, I saw a dog, frozen in time. His eyes were open, and his tongue was hanging out of his mouth. My fear and sadness were so intense that I choked on the emotions. Dad thought I was choking on my gum, so he slapped me on the back.

When I could breathe again, I asked him why my uncle had a dog in the trunk. Dad said it was a fox. He told me that Uncle Terry had shot the fox and was going to stuff it. I didn't understand what that meant, but it sounded awful. I began to cry. My love of animals was wounded deeply. It upset me that my dad was displaying such excitement over the death of that poor fox.

The vision of that dead, furry creature left a lasting scar in the hard drive of my memories. I was afraid to fall asleep that night because I kept thinking of that fox. His life had been stopped, and I was sad for him. I was sad for me, too. Like the fox, I was defenseless and helpless.

I knew how it felt to be overcome by the kind of power and dominance that transforms light into dark. My dad's control suffocated me, leaving me unable to breathe through my own identity, just as a bullet from my uncle's gun had left the fox without breath.

The next morning, I tried to stop thinking about the fox as we drove the seven miles to a small town called Upper Port Latour. It's so tiny that you'll miss it if you blink. We were going to visit Aunt Viola, Nan, and Dad's father, Grandpa Adams. We started at Aunt Viola's. She was very nice and quite attentive to me. She was the only sibling out of the six who never smoked or drank a day in her life.

Dad loved Viola, but he would never give up his smokes and drinking long enough to stay with her when we visited Nova Scotia. Aunt Viola lived alone. Her husband had a heart attack and died when Dad was a teenager. She had a married daughter named Pat. Dad said Pat was his favorite niece, and he loved to pick on her. Every time we got together with Aunt Viola, he told the same story. I thought it was funny until I got older. Then I thought it was just cruel.

Pat's beautiful red hair had been perfectly curled in preparation for the Saturday night dance. She wore it in an up do with gloriously cascading curls. Her makeup was flawless. Her dress was beautiful. She thought her date had arrived, but it turned out to be Uncle Clyde instead. He looked at Pat in her fancy dress and smiled devilishly as his prankster side emerged. Without a word, he picked her up and carried her into the bathroom where he held her head under the tub faucet. Pat screamed as he turned it on. Her red-headed temper flared and choice four-letter words flowed like Niagara Falls. I don't think Pat ever spoke to my dad again.

From Viola's, we drove down the hill to Nan's house. It looked like a tiny dollhouse and was absolutely adorable! I didn't know it then, but it's customary in that area of Nova Scotia to paint buildings vivid colors in order to see them in the fog. Nan's house was a light teal with red trim. Wild lupines sprouted all over the slope in front. The winding walkway leading to the house reminded me of Goldilocks and the three bears. The entire place had been hand built by Nan. It was a tiny plantation that symbolized her strength and love of life, all of it wrapped in the serenity of the ocean breeze.

When we walked into the house, it smelled like cats. I was thrilled! Nan had cats, cats, and more cats. When I first saw her, I was a little scared. She was dressed like a tiny man, and her hair was pulled into a bun. She couldn't have weighed more than 110 pounds. Nan's face was wrinkled, and her tiny blue eyes sparkled. My father told me to give her a kiss. When I did as I was told, I discovered that her skin was as soft and sweet as nurturing nectar. She wrapped her loving arms around me, and I could feel the energy of her love. It was my special moment with my Nan, and we connected instantly and permanently. It was a familiar bond that I couldn't place, as if I had known her before.

I'm not sure if the connection between my dad and his mother was on the same level as my bond with her. I do know that Dad loved Nan with all the love he was capable of giving. If he had allowed her nurturing to penetrate deeper, he might have been able to draw on that strength to reach a more spiritual level. She knew he was troubled, but she was never able to help him. Healing comes from the seed of desire within oneself.

When we visited Nova Scotia in later years, I always stayed with Nan. My father left me there so he could drink, play his guitar, and sing without having to worry about taking care of me. He knew I was in perfect hands, and so did I. I loved being with my Nan because I felt safe from the darkness.

Her energy was holy and pure. She spoke to me about her psychic gifts and introduced me to her simple way of life. Nan shone with a heavenly luster and brought me into her light when I was with her.

The inside of Nan's home was as adorable as the outside. A wood stove sat in the kitchen, and the living room featured an antique organ and harmonica. Upstairs were two tiny bedrooms. There was no bathroom. Instead, she used an outhouse. It was creepy and smelled bad. Even though I gagged every time I used it, the outhouse was an adventure that I welcomed.

Nan had built a small barn where her many cats could come and go, and she tended a huge garden overlooking spectacular views of the ocean. It felt like the most peaceful place on earth! Today, all I have to do is close my eyes and picture my Nan and her humble home in my third eye. Then I can instantly breathe in peace and feel the warmth of her light, which surrounds me always.

During my first visit, Nan noticed the belt marks on the back of my legs. She knew exactly what had happened. "What have you done to this child, Clyde?" she asked. "You should be ashamed of yourself. How could you ever beat that tiny little thing? You stop it! Don't let me find out that you've ever done that again."

My father laughed it off. "She was bad, Mom, and I punished her. She's fine. Don't worry."

When I heard her stick up for me, I loved her for defending me. My dad didn't dare argue with his mom. He had respect for her, a respect I yearned for most of my life.

Dad talked Nan into playing her accordion and harmonica. The harmonica sounded as awesome as the bagpipes, and I knew then where Dad's and Aunt Faye's musical talents came from. Dad's not-so-good traits probably came from the person we visited next.

While Mom stayed to chat with Nan, Dad took me for a short ride to visit his father. It was the only time I saw Grandpa Adams because he died shortly after our visit. He looked like an ancient version of my dad. He was in bed, and my dad knelt down beside him. Dad tried to introduce me, but Grandpa was too sick to acknowledge me.

As I stood there, feeling scared and confused, my grandfather threw up all over the floor. My dad held his father's face between his hands and wept. I began to cry, too. I watched my dad lean over and kiss Grandpa on the cheek and say goodbye. Our hearts cracked with sorrow at the same time.

Seeing my father in that emotional state broke my heart. Remembering brings tears to my eyes even now. For a moment, Dad let his protective façade melt away. It soon turned solid again, and the door to his heart closed tighter than before.

He didn't know that embracing our emotions frees us while ignoring them can paralyze us. I'm not sure who my dad said goodbye to that day, the father he loved or the man who had stolen a piece of his soul. In either case, Dad did not leave the sadness and anger there. He carried them with him, deep inside, throughout his life. But he never spoke of that last visit to his father's house, and he never mentioned his father again.

That was one of the few times I witnessed my father's vulnerability. The other moments that brought my father to his knees were when his brother Carl drowned and when his mom passed.

When the vacation ended and we returned to Hamilton after visiting Dad's family in Nova Scotia, the darkness overtook Dad again. Mom and I went back to adjusting our emotions to accommodate his.

One day when Dad was working at his service station, Mom and I visited her friend Eileen. As they were having coffee, Eileen asked me if I was excited about starting kindergarten, and I said I was.

She looked at my mom and asked, "Is Debbie going to be an only child forever?"

Hanging her head, Mom said, "Clyde doesn't want any more children."

"She needs a brother or sister, Wendy. What's the matter with Clyde?"

That evening, Dad was in a good mood, so Mom got up her courage and mentioned the conversation to him. Just as she suspected, he said, "One child is enough."

"No, it isn't. I don't want this dear, sweet little girl growing up alone. We need to have just one more child."

By standing up to him, my mother allowed her honesty to surface and strengthened her strand.

In the winter of 1968, Mom became convinced she was pregnant. She went to the doctor, but he said, "I don't think so. Come back in a couple of months and I will re-evaluate your condition." Mom's belly grew bigger and bigger, and she was so excited. She returned to the doctor, expecting him to confirm that she was going to have another baby. But he told her it was a false pregnancy.

When Mom got home from the doctor's office, Eileen dashed over to hear the good news and found my mother sobbing. When she couldn't get Mom to stop crying, Eileen called Dad and told him to come home from work.

Emotional rescue was not my dad's thing, not even for himself. His quick fix was to go back home to Nova Scotia instead of dealing with Mom's feelings.

Running back home seems to have been a pattern for both my parents. Don't we all want to run home when life gets tough? Home is a feeling deep

within us. We all seek feelings of security and safety. Home is a feeling we can reach once we have surrendered. It is wherever the heart is, no matter where we are.

The night before we left for Nova Scotia, I spilled my milk because I was so nervous. Dad never allowed me to drink anything until my plate was completely clean. The glass was full, and I accidentally hit it with my elbow. I watched as the glass tipped over and landed on its side. The milk seemed to spill out onto the table and roll onto the floor in slow motion. I was terrified, and for good reason. Dad did not like mistakes.

"What did you do that for, stupid?"

I was so scared that I got a little sassy with him. "I didn't do it. You're stupid!"

That made him so angry that he pulled me out of my chair and whipped the back of my legs with his belt. Then he sent me to my room without the rest of my dinner. I went to my room physically and emotionally undernourished.

When we got to Nan's house, she noticed my legs and said to my mom, "You shouldn't let him hurt her like that."

Mom replied, "Nan, you of all people should know you can't tell Clyde anything. It just makes him angrier. I've tried to tell him. He doesn't stop hitting Deborah. He just gets violent with me, too."

Today Mom has labeled herself an unfit mother for allowing those beatings to happen. When I was a child, I blamed her for not saving me. I've assured her that I no longer blame her. Forgiveness softens us and others. Now that I am an adult, I understand the position Mom was in. I don't even blame my dad, because he was sick and didn't know how to recover. I forgave him and have compassion for him.

Christmas of 1969 was difficult for my mom. She had finally gotten pregnant and was very large and uncomfortable. On New Year's Eve, she felt labor pains and went to the hospital. It turned out to be false labor, so she was sent home. One week later, the pain returned. That time they were definitely labor pains.

Dad had just had his car detailed, because he was neurotic about keeping it clean. As they pulled out of the trailer park, Mom's water broke all over my dad's precious, clean car. It was so cold that day that the fluid started freezing to the seat and floor of Dad's no-longer-spotless car. Dad gasped in dismay. Mom was in so much pain that she didn't pay any attention to him.

Half an hour after my mom arrived at the hospital on January 7, 1970, my little sister was born. After the car mishap, I'm sure that learning he had another daughter instead of the son he'd hoped for threw Dad over the edge. Mom said he turned as white as a ghost when he heard the news. He made it clear to her just how unhappy he was, but he said he'd come up with the perfect name. While driving into the hospital parking lot, he'd noticed that the movie theatre across the street was playing *Bonnie and Clyde.*

"As long as we have another girl, we might as well name her Bonnie." he told Mom. "Then we'll have our own Bonnie and Clyde!"

Mom thought it was clever and suggested that my sister's middle name be Mae, for her mother. Dad agreed since my middle name came from his mother.

Mom was at the hospital for a long time, and I was getting scared she might never come back. I knew my mother had gone there to get a baby, but I wasn't sure I liked the idea. I was afraid she would like that baby more than me, and I would be alone.

When she finally came home, I was giddy with excitement. But my mother was paying way too much attention to the big blanket she was carrying. She carefully laid it on the couch. When I tried to squeeze in next to her, she wouldn't let me.

Just then, I saw the blanket move. I asked her, "What's in there?"

"She's your baby sister," she said as she parted the blanket so that I could see the baby's face.

As I leaned toward the little creature and made eye-to-eye contact with her, I thought to myself, *She is not getting any of my toys!* I was going to protect my stuff just like Dad taught me. I would not share my toys, my room, or my parents with her. I especially wasn't going to let her play with my mama panda teddy or her panda babies that Dad bought me when I was born.

The selfishness and lack of trust that my dad had literally beat into me was taking shape. Dad had been molding me like a piece of clay not to touch anything unless it was mine. My stuff was mine and nobody else was allowed to touch it. Mom used to tell me that I was a stingy child and that it was my father's fault.

As a child, I had a friend named Ray. Ray came to play at my house almost every day. I was cruel to him. I told him he wasn't allowed to touch other people's toys, including mine. He could only watch. I wouldn't let him talk unless I told him to. In contrast, when we played at his house, he was a great host. He gave me anything of his that I wanted to play with. I especially loved his swing set, because I didn't have one of my own. I don't know why poor Ray put up with me. He was such a sweet, giving boy, and I was such a mean, stingy brat. I was my father's little girl. His inner life had created my outer life.

The mold of those weaknesses took me a long time to break. My willingness to acknowledge them strengthened my spirit and freed me forever.

After spinning and twirling and showing off the best I knew how to get my mother's attention, I approached the baby again. I leaned over and gawked at her, looked up at my mom, looked at the baby again, and yelled, "I hate her! Take her back!"

Mom picked up my sister and sat down on the couch. She patted the cushion next to her and asked me to please sit so we could have a little talk. She tried to explain to me that the baby was my new sister and that her name was Bonnie. She explained that people don't take babies back to the hospital and that Bonnie was there to stay. She told me babies are not possessions like toys. They are people.

I heard Mom, but I wasn't going to change my mind. I was afraid of Bonnie's presence because I didn't want to share Mom. I was a selfish little girl.

Mom thought she had convinced me that Bon was there to stay and that I was getting used to having a sister. About a week after our mother-daughter talk, she learned that I still wanted Bonnie gone. Mom caught me with my two little fingers aimed and ready to poke my sister's eyes out.

Mom couldn't believe it. She ran over and grabbed my hand to stop me. That time her tone got very serious. She talked to me about what a bad and mean thing I was about to do. She said, "Don't let me ever see you trying to hurt her again."

I never again tried to poke my sister's eyes out, but I did write all over her face with a pen one day. I did a marvelous job! Of course I got caught. That time I was severely punished. Mom told Dad, and I got the belt and the corner once again. I never tried to physically hurt my sister after that. Instead, I played practical jokes on a baby who had no idea what was going on. It made me laugh.

Today my sister is one of my best friends. I transformed my jealousy and anger from our childhood into love and acceptance.

As a baby, Bonnie cried most of the night and day. Mom tried everything to soothe her. Nothing worked. When Bonnie finally cried herself to sleep, Mom got a little break to do housework or get some rest. It's understandable that she was inpatient with me and yelled when I got home from school and woke the baby by talking too loud. Over the weeks, my mother became overwhelmed. She had a crying baby, a little girl in kindergarten who was relentless in disturbing her baby sister, and a husband who was no help at all.

No matter what happened, big or small, Mom would react by crying. She was diagnosed with postpartum depression. Of course, that was more than my dad could handle. His solution was to soothe his own inner madness by drinking. The more Mom cried, the more Dad drank. He didn't know how to support and love any of us. He came home only to sleep, eat, and drink.

Aunt Faye called one day to see how we were all doing with the new addition to our family. Dad didn't sugarcoat the situation. He told her it was a disaster. He said it was all too much for Mom, who was losing her mind. She told him to calm down and tell her how she could help. He begged Aunt Faye to come.

One week later, Aunt Faye was at the front door. She stayed for two weeks, but Mom got no better. Her body, mind, and soul were overcome by the symptoms of postpartum depression. Dad wanted to escape the overwhelming responsibilities of family life that he was unequipped to handle. He announced that he had to take Aunt Faye home and said the best place for his wife and children would be in Nahant. Dad had a mind for fixing things mechanically, but he lacked in the emotional rescue area of compassion.

For 10 days at her parents' in Nahant, Mom paced with my little sister as they both cried. Bonnie's crying was relentless, and it was wearing on Grandpa's nerves. The entire situation became ridiculous. Dad was back at home, drowning his emotions in beer, because he couldn't handle the challenges of family life. He was weak.

The energy we put out, whether positive or negative, is what we attract.

One day while Mom, Bonnie, and I were in Nahant, Dad was preparing to work on a car. He had some trouble with the automatic lift that raised the cars overhead so he could stand while working underneath them. It was stuck, and he kept playing with the lever. While he was trying to move it manually, the lift suddenly released, pinning his leg under the machinery.

Was the accident the work of the universe, making him a prisoner of the home he so often tried to escape? How could he handle his family's problems and his own while he was trapped at home as his leg healed? He was in tremendous physical and emotional pain.

It was years before he was able to return to fixing cars. The accident was devastating financially and a blow to his ego. My father's strand weakened even further.

Everything happened quickly after Dad got hurt. Grandpa offered us a chance to move to Nahant. He told my mother that he would sponsor Dad so that he could enter the United States to live. He also offered Dad a generous job. As soon as Dad could stand on his leg, he would have a job working at Macomber Looms. My parents didn't have much choice. There was no money coming in, and we couldn't stay where we were. Mom and Dad decided that it was a great offer and a smart choice to make.

Dad put our mobile home on the market, and it sold immediately. The furniture sold with the house, so all we needed to move were our personal belongings. Grandpa drove to Hamilton with his station wagon to help us make the move.

The night before we left, Eileen and Lloyd had a going-away party for us. I remember how sad I felt to leave them, but I was thrilled about living at my Gramma and Grampa Hart's house. The party was the kickoff for a series of synchronistic events that would lead me to a spiritual awakening.

Chapter Four

The All American Boy and
The Troubled Yankee

If men as individuals surrender to the call of their elementary instincts, avoiding pain and seeking satisfaction only for their own selves, the result for them all taken together must be a state of insecurity, of fear, and of promiscuous misery.

~ Albert Einstein ~

Life on Pond Street in Nahant, Massachusetts, was completely different from living in Hamilton, Ontario. We all breathed a little easier. Mom had suffered through challenging times during her first six years of marriage. At home with her parents, she finally felt secure. She was still suffering from postpartum depression and dealing with a colicky baby, but it was easier to cope when she had the support of her caring, loving parents.

Dad was grateful to my grandparents, too, but his pride was injured. His leg laid him up for weeks. He was forced to be on his best behavior all the time, and that was torture for him.

I was delighted to be in Nahant. I loved my grandparents and their home, and I enjoyed a newfound sense of security. I knew that Dad wouldn't punish me in front of them. However, the dysfunctional family life that I had endured from a very early age was manifesting in my six-year-old body. I had terrible digestive issues, so my father forced me to drink cod liver oil in orange juice every morning. I held my nose shut, closed my eyes, and drank it down, gagging until I almost threw up. If that treatment didn't work, he made my mother insert a suppository into my bottom. I had to sit in my rocking chair until it worked its magic.

When we were in Nahant, any unpleasant experiences seemed to evaporate under my grandmother's sweet, tender, loving care. Manifestations of negative emotions disappear when you're willing to let go.

My grandparent's house was a wonderland for me, where each room held a different meaning. The living room tapped into my curiosity because I wasn't supposed to go in there. Brocade couches, tasseled pillows, and crystal antiques that turned the sun into rainbows created the perfect setting for a pretend princess.

I loved sneaking into that room after dark because it was the best place in the house to watch the lights on airplanes as they flew over the ocean and landed in Boston. I couldn't hear the planes, so they seemed magical. In the distant city, tall buildings displayed even more twinkling lights. I wondered about the people that lived there and what they were doing. Could they see our house in Nahant?

The Sugar House was my favorite room. It embodied the character of everyone who had ever spent time there. I don't know why Grandma called it the Sugar House, but I liked the sound of it. That's where I went to read, paint, daydream, or just sit in front of the fireplace. It was a room where self-expression came alive, the room where everyone loved to be. The energy of family bonding lived there.

The kitchen was the heart of the house. My grandmother was a wonderful cook, and she made the fluffiest, most delicious scrambled eggs!

I view my heart as an egg, while my soul is the tiny embryo deep in the center. The embryo wasn't able to grow because my heart had been thoroughly cracked, beaten, and scrambled by the age of six. The only way to survive was to grow my protective ego shell thicker and thicker, keeping myself from being born. Today, after peeling back the protective layers, I have been reborn. I am now able to receive gifts and treasures to string on the strand of my life.

My grandparents' guest room was fit for a princess. It was every little girl's dream. Beautiful dolls in silk and lace sat on the pillows, waiting for me to play with them. They were Mom's old dolls. The room was bright and sunny, with a mahogany four-poster bed that had been my great grandmother's. A gorgeous handmade lace doily protected the top of the dresser, which was decorated with darling little antique tea sets and vases. Next to them were photos proudly displaying me and my cousins.

I wanted so much to pick up the beautiful dolls and brush their hair, but my grandma said they were too old to touch. I loved to creep into the guest room and stare at them, pretending they were mine. I almost always got caught.

My dad would hit me with his belt if I touched something that didn't belong to me. Grandma never did that. She just asked me in a kind voice to please come out of the guest room. I always listened to her and did what she asked me to do. It's easier to listen when someone speaks in a calm, kind voice.

When summer came, I made a new friend. Every day my heart would beat fast from the anticipation of playing with her. I can't remember her name, but I remember that she had long, curly brown hair and a beautiful face. My hair was straight and yellow, and l longed to look like her.

She had older brothers who treated her like a princess. I had always wanted big brothers to protect me. I'm not sure if I was giddy from our friendship or from yearning for the kind of life she lived. Her home was a huge New England house perched on a secluded piece of land. It was surrounded by a luscious green lawn where we played all kinds of games. The large windows in the front of the house framed a picturesque view of the ocean and Boston. It looked like a mansion to me.

I would wait and wait, looking out the window until I saw a sign that someone was home. Then I raced down their steep driveway as fast as I could and knocked on the door. I was willing to wait forever for them to come home because they accepted me for me. They never judged me.

When I couldn't play with my friend, Mom let me go outside to play alone. I loved to wander down the street until I came upon a delightful new smell. The memories of nature in Nahant are still fresh. I remember the sweet smell of honeysuckle and wild pink roses, the sound of the ocean crashing on the rocks, and the clear blue sky reflecting off the water. As the warmth of the bright golden sun seeped into my skin and clean ocean air filled my lungs, I felt a sense of peace. Those beautiful days brought the child in me back to life.

Even at such a young age, I had a connection to nature that made me feel free. Freedom and peace are within us all. They wait there for each of us to uncover them through self-realization.

Some memories of that summer in Nahant make me laugh. Almost every day as I walked along, sniffing freshly picked honeysuckle and talking to my invisible friends, two huge, hairy dogs would start following me. Every time it happened, it scared me silly. I loved animals, but those dogs were bigger than I was, and they had so much hair that I thought they had no eyes. I didn't know how they could find me without eyes, so I ran all the way home every time I saw them. I was too young to understand that they were sheepdogs, and their long hair covered their eyes. I never told anyone about them, because I wasn't supposed to leave the yard.

Dad's leg finally healed, and he started his new job in an unfamiliar industry, building new looms at Macomber Looms in Saugus, Massachusetts. Della Macomber, my grandpa's aunt, owned the company at the time. Dad rode to work every day with Grandpa. I'm sure he was feeling the loss of his independence. Dad was a creature of control, so maintaining normal composure must have taken a lot of energy.

Because he couldn't express his emotions, he stored them with all the other unexpressed feelings that fueled his rage. I have compassion for my dad today, because I lived through a similar phase in my own life before I attained the more peaceful stage I inhabit today.

Bonnie was a difficult baby to care for because she still cried a lot of the time. It weighed on Grandpa's patience, and Grandma worried about him. The situation presented Dad with the perfect opportunity to take control again. He drove to Salem, New Hampshire, to look for a place for us to live and found a company that built custom-designed mobile homes. Mom wasn't too happy about living in another trailer, but Dad told her it's all he could afford. As usual, the discussion ended there, and Dad used part of the profit from the sale of our home in Canada to buy a built-to-suit mobile home.

My summer of peace ended in late August when we moved to Salem. I started first grade there, but I don't remember much about it. The only clear memories I have of that year are about being picked on by the other kids. They made fun of my Canadian accent and called me stupid during alphabet lessons. Dad told me I was stupid almost every day, and I started to wonder if he was right.

I knew the alphabet because I had learned it when we lived in Canada, but the kids in Salem made fun of the way I pronounced the letters, especially the letter Z. In Canada, the letter Z was pronounced zed. In my new school, they pronounced it zee.

Being different doesn't make someone stupid, but I didn't know that when I was six. I would go home crying every day. Every morning, I trudged back to school, feeling sad and hopeless. I felt as if I wore a giant bull's-eye on my back. I was the target of the other students' darts of meanness. They stole my self-esteem and further weakened my strand.

I wasn't the only one coming home upset. Dad had to drive to Saugus every day to work with my uncle Rick and Grandpa. It was a long way from our home in New Hampshire. He complained that everyone at work made fun of him because of his severe limp. He wore his good clothes on the way to work and changed into his uniform once he got there. They teased him because he had to hop around on one leg to get into the uniform. Sometimes he saw them whispering together, and they would snicker when they looked at him.

Mom didn't know what to make of Dad's accusations. That kind of behavior was uncharacteristic for her brother and father, but it wasn't like Dad to make up stories.

He was self-conscious because of his limitations and his limp. His co-workers probably weren't trying to be cruel. But Dad's already impaired mind and soul rejected any kind of joking about him. He just wasn't capable of embracing the challenges in life and letting them go. He lived in denial.

Although his fellow workers teased Dad, Aunt Della took a real shine to his work and personality. She invited him to do some odd jobs for extra pay. Her acceptance definitely fed his ego, so our family life became almost normal. Dad wasn't mean, cruel, or abusive to Mom or me. He was too busy working for and pleasing Aunt Della.

We stayed in Salem less than a year. Ginger, Mom's childhood friend, heard about some land in Kingston, New Hampshire, that was being sold for unbelievably low prices. Dad was ecstatic because it would give him a project to work on. He used the rest of the money from the Hamilton home sale and bought a piece of land. Before long, our new address was New Boston Road, Kingston.

Just saying the name of that place used to give me chills. Moving to Kingston was the beginning of the worst years of my life. I thought I would never escape from that place. It was hell, and I prayed every night for a way out.

If I have learned anything from my awakening into peace, it is that nothing is permanent. Impermanence enables evolution on every level, which makes each day an opportunity for transformation. The only requirement is desire.

I started the second grade at the DJ Bakie Elementary school. My teacher, Mrs. Amazine, was an elderly lady and not very patient with young minds. One day, she was trying to teach us how to tell time, and it wasn't working. She became frustrated and screamed at us like crazy. I closed my eyes and covered my ears with my hands because the yelling transported me to our living room where I stood with my pants down, waiting for a beating from Dad. I was always on edge as I waited for Mrs. Amazine to hit me, but she never did.

Teachers should serve as sources of inspiration that help light our paths with their experience. It wasn't until 41 years later that my experience with Mrs. Amazine taught me about timing and patience.

Our lives shifted again in the fall of 1972. My dad was fed up with working in Saugus for Mom's family. His leg was as good as it was going to be, and he was ready to work on cars again. Mom had started a small daycare and watched two other toddlers in addition to my sister. It helped her earn some money and kept Bonnie occupied.

Dad saw an ad for a head mechanic's position at a service station in Seabrook. He drove there to meet the owner, who turned out to be another old guy looking for someone to take over his lease. History repeated itself. Shortly after my dad started working there, the owner came to appreciate his mechanical ability and work ethic. When the old gentleman retired, Dad took over. He had regained control. Dad was back in his element, doing what came easily to him.

A part of me wishes my father could have channeled that mechanical knowledge into fixing himself. What kind of a man would he have grown into had he been able to repair himself through self-realization and acceptance?

Dad and the other guys from work would go down the street to the Chinese restaurant for a few drinks after work, which usually lasted through dinnertime. When he got home, he would have a few more beers. It became a daily habit after the old guy gave Dad the service station. Mom finally got fed up and told him he was drinking too much. She said it wasn't healthy emotionally or physically. He responded by saying, "What the hell do you think you know about me? Just because you're a college graduate doesn't mean you know a goddamn thing."

Mom's fragile self-confidence was repeatedly shot down by my dad. He resented her education. His resentments were suffocating him, and his only way out was through drinking. I know from firsthand experience that hiding behind alcohol progressively evolves into alcoholism. Alcoholism is a disease of the body and mind, which ultimately affects the spirit. The solution is to transcend the mind and heal the body. The miracle of spirit is restored and the gifts of life's treasures can be strung upon the strand of life.

Poor Mom was not a good cook, but she tried. Dad was selfish, ungrateful, and disrespectful. On a good night, he ate in silence as if he wasn't even in his body. On bad nights, he would pitch his dinner across the room, smashing the plate and flinging food everywhere.

On the nights when he decided dinner was edible, we breathed a sigh of relief. He had a rule that once he ate, his drinking was done. If he tossed the food around the room, alcohol became his dinner, and he would have us for dessert. On those nights, Mom would sob quietly while she cleaned up his mess and then go into their bedroom and shut the door.

At first, Mom tried to make sure Bonnie and I were in our rooms when Dad's truck came roaring up the driveway. But I was an energetic kid, and I didn't want to go to my room every night when he got home. When I didn't retreat to my room, Dad would stumble around until he saw me and then stop and stare. If I said anything at all, Dad would point his finger at me and say, "Shut your fucking mouth! Don't you know kids are meant to be seen and not heard? You're to speak only when spoken to. Do you understand me?"

I knew that my answer had to be word-for-word what he wanted to hear or he would grab for me. If he missed, I would run down the hall to my room. Depending on his mood, he would either forget about hitting me or drag me out of my room and hit me upside the head. If my answer processed as the correct one in his alcohol-soaked mind, he would order me to get him a beer. He treated me for years like his private bar maid.

Some nights I stayed in my room and avoided his abusive behavior. But when I was unavailable, he turned his anger on my mother. I would hear her crying as he abused her either verbally or physically. I prayed for help as I cried myself to sleep on those nights.

The first phase of my healing journey was experiencing life as a victim and witnessing my parent's struggles. *The miseries of our past are invitations to change our present.*

∿☙

In the third grade, my assigned seat was next to a boy named Benjamin Franklin. The things he did grossed me out. He was always picking his nose and lifting his rear at me and farting. Then he would laugh with a snort. One day he said something real fresh to the teacher. She grabbed him out of his chair and tried to escort him to the hall for a time out. He screamed, "Let go of me, you fat pig," and ripped the scarf out of her pony tail. He was punching her with all his might to intentionally hurt her. Witnessing him verbally and physically hurting my teacher brought up strong emotions, and I began to cry.

Two minutes after that upsetting drama, the principle came in to tell me I was being dismissed early because my grandparents were there to pick me up. Mom was in the hospital having my little brother, so Bonnie and I would be staying in Nahant over Thanksgiving break.

Dad had never wanted children, and he certainly didn't want another girl. He watched my mother take her birth control pill every single night to make sure she wouldn't get pregnant. In January of 1973, my mom had pneumonia. The doctor put her on an antibiotic, but he didn't give her any drug warnings. Mom had no way of knowing that the prescription could interfere with her birth control pills.

Mom was consumed with panic at the thought of telling Dad she was pregnant again. She had become friends with a woman named Carol who lived on the street behind us. Carol was a fabulous cook, and she loved having us over for Sunday meals. Mom told Carol her secret and shared her concern about telling my dad. Carol came up with the idea of having us over for one of her fantastic meals the following Sunday, which was Mother's Day. She told my mom to bring the coffee brandy, and she would supply the milk. They planned to tell Dad the news after they'd gotten a few drinks into him.

When the time came, Mom nervously blurted out, "I'm pregnant." Dad's behavior shifted in an instant. Dinner was over before it began, and Dad left without saying a word. His way of teaching Mom a lesson was giving all of us the silent treatment for the next two months. He got up every day in silence and came home drunk most nights. It didn't matter to him that the pregnancy wasn't Mom's fault.

Mom was no stranger to Dad's erratic behavior patterns. She had been down that all-too-familiar road before. She would no longer be subjected to living in silence or be the victim of his constant drunkenness.

Once school was out for the summer, Mom packed us up to spend the summer in Nahant. My grandparents were in Nova Scotia, but they said we could use their house. When we were ready to leave, Mom tried to start the car. Nothing happened. She had made the mistake of telling Dad about our plans to leave, and he had removed the starter cable so that we would be stranded. It was yet another way he tried to control our lives. He wouldn't communicate. He drank too much. He beat us. Why did he try to keep us as prisoners? Was he turning into a replica of his own father?

Mom's parents picked us up three hours later and drove us to Nahant. I'm sure that must have blown my dad's ego to kingdom come, especially after receiving Mom's note. She told him she was leaving him because his abuse was affecting all of us on a physical, mental, and emotional level.

It was Dad's chance to soul search. Taking responsibility for your actions is a sign of strength.

Once I was back in the comfort of my grandparent's home, a sense of relief poured through me. We had all finally begun to relax toward the end of July when my dad started calling to beg Mom to come home. I prayed every night that she would never go back there. When Dad said he would gladly come to pick us up, Mom said, "No. Don't waste your gas or your time, because I am not going back!" When I heard her say that, I put my hands together in prayer and thanked God.

The third weekend in August, Dad showed up without any warning. He seemed remorseful. When he leaned toward me with a hug instead of a slap, I flinched anyway. He had a pleasant smile on his face as we drove down the hill for dinner that evening. After we ate, Bonnie and I played on the beach while my parents sat on a bench and had a serious talk. Dad told Mom how deeply sorry he was. He promised he would never do it again.

Mom said those were always his famous last words. When I asked her why she believed him that time, she said his sincerity was real. She decided we would go back on a trial basis to see if things would work. If she hadn't been pregnant, she might have made a different decision.

Did he want us back because he really loved us or because his difficulties in life were too torturous for him to face alone? How long could he resist his difficulties before his strand would break again?

Dad was under extreme stress, trying to perform his mechanic duties and run the gas station at the same time. On top of that, the old guy's wife retired from doing the bookkeeping. Dad asked Mom to take over the bookkeeping job. It must have been very difficult for my father to ask, because he had always put Mom down and called her stupid. He had to swallow his pride because he needed her office skills. Mom thought it might earn her the respect she deserved if Dad saw her doing the trade she had learned, so she said yes.

I don't know how she did it, but Mom became a woman of all trades. Even though she was pregnant, she filled in for employees who didn't show for work. She learned how to pump gas, check the oil, and wash windshields. She spent long days keeping the accounts for the business and doing anything else Dad needed her to do. At first everything ran smoothly between them at home and at work.

Of course, it wasn't long before Dad returned to his old patterns. He began to accuse Mom of stealing money and robbing his business blind. She kept trying to prove herself to him. One Friday, my mom had to open the service station because the employee who was scheduled to open that day didn't show. She was nine months pregnant and ready to deliver at any time, but Dad had gotten drunk the night before and was so hung over that he was sick.

Dad was so self-centered that he couldn't take responsibility for himself, his business, or his pregnant wife. Mom was pumping gas in the cold with snow flurries coming down while Dad nursed a hangover. He had conned her into going by saying that if anyone from Souza, the owners of British Petroleum, were to drive by and see the station closed, they could pull their product and that would end their income. After repeatedly accusing her of stealing from him, he persuaded her to bail him out by saying, "After all, it is our business now."

How could my dad send his pregnant wife to perform manual labor in winter weather? Dad's weaknesses were progressively injuring him and those around him. Injury leads to despair. Despair leads to anger. Grab for the pearl of bravery. Hear the injury as a message and listen.

At 3:00 a.m. the next morning, Mom was awakened by labor pains. Dad must have won the battle with his self-induced hangover, because he took Mom to Exeter hospital. At 7:00 a.m. on November 19, 1973, Dad finally got his wish. Their third child was a boy. They named him Scott Allen Clyde Adams. Scott would later take on the nickname that Dad's family gave him: Damn Yankee.

Dad pulled a fast one on Mom while she was in the hospital. She found out from the doctor that Dad had signed a paper giving permission for the doctor to tie Mom's tubes, preventing her from ever getting pregnant again. She was furious, but she let the incident go. Maybe she thought that life with Dad would become better since he finally had his son. If so, it was the biggest lie she ever told herself.

The only way we had a chance for a normal life was for my dad to discover his higher self through facing his weaknesses. Normalcy would also require that Mom let the dignity of her soul rise high enough that she would flatly refuse to be a victim.

But Dad was too stubborn, and Mom had too many fears and doubts. My hope and prayer was to someday be free of their calamities. I knew there were more pearls to add to the strand of life, including true love, joy, and laughter.

Mom knew her dream of a normal family life had been crushed before she even left the hospital. During her week-long stay, Dad's routine was typical. He went to work every morning and showed up at the hospital drunk every night. Mom had become friends with her roommate,

Melinda. They had given birth to their baby boys on the same day. When Dad showed up wearing his greasy green uniform, barely able to walk and slurring his words, Mom slouched down in the bed and tried to hide under the blankets.

Mom envied Melinda. Wayne was an adoring husband who brought flowers, talked with his wife, and treated her with respect. It made Mom smile to see them together until her own husband stumbled in, smelling of whisky and cigarettes and falling all over the bed. The nurses knew exactly what was going on. They had to come in frequently to ask him to settle down and lower his voice.

One night Dad decided to ask the nurses some questions about the baby, and they ignored him because he was filthy drunk. His foul-mouthed yelling started after he noticed that his son's body would quiver every few seconds while Mom was holding him. It turned out that Scott had been born with an underdeveloped nervous system. Dad's behavior got so bad that he was asked to leave. He did as they asked, but not without making a scene on his way out the door.

Mom spent Thanksgiving in the hospital. The nurses put linens on the tables, lit candles, and shut off the industrial lights. Of course, Dad spent the entire day with his friend John, doing what they did best. He drove to the hospital drunk. He wasn't embarrassed by his behavior, but Mom was.

It was clear that he hadn't eaten all day. The nurses were about to serve dinner, and Dad said, "Well, I'm not staying looong and I'm not haaaving dinner." Then he stood there, wobbling back and forth. The nurses were in no mood for his shenanigans. That time they asked him to leave immediately. Mom was so humiliated that she started to cry. Melinda's family saw the whole drunken mess.

Why was my dad still hiding behind alcohol? He finally had the son he always wanted. Maybe he was afraid to be a real father. *Fear is the enemy if not embraced.*

On the day Mom and my baby brother were to be discharged from the hospital, Mom waited and waited, but Dad didn't show up. Eventually, John's wife Beverly arrived to drive them home. Beverly told Mom that Clyde had called her because he had no one to cover work for him.

Mom said, "I wouldn't expect anything more from him. All he has done since Scott was born is disappoint and embarrass me." Mom never got over it. She had given Dad plenty of time to make arrangements to pick them up and take them home from the hospital.

When a mother takes her child home for the first time, it's a special moment. It's a time for family bonding and a celebration of life. Dad dismantled that day and lowered it to an inconvenience and a favor performed by a friend. Mom's disappointments and embarrassments turned to anger when my dad was unable to participate in that milestone. He wasn't reliable, and he was weak. He was no longer capable of being his best. He wasn't willing to view his pain as an opportunity to prosper.

Grandma drove me and my sister home from Nahant the next day. When we got there, Dad was having a party. The house was cloudy with cigarette smoke and filled with beer-swilling, loud-mouthed fools. Mom said Grandma was so disgusted by the scene that she gracefully ripped him a new one. Dad was a little afraid of her for some reason. Maybe she reminded him of his own mother, who was a tough cookie. In front of all my dad's friends, Grandma chastised her son-in-law.

"What is wrong with you?" she asked. "This isn't the men's club. This is the home where your wife and children live, and you're disrespecting them. You will not drink and smoke around my granddaughters and new grandson. Do you understand that?" He laughed at first and then realized she meant business. "Please ask your friends to leave," she said.

He was acting like a boy trapped in a man's body. He needed the discipline that he was unable to give himself.

While Grandma helped Mom with the baby, Dad shuffled his buddies out the front door. Grandma stayed for a couple of days to help Mom, and Dad was on his best behavior. After Grandma left, Mom and Dad fought every day.

The strand of their relationship was broken and unhealthy. Dad didn't have a sensitive bone in his body. All he cared about was his business. His only goal was to make money so he could buy toys to show off to his family in Canada. He was vain and lacked humility.

Dad coerced Mom into going back to work as soon as her mother left. She had no time to recover or bond with the baby. Mom put Bonnie and Scott into daycare, and she worked while I was at school. During school vacations, I went to daycare at Pat Bralesford's house with my brother and sister. Mrs. Bralesford lived on a farm and had nine children. I pretended I was one of her kids. She was physically tough but also soft and feminine. She had a gentle voice and a smile on her face. Mrs. Bralesford conducted her household duties with ease and calmness.

Bonnie and I loved to play in the barn. I remember the smell of the hay and the exhilarating scariness of the cobweb-infested loft. Most of all, I loved all the farm animals. I was in heaven. When we are unhappy and constantly feel insecure, our spirit protects us by allowing us to pretend and fantasize about what we really want and need. It satisfies us for a while.

All through the fourth and fifth grades, I looked forward to getting on the school bus. My bus driver, Mrs. Doliver, was wonderful. She was beautiful and wore her hair like Jackie Kennedy's. Her caring smile welcomed me when I boarded her bus, and I often wished she would adopt me and drive me far away.

Mrs. Sykes, my music teacher, was a tiny little thing who looked older than the hills. Her skin seemed to be falling off her body. But her tiny little fingers played the piano like she was born for that purpose. I loved Mrs. Sykes and Mrs. Doliver because they treated me with kindness and patience. They didn't yell at me or hit me when I made a mistake. Going to school kept my spirit alive. It was far better than my dysfunctional life at home where I could feel tension in the air every minute. When the bus stopped at my driveway at the end of a school day and I began the walk to the front door, it was like breathing poison into my lungs.

My little red-headed, bratty brother was treated like the golden child. I had finally been replaced by the boy Dad always wanted. The only benefit I gained was that I was allowed to grow my hair long. Scott was a sickly little boy, so he could do no wrong in Dad's eyes. His life as a child was the opposite of mine. Scott received love, nurturing, and joy from my dad.

I was still my dad's slave. He no longer referred to me as his pride and joy or his sunshine. I was nothing more than a handy target when he needed to release his anger. He yelled at me ferociously and beat me with a belt on a regular basis.

Even though my brother could bring my dad out of the dark and into the light, it never lasted. What was so dark for Dad that his darkness stole my light? I grew up wondering if that was how life was supposed to be. I didn't want to believe it, so I prayed every night for the day when I could leave and strengthen my strand, freeing myself so I could explore what life really was.

1976 was the Bicentennial to celebrate the Declaration of Independence. The irony is remarkable, because independence was something that I yearned for. I wanted to be free to navigate my own soul on the path of independence. I remember feeling as if my whole world was spiraling downward because I was my father's daughter.

From the age of three, my life was like watching my mother's pearls fall, bounce, and roll away in slow motion. It was a constant struggle for survival. I was never able to achieve my father's standards of perfection. I buried myself deeper and deeper within a shell for survival. I lived in constant fear and sadness. Yet, dealing with my dad's tumultuous moods, which were caused by his own buried truths and demons, has become the most wonderful gift of my life. His inability to free himself from his self-made prison became the catalyst for my own rebirth.

Chapter Five

Growing Pains

Children are living messages we send to a time
we will not see.

~ Neil Postman ~

In the fall of 1976, I finally made it to Sanborn Regional Middle School. I felt less enthusiasm than the other kids that year because I was grieving the loss of a friend. The previous winter had not only taken someone from me, but it had also blindsided me with the reality of tragedy at a vulnerable age.

I was already experiencing the effects of daily trauma to my body, mind, and soul. The senseless death of a close friend compounded the trauma by leaving a hole in my heart. I can still picture those beautiful brown eyes peeking over her glasses and that mile-wide smile.

It had been a typical winter for New Hampshire, very cold with lots of snow. Most kids my age loved sledding, snowmobiling, and ice skating, but my dad seldom allowed me to play in the snow with my friends. I was an inmate in his prison. That's why I looked forward to school and seeing my friends every day.

I had two special girlfriends, Barbara and Sandra. We were a threesome, at least in school. They stopped inviting me to play after school because they knew the answer would be no. I never invited them to my house because I was too embarrassed to expose them to my dad. Sandra and Barbara became close because they spent all of their free time together, and I felt left out.

They were nice girls who were always very kind to me, especially during school lunch time. My nerves always spiked right before lunch. Everyone else had lovely and convenient sandwich bags that folded over neatly or they had a hot lunch pass. I unwrapped my ketchup and cheese sandwich under the table because Mom wrapped my lunch in waxed paper. When the kids made fun of me or made remarks about how poor I was, Barbara and Sandra comforted me. They were my true friends.

One Monday morning in Mr. Cole's fifth-grade home room, an announcement broadcast over the intercom had a devastating effect on me. The principle said that our school had experienced a loss over the weekend. When he said Sandra's full name, my heart began to ache so much that I thought it would stop beating. I couldn't swallow, my arms and legs went numb, and I couldn't speak. I stared straight ahead as tears rolled down my face and into my mouth, salty waterfalls coming from the hole that had just opened in my heart. I had never experienced the grief of losing someone close before. I remember thinking it had to be a mistake.

As tears splashed into my lap, I whispered, "How could you be gone? You're one of my best friends. Why did this happen to you?" I would never get to tell her that I loved her. How would I ever get over the loss of my friend?

I didn't know that the glory of allowing yourself to experience grief can shake the pearls of your soul loose.

The memory of Sandra's smile was fresh in my mind's eye that day, but for how long? Would I forget her smile, the sound of her laugh, and her generous kindness? She had made me feel liked—even loved. I have never forgotten Sandra. She taught me how to smile in difficult times.

The moment I heard that she was gone, I learned that human life is impermanent. I was too young to contemplate the real life challenge and lesson, but that experience planted the seed. That seed would sprout and grow once it was watered with additional experiences.

Barbara must already have known about Sandra because she didn't say a word after the announcement. She didn't even look up. She was clutching an eraser on which she had written Sandra's name in ink. I tried to get her attention, but she had shut down. Barbara and I had only each other, and she wouldn't even look at me. I thought she blamed me. Having Barbara shut me out made me cry even harder. My sobbing became uncontrollable, and I cried so much and so hard that I began to hyperventilate.

Later that day, I learned the horrific details of my beloved friend's passing. She was an amazing ice skater, and she had gone to her favorite place to practice. On the way home, she was walking on the side of the road because the sidewalks were covered with snow. The road was slippery that day, and a car lost control and hit her.

Sandra always tied her skate laces together and draped the skates around her neck. She must have left the blade guards off, because one of the skate blades struck her head when the car hit her. Sandra died on the spot. It happened so quickly that she really never knew what hit her. Thank goodness she didn't suffer.

Even though it was hard for me to think about her tragic death, it was all I could think about. It consumed me, and I had nightmares for weeks. I know it was even harder for Barbara. I never saw her smile again. I tried very hard to be a good friend to her, but she couldn't open her heart and let me in. She was afraid to get hurt again.

Something about that life event must have touched my dad's heart, because the following weekend he offered to take Barbara and me out for Chinese food. I jumped at the opportunity to have Barbara see that my dad had a compassionate side. That dinner was the last time Barbara and I did anything together. Sandra had been the glue in our threesome. With Sandra gone, my friendship with Barbara couldn't survive. I grieved for months.

My relationship with Sandra and Barbara had served as a temporary reprieve from a hellish home life. They accepted me for me. They allowed me to express myself without judgment. They didn't steal or squash the essence of my being. I didn't have to wear a protective mask around them, which is how I had to live at home. I am forever thankful to Sandra and Barbara for giving me the gift of friendship and an open heart. I am happy to say my heart today is healed and wide open. Those two precious pearls taught me about a love for life that I could only truly experience after finding myself.

When I turned 11, I started to notice that other parents didn't threaten their kids. I realized how dysfunctional my family life was, but there was no escape. It was only when I was out of the house that I felt alive and free. As I transitioned into my teen years, I was always in survival mode. I did what I had to do to satisfy and serve my father. It was my only option. When I deviated from his tyrannical ways, I suffered his wrath. I didn't speak unless he told me to. I was an inmate in the prison of my own home, where I was verbally, physically, and emotionally abused on a regular basis.

The repeated abuse affected me on the deepest levels imaginable. It left me heartless and numb for years. The witness of my conscious took over during each episode of abuse to protect me from fully feeling anything.

When I was in the third grade, Bonnie was in the first. Scott was three years old and still staying with Mrs. Bralesford during the day. Mom and Dad were still at each other's throats at the service station. I was alone in the house every morning until the bus came to pick me up for school at 11:30 a.m. I always had a list of house chores from my mom and a ton of outdoor work to do for my father. On top of that, I had to finish my homework.

For lunch, I would make Kraft macaroni and cheese with ketchup. I loved the smell of macaroni cooking while I vacuumed the living room floor. If I had time after my chores were done, I'd sit in Dad's chair and watch TV. The lineup included "Happy Days," "Sanford and Son," "Hollywood Squares," and "The Price is Right." I'd watch as many as I could before the bus showed up.

Mom needed my help because she spent every day working at the service station. She had me do the laundry, dishes, vacuuming, and dusting. A part of me resented her for that. I was just a kid. Why was I doing my mom's jobs? The other part of me grinned at the idea of being alone without a warden. Dad's chores for me included raking the leaves, mowing the lawn, and tending the garden. At the time, I hated him for it, because everything had to meet his ridiculous standards of perfection.

What was the source of his obsession with perfection? It was the illusion of a scared man's ego and of a mind that wasn't open. Today, I view his perfectionism as part of a perfect plan, the spiritual plan for teaching me how not to be. There is no room on my strand for closed-minded perceptions of perfectionism. The person I am now is accepting and open-minded, and that is perfect enough for me.

If I missed one leaf on the lawn or didn't finish everything on his list, Dad went ballistic. He would throw things at me and turn red in the face. The veins in his neck would pop out as he dashed at me with his arm cocked to strike. He screamed, "You stupid, little, fucking bitch. I thought I told you to rake every leaf, not leaving a single one!" By the time he finished the sentence, he would have struck me in the head at least twice, hitting hard enough to knock the saliva right out of my mouth.

I wanted to run away as fast as I could or sprout wings and fly away, because he usually finished his outbursts by beating me in the head all the way to the corner of the living room, where he shoved my face into the wall. He often made me stand there for hours. The whole time I stood there, I wished he would disappear and never come back.

He was so crazy that he made me feel crazy. I couldn't remember anything. I lost the ability to think. He kept telling me to repeat back to him what he'd told me to do. I didn't want to answer him because my answer was always wrong. I just wanted to be allowed to explain or express myself. It was so frustrating that I felt my own rage building toward him.

Sometimes I resorted to lying to avoid trouble. I learned very fast that was not the best strategy. He had always told me, "You better not lie to me. I'll know if you do. I have eyes in the back of my head." I believed him. If I did lie, I got the belt across my bare legs and then had to stand in the corner. He said if I told the truth, I would still be in trouble, but he wouldn't hit me. All that meant was that I wouldn't have belt marks on my legs to cover up.

As I stood in the corner and sobbed, I asked myself why. What had I done to deserve the way he treated me? I became so angry that I wanted to beat him in the head and see how he liked it. All the while, he arrogantly sat in his chair, sipping beer and smoking cigarettes. From his throne, King Clyde would order me to stop crying or he'd give me something to cry about.

I had to cry. It was the only way I could release some of the negative energy he beat into me. The more I cried, the more he abused me by calling me a "fucking stupid meathead," among other gross names. He told me I would never make anything of myself because I was too stupid, just like my mother. One of his favorite lines was, "You're a nothing. You're good for nothing. You will be nothing. You're a good-for-nothing, stupid little bitch!"

When the tears ran dry, all I could hear was his voice flowing through me as the horrible names he called me repeated with the ebb and flow of my blood. I spent years trying to prove my worthiness to him and myself, because I carried his voice in my head.

Today I am free. Inner peace has quieted my mind. The acceptance of my experience of misery has fashioned me with pearls of wisdom.

While young girls in normal families enjoyed movie nights and popcorn, I endured random acts of rage and violence. I heard and felt everything he said and did to me, but I dumped it all deep inside my cells in order to survive. I made sure it stayed so deep that it blocked my reactions. It was easier to be the witness of my own abuse.

Sometimes Dad's dark side was hidden away for a while. He would tell jokes, play jokes, and be filled with laughter. When he was like that, his laugh came from the little boy inside him, and it was genuine and captivating. I enjoyed that side of my father, and I gobbled it up and held it tight inside until the next time.

Dad and I shared one common interest, a love for animals, which made me wonder why he liked to hunt. However, his relationship with animals was much different from mine. He considered them possessions that must obey him, which was similar to the way he treated his family. My approach was to love animals for their pure innocence, their ability to live in the present moment, and their willingness to love unconditionally.

One day, Dad surprised me with a dog just for me. He was a German shepherd puppy about eight months old, and he was already huge. He had unusual coloring for a German shepherd, mostly rust with a streak of black down his back to the end of his tail. We named him Randy. He had a very dominant personality, and he was much too big for the house. When he would lie down, he covered the entire length of the living room floor from the tip of his nose to the tip of his tail.

When he first came to us, Randy was a sweet dog, but he challenged my father. Mom kept a bowl of fake fruit on the coffee table, and Randy grabbed the orange and started chewing it like a toy. Mom yelled at Dad to take it away before Randy destroyed it. When my father reached for the orange, Randy growled at him.

With Dad's warped sense of humor, he thought the growling was funny, so he kept taunting Randy to make him growl even more. It took my dad nearly an hour to get that orange. After that, he showed all of his friends the game to demonstrate what a vicious dog he had. Eventually, I became as afraid of Randy as I was of Dad.

It was the beginning of a new nightmare for me. I had to take care of that dog by myself. He scared the crap out of me every day. My father installed a dog run, and Randy was chained to it all the time. It turned him into a psychologically deranged horror. I felt so sad about what had happened to Randy that it made me cry. But I was so afraid of him that I would sneak out with his food when he was at the far end of the run. He always saw me coming and speed toward me with his ears pinned back. When he reached the end of the run, he lunged at me. I threw his food down and ran.

Filling Randy's water bowl posed a whole different challenge. It was a huge trough, the kind that horses use. Of course, it was smack dab in the middle of Randy's yard where I couldn't get to it without him jumping on me and knocking me down. My father wouldn't help me even though he knew I was terrified of the dog. He forced me to change the water, and I hated him for it.

My next surprise was a horse named Mitsy. I adored horses, so I was thrilled. I loved spending time with Mitsy until the day she kicked me so hard I nearly stopped breathing. After that, I was afraid to clean her stall again. My reluctance to do my horse chores earned me another blow to the head from my father as he again called me a stupid bitch.

My other middle-school pets were a cat named Squiggy and a parakeet. One day, my dad screamed at me because he saw a few shells in the bottom of the birdcage. "Damn it, I told you if you want these animals, you need to take care of them. I'm sick and tired of telling you. Now do it!"

"Okay! I will," I said.

I was so mad that I took the cage outside and shook it upside down. The door came open and out flew my pretty bird. I cried and cried. Finally, I went inside and reluctantly told Dad that I'd lost my birdie. He smirked and said, "That'll teach ya. He'll probably get eaten by something bigger."

I don't know why I'd expected some comfort from him, but his unfeeling reaction hurt. I cried myself to sleep that night, knowing that if I hadn't overreacted, I would still have my bird.

Even though my dad's lack of empathy led to experiences with pets that left me with internal scars, my soul holds a huge amount of love and compassion for all animals. Animals reach the part of my core that brings me peace. Scars are the beauty marks of old wounds that have healed. They are the pearls that never lose their brilliance.

The concept of hunting animals has always sent panic through my body. I could never understand how my father could go into the woods and shoot at a defenseless, innocent creature. How could he look up into the sky and shoot a duck or a Canadian goose?

I didn't want any part of hunting, but my dad was still trying to groom me as a son even though he finally had a real one. My little brother Scott was a toddler during my middle-school years, so he was too young to join Dad in his Grizzly Adams adventures. That left me. It's no wonder I ended up a tomboy.

I was often summoned to walk through the woods at ridiculous times of the day so my father could shoot a deer or something. The only part of hunting that I enjoyed was setting up targets and learning how to shoot. Dad was teaching me something and spending time with me. I was pretty good at hitting the targets, so he had no reason to yell. But he stopped taking me hunting once he found guys from work to go with him.

As much as I hated the thought of him shooting an animal, I'd cherished the opportunity to spend time with him, even if it was on his terms. It was one of the few times my father made me feel that he cared. I felt that he accepted me in those precious moments. Every child needs the accepting love of a parent who can show love and supportive guidance.

Even though he no longer took me hunting with him, Dad still got me involved. It makes me feel sick when I remember the times he forced me to pluck wild birds and gut them or scale, debone, and filet the fish he caught. I drew the line when he told me to skin and gut a rabbit, and I was severely punished for it. I didn't care. I was not going to dismantle that beautiful, defenseless rabbit.

Did my reaction come from the way he treated me, his defenseless daughter? The damage he did to me as I stood on the cusp of becoming a young woman was dreadful. Yet, my long history of damage became the beauty of today's pearls.

My father controlled every single aspect of my life during my middle school years and through the first years in high school. He dictated what and how I ate. He told me when and for how long I could groom myself. He told me how to wash dishes and cook food. He dictated when I could speak and limited what I was allowed to say. He controlled who I spent time with and what I did in my spare time. If I didn't live within his rules and live up to his expectations and commands, I was punished.

The chronic misery of his tyranny has now been transformed into my strand of empowerment. It feels grand to be alive, and I wear a pearl of gratitude for my dad.

During the Carter administration when our country was in a fuel crisis, cars lined up for miles waiting for fuel at Dad's service station. He was working all the time and making pretty good money from the used car lot he'd added to his business. By then, he had taught me how to roll myself under a car to change an oil filter, the oil, and the spark plugs. I didn't mind learning some of his trade. Sometimes he even treated me with a tiny bit of respect, especially when I stopped handing him a wrench when he asked for pliers or vice grips. He showed me all the tools and told me their names just once. If I handed him the wrong one, he told me I was stupid. I started rolling my eyes when I knew he couldn't see me.

The older I got, the more I realized there was something seriously wrong, unethical, demoralizing, and frightening in our family. It was creating total disharmony in my upbringing, which would ultimately leave scars that penetrated into every cell in my body. His unthinkable actions forced me to surrender my identity.

As I repeatedly struggled to meet my dad's yearning for unachievable perfection, Mom turned a deaf ear and blind eye to my plight. I blamed her for not stepping in and saving me, but I didn't understand the position she was in. The older I got, the more disturbing he became. I cried myself to sleep most nights, and I often wished him dead.

Thomas Carlyle said, "Adversity is the diamond dust Heaven polishes its jewels with." That quote is bittersweet to me now. As I lived through the hardships, I didn't think I would ever escape them, let alone become polished by them. When we're exposed to ugly situations that appear as if they will never end, it's important to remember that nothing is permanent. Every seemingly negative circumstance can be used to improve and refine. Pearls don't shine without the frictions of life.

Dad's mood shifted as quickly as the wind in a storm. At home, things were progressively getting worse. Mealtimes had always been grueling.

I wasn't allowed to drink anything until my food was gone. When I had eaten everything on my plate and every drop of milk was gone, I could ask to be excused. He would inspect my plate and cup to make sure they were empty before allowing me to leave the table.

Dad started to cook, and he made foods that I didn't like. One stands out in my memory. His disgusting fish cakes were loaded with onions. The fishy onion smell made me gag. If I threw up, I would be punished and sent to bed with no dinner that night and, perhaps, none the next night. I didn't mind, because avoiding him and his lousy cooking was worth going hungry.

We had a well for our water supply in Kingston. When I washed the dishes, Dad had me fill one sink with soapy water and the other sink with clean water. If I ever got caught letting the water run while rinsing the dishes, I wasn't allowed to shower for a month.

As it was, he only let me shower once a week. The rest of the time, I had to take a bath in no more than two or three inches of water. I was expected to bathe, shave my legs, and wash and rinse my hair in that small amount of water. I was so embarrassed to go to school with greasy hair. Always feeling dirty made my self-esteem plummet even further. I resented being deprived of the simple pleasure of a hot shower and soap.

Dad followed the same bath regimen he prescribed for me, with one exception. After he'd run his bath, he would call my name. That's all he had to say. I took a deep breath, and my legs carried me to the bathroom. As my father sat naked in a puddle of water in the tub, I was forced to wash his hair. He tried to cover his privates with a face cloth, but it wasn't an effective method. It was an unnatural, unhealthy situation that no father should impose on his impressionable young daughter.

I knew it was wrong, but he left me no other option. It was the most repulsive, filthy, revolting task I ever performed for him. That was when I knew he had some serious issues. He degraded me and sickened me. I filled the cup in the only place I could find enough water without reaching in front of him. The water was grey with filth. As I poured soapy water over his head, I purposely aimed the stream toward his eyes.

He didn't know I did it intentionally, but it made him mad anyway. "What the fuck is the matter with you? Can't you aim? I'm going to slap the stupidness out of you when I get out of here!"

My mother was too scared to stop his deranged behavior. I resented her for that. I acted out and misbehaved for her every chance I got when my father wasn't around. Of course, I would usually get in trouble for that, too, because she tattled on me.

I was getting older, but my spirit was shrinking. My behavior was a direct result of how I was being raised. Subconsciously, I was getting even with my parents while my ego continued to strive for acceptance.

For years, I had tried to impress my father when I learned something new. His reaction was usually to make fun of me. I took ballet lessons and showed him the positions. He laughed and said, "You look like a stupid dancing crane." I stood there in tears, my mixed emotions swirling and shifting. I despised him for making me feel that way, but I loved him because he was my father.

The excitement that had filled and uplifted me as I learned to dance was replaced in an instant by a heavy fog of defeat that burdened my spirit. I craved acceptance from him. I needed his approval. I wanted him to tell me what a great job I'd done and hug and kiss me. I longed for his smile to come from his heart and not his ego.

Instead, he said, "What am I paying for? These aren't dance lessons. You look ridiculous!" When he judged and humiliated me, I wanted to smack him in the head for hurting me. My ballet and tap shoes were retired very quickly and so was my self esteem.

As horrible as Dad made me feel, I was aware of a little flicker of hope burning within me. He tried and tried to blow it out. Sometimes he succeeded, but as soon as I was away from him, that flicker ignited again like birthday candles that won't blow out. It has stayed with me, sometimes burning low and sometimes burning high. The experience of both the highs and lows has made my strand grow stronger through courage.

❧

Mom lived in her own world of survival, but I still needed her during my vulnerable years. Her involvement in my introduction to the birds and the bees didn't exist. I felt abandoned. At the age of twelve, I got my first period. It scared me because no one had told me what happened as girls matured.

Bonnie and Scott wanted to have a slumber party in Dad's fish and game room, but they were too scared to sleep in there alone. It was not my favorite place in the house, because it's where he kept the stuffed animals he had killed. That room was creepy. But I gave in to my brother and sister and spent the night there.

The next morning when I woke with all those eyes looking at me, I felt awful. I had massive pains in my lower abdomen, and I was nauseated. When I unzipped my sleeping bag, I realized that I was soaking wet. I flipped it open and panicked. I was sitting in a pool of blood. I thought that I was bleeding to death.

I got up, tore off my pajamas, and threw them away. I hurriedly put on clean pajamas, but I was petrified to tell anyone what had happened because I thought I would get into trouble. The blood had saturated through the sleeping bag and into my father's carpet. I didn't know what to do. I just sat on the couch nervously rocking back and forth, holding my aching belly.

Thank goodness my mother woke first. When she realized what had happened, she told me what was going on with my body and showed me how to use what I called a mouse mattress (aka Kotex pads).

As I grew from child to teenager, music became one of my strengthening tools. It helped me cope with Dad's belittling, commands, and beatings. Sometimes it kept me from getting into trouble. Music saved my sanity.

I got an orange record player for Christmas one year. It was my favorite gift. My favorite 45 record was Elton John's "Goodbye Yellow Brick Road." I played it over and over and memorized the words: "You know you can't hold me forever. I didn't sign up with you...Oh, I've finally decided my future lies beyond the yellow brick road." For obvious reasons, that song held significant meaning for me, and I belted it out in my room. When I finally listened to the flip side, the words in "Screw You" ("Young Man's Blue") resonated with me, too.

I played that record until I wore it out. Elton John's lyrics made me realize I wasn't alone. Most of my life was spent in constant mayhem. It was the music of my favorite artists that enabled me to escape, if only temporarily. Fleetwood Mac, the Rolling Stones, KISS, and KC and the Sunshine Band were among my favorites.

Someone once said, "Music is what feelings sound like." I know that to be true. Growing pains shaped my pearls. My music smoothed and soothed them. I grew spiritually when I made time to listen to my feelings.

As a young girl, I detested the music my dad listened to. When I was 13, he could have killed us both one evening while listening to George Jones as he sped down the highway. Dad had purchased a 1969 blue Ford Mustang Mach I. It was in mint condition. Dad's mission in life was showing his mom and siblings how well he was doing. He decided to drive to Nova Scotia to show it off one Friday evening. I was his only choice for company because my brother and sister were too young, and he needed Mom to stay home and manage the service station for him.

He had been drinking before we left, and he was in an amazingly splendid mood. The trip was a last-minute decision, and he was trying to beat the clock so that we wouldn't be late for the ferry. I had no idea how fast he was going, but I was enjoying it and encouraged him to go faster.

"Go faster, Daddy. Go faster!"

With a smile on his face, he said, "You got it, sunshine."

With both of us laughing, he punched the pedal to the floor. The car handled smoothly, like silk on skin. I shared my dad's love of cars back then, and I still do. The thought that something bad could happen to us never crossed my mind that night. I think I was enjoying his high mood more than the high speed.

The high from that joy ride ended with blue lights signaling Dad to pull over. The flashing blue lights and blaring siren behind us were pretty scary to me. The officer approached the car and shone his flashlight in my face and then Dad's.

"Can I help you, officer?" Dad asked.

The officer ignored his question and said, "License and registration, sir. Do you know how fast you were going?" Dad gestured to me to look for his registration. I began fumbling through his papers and pulled it out. As I started to hand it to him, the officer said, "Please step out of the car, sir. Have you been drinking tonight?"

Dad didn't lie, but he minimized the amount he'd had. "Yes, officer. I had a beer or two before leaving for an emergency trip home."

They both walked away from our car, and I couldn't hear them any longer. I didn't know what was happening. Was my dad getting arrested? I would be alone. It seemed like an eternity as I sat in the car watching the traffic whiz by. I felt as if our lives were on public display. The spotlight from the squad car showed everything.

When they walked back to our car, the officer told me I was my dad's lucky charm. He said to my father, "Thank your daughter. If it wasn't for her, you would be going off to jail right now."

Dad had given the officer a sob story about being a single father. If he went to jail, I would have nowhere to go. He was very proud of putting one over on the law. He and his family thought it was hilarious. I was my father's pride and joy during that trip. Although it made me feel I was important to my dad, in reality, he had used me to get himself out of trouble.

He set the standards very high for me, but he didn't live by them himself. I wonder now if he wanted more for me than he was able to give himself. He was the foundation for repairing my strand even though he was also responsible for breaking it. It was up to me to cultivate the pearls to string on it.

Chapter Six

Sweet Sixteen

Life beats down and crushes the soul,
and art reminds you that you had one.

~ Stella Adler ~

For some people, their high school years are their best years. Not for me. My life got steadily worse. I walked through each day like a robot, doing only what I was told to do. I had succumbed to an unacceptable way of life, and I was just going through the motions. It was like living in black and white, unable to enjoy the lovely colors of the world.

While part of me was shut off to the world, another part was wide open and searching for something. There had to be more. I looked and looked until I realized that what I was searching for came from within. I had all I needed to become what Jane Fonda called "broken open."

At 14, I was fully developed physically. I became extremely self-conscious because my father teased me about what he called my "boobies." He giggled like a schoolboy whenever I walked into the room. "What are those things? Did you get bit by a mosquito? Look at those mosquito bites on your daughter, Wendy!"

Under my breath, I whispered, "Leave me alone. Don't look at me. I hate you!" If he'd heard me, he would have leaped down from his throne to punish me for talking back.

Mom never acknowledged his remarks, but she didn't stop them from happening either. I silently begged her to make him quit, but she never did. He would yell for me to come from my room while he lounged in his chair. "Deborah! Get your ass out here and get me a beer! Run! Don't walk! Will you look at those mosquito bites?" He would laugh hysterically as I ran to do his bidding.

His degrading treatment made me feel ashamed and insecure. I detested him. Every day my soul was buried a little deeper, and my hatred for him grew. I felt so alone. When I poured his beer, I had to do it just right so there would be no head. If it ended up with a mushroom cap of foam, I got a slap in the head. It took a lot of practice to pour his beer perfectly, especially when he taunted me while I poured by reaching up to pinch me or flick my breast. I wanted nothing more than to throw the beer in his face.

The molestation and degradation continued the entire time I lived there.

I felt invaded and exploited. I was so self-conscious about my body that I began to hunch forward to protect my heart and my breasts.

My poor posture became as much a part of me as my insecurities. Herbert Gold wrote: "He carried his childhood like a hurt warm bird held to his middle-aged breast." When I read those words, I cried because I had lived them. My father repeatedly stole my youthful energy to replace his own. After breaking myself open years later, I learned to accept love. Without love, the best pearl of all, my strand would have died.

It was very difficult to do my outside chores because I had no self-confidence. Every time I heard a car, I would hide behind a bush or a tree and wait until it passed by. But I had to finish. Completing my chores was my ticket to get away from the house, where I could socialize and find myself.

I had no idea who I was or who might like me, so I tried to make friends with every clique and group in school. I hung with the jocks, the popular kids, and the rebellious cigarette smokers. As I spent time with each group, I tried to figure out who I was and where I belonged.

The cigarette-smoking group wasn't a good choice, because I started smoking with them. My parents didn't know at first, but Dad caught on when he realized cigarettes were missing from the machine he kept in our garage. At first, he blamed my sister. He made her smoke one after another until she turned green and threw up in the ashtray. I felt guilty and ashamed of myself for allowing her to take the blame. Later, I found out he had caught her smoking behind the garage. That's why he thought she was responsible for stealing his packs.

One day at school, I was in the smoking area having a cigarette between classes. For no reason other than she thought it would be funny, another student flicked a lit cigarette at my face. It hit me in the corner of my eye. My temper flared. It was bad enough to have my dad hit me in the head. No one else was going to treat me that way. I lost my cool and punched her in the face, but I wasn't a fighter, and she kicked my ass. I was the one who got suspended because I had thrown the first punch. No one was brave enough to tell the principle that she had flicked a cigarette in my face. The girl was a bully, and she would have taken care of them after school.

The school called home and told Mom what had happened. I was suspended. After Mom told Dad, he grounded me. I was used to being grounded, so it wasn't much of a punishment. However, he hadn't grounded me because I got suspended. I was punished because I lost the fight with the bully.

While I waited out my suspension, Dad decided to teach me how to fight. He was staying home a lot because he had developed a debilitating condition that limited the use of his hands. He couldn't work on cars very well, so Mom was running the station by herself. If I threw a good punch, he allowed me to go for a bike ride. I know now that teaching me to defend myself was his way of preparing me to be independent and able to take care of myself.

During my teen years, the Donahues, an older couple who lived nearby, became a safe haven for me. They helped me survive and keep my sanity. When I could get away for a bike ride, I'd go straight to their house and stay for about an hour. They looked forward to my visits as much as I looked forward to seeing them. Their children were grown, and they were lonely. Our routine was sweet. They served me a snack and a beverage, and I listened to their dreamy stories about traveling the world. They described the countryside and culture of each place so well that I thought I was there with them.

I think the Donahues reminded me of my grandparents, who had moved from Nahant to York Beach, Maine. I didn't see them very often because Dad didn't like them anymore. He had told them off, so they stayed away unless Mom needed them.

Mr. and Mrs. Donahue were kind and respectful. They were great role models for a normal life, and I will always be grateful for their friendship. Those precious visits with the Donahues showed me that there are gifts in life waiting to be experienced.

At home, my only safe haven was my artwork. I discovered in high school that I had a talent. I could draw anything in any medium, and I loved it. My art teacher was brilliant and patient, and he had a delightful, peaceful energy about him. When I was creating something beautiful in his class, I could feel all those qualities come to life in me.

My favorite subjects were flowers. Every flower was unique in an aromatic and colorful way. His class fed my soul. My strand absorbed the nourishment that came from the freedom to express myself.

I often used art to block out my parent's arguments. They usually started with my dad accusing Mom of stealing from him. He was so paranoid that he had started hiding his money in the luxury car that he had selfishly purchased. It was a brand new black Lincoln Continental Mach IV with white leather interior. He hid his money under the floorboards of the trunk and kept the car doors locked while it sat inside our garage. He locked the garage, too, so that nobody could take the money from him. He was sure that everyone was out to get him.

Dad spent a lot of time at his friend John's house. John was a fellow mechanic who worked out of his own garage. Dad sat there all day gabbing with John and drinking, while John's talking mynah bird swore at the customers. One night he came home from John's and starting falsely accusing Mom again. He really went crazy. "What are you spending my hard-earned money on today, you stupid bitch?" he asked, slurring his words. "Where's my gun? I'm gonna put it to good use and rid this world of you!"

Without looking away from Mom, Dad said, "Deborah, go get Bonnie and Scott, and all of you get your asses out here."

I ran down the hall and got my brother and sister. When we reached the living room, Dad was mumbling something about blaming Mom for what he was going to do next. His hair was disheveled, and he was waving a gun around like a pointer stick. He ordered us to line up next to each other. *What the hell is he doing?* I thought. I knew he was crazy, but I couldn't believe he would kill us.

Mom started pleading with him to stop. She said, "You can do anything to me, but leave my kids alone!"

With tears streaming down his face, Dad said, "I'm going to fix everyone's problem."

The circumstances were shredding him to his core. Sri Aurobindo said, "What we have within us creates the circumstances outside of us."

I couldn't figure out why Dad was crying when he was the one with a gun. My sister and brother started crying and calling for Mom to help us. I was beyond terrified, but I tried not to show it. I was shaking from head to toe and even peed in my pants a little. Sweat broke out on my upper lip.

Something deep inside told me not to panic, that everything would be all right. My dad looked confused, trapped, and powerless. He was clearly suffering from something much deeper than an out-of-control argument with my mother.

Mom jumped in front of us and told him to stop. She said, "Oh, no, you're not." Then she shoved him. He stumbled backward and, at that moment, I saw the pain behind the tears in his eyes. That was all I had time to see because my mother was pushing us down the hallway toward the back door.

He realized what her plan was and yelled, "Don't you dare, Wendy. You're not going anywhere. Don't you listen to her, kids! She's going to get you all in trouble."

Mom ignored him and continued to push us right out the back door into the dark. We scampered down the stairs and into the night wearing our pajamas. Mom was right behind us. We ran to a friend's house, and Mom used the phone to call Neil Parker, the Chief of Police. She reported Dad's unstable behavior. Mom had called him before when fights got out of control, so he wasn't surprised until she explained that Dad had threatened us with a gun. Chief Parker went to our house and collected all of my dad's guns and threw him in jail for the night.

Mom hated to do it, but she called my grandfather. She wouldn't take us back home when Dad was acting so crazy. My poor grandparents drove down to pick us up and take us to their house in Maine.

Even though she knew Dad hated her, Grandma never said a negative word about him to me. Instead, she tried to point out his good qualities. She took me into her garden where we got lost in the scents of flowers and herbs. I would sit and watch her while she grounded herself by tending her plants. She taught me how to feed the wild birds from the palm of my hand. The feeling of their tiny feet gripping my finger and their sweet little beaks taking seeds from my hand is something I'll never forget. There was a mutual feeling of trust between us. They instinctively knew I would never hurt them. It was lovely moment of harmony.

Through all the sheer terrors in life, we have the ability to return to peace.

Every time we left after a visit, Grandma stood in her front yard blowing kisses and doing a solo waltz to make us laugh. She was another brilliant role model for me. She knew how to bring a little of my soul to the surface. From her, I received the gifts of my artistic ability and my love for flowers. I now carry them with me on my strand.

We only stayed with my grandparents for a few days before Mom took us back home again. I didn't want to go because I felt uneasy about how Dad would act. I was surprised to find that he was filled with remorse for what he had done. Our lives were overshadowed by his depressions as much as his obsessions. His emotions were like a rollercoaster. That time he was at the bottom of down and stuck there. He focused all his energy on us and making up for his wrongdoing. He couldn't apologize enough. He seemed sincere, but I knew that his old patterns would sneak back in once he felt comfortable with himself again.

He tried to make up with me by being my friend. He even offered to teach me how to drive. He decided that I should learn to drive like a pro. He took me to the sand pit in his four-speed truck and let me drive around like a NASCAR driver. It was tough at first, but once I figured out how to synchronize the clutch with the gas pedal, I had a blast. There were no rules and no boundaries. It was pure adrenaline, dirt, donuts, and fun. To be allowed to drive Dad's truck was an honor. It is one of my most memorable moments with him. For once, he let me be me. Dad was an amazing driver, and that day I was my father's daughter.

Every weekend, we went to the sand pit together. Dad took his beer and sat on a rock where he watched me shift in and out of four-wheel drive, drive in reverse all the way around the pit, and do a figure-eight pattern while driving forward. He told me I was awesome. Bouncing around in that truck with the wind blowing across my face allowed my confidence and my smile to bloom.

One day, Dad announced that I was ready. He pulled his Lincoln out of the garage and climbed into the passenger side. I was so nervous that my knees were knocking. I listened to his instructions and nervously put the car into drive. A few minutes later, I was driving his beautiful car on the road without a license. I enjoyed having a real dad that afternoon. But soon after we got home, his mean side returned.

Today, I view Dad's erratic behavior as his way of getting his roller coaster back on top. He was always putting band aids on his wounds after crashing. Band aids don't treat. They just cover up the wounds, leaving the pain beneath. Take off the band aid. Be willing to air out your wounds. The rewards you gather will be pearls for your strand.

The biggest band aid Dad ever used was trying to build a big, white house with pillars on the front and move us into it. He bought some land and decided to cut down the trees and haul them away with his unpaid helper—me! We worked 14-hour days, cutting trees and making piles of branches. We had to drag them through thickets and load them all onto the stinking truck he had taught me how to drive. My hands became blistered, raw, and red. My arms and legs were covered in cuts from the brambles. I itched from numerous mosquito bites, and my feet hurt terribly. I would go to bed at night wishing I would never wake up.

Dad worked me as if I were a 300-pound lumberjack instead of a teenage girl. I hated him and lied to my friends about what I was doing after school and on weekends. After all the work I was forced to do, the house was never built. I was relieved when Dad decided to stop working on the house, but he just found another way to torment me.

I had asked him weeks in advance if I could go to the school dance, and he said yes. The day before the dance, he started calling me boy crazy. Then he made up an excuse to punish me, whipping me with the belt so hard that it kept me from going to the dance or anywhere else.

Mom and Dad went out with their friends almost every weekend. I enjoyed having Dad gone, but I had to babysit for my brother and sister. One weekend I got so bored that I decided to try Dad's whisky and crank up his stereo. My younger sister and brother were clever enough to threaten to tell on me if I didn't give them some, too. I knew it was wrong, but I gave them each a tiny sip.

They were dancing around and laughing like hyenas before both of them went to bed and passed out. I was relieved when they went to bed because I panicked at the thought of Mom and Dad coming home while they were acting like miniature drunks. I was smart enough to cover my tracks. I made dark, steeped tea and added it to Dad's whisky bottle. Dad never noticed the difference.

On Easter Sunday in 1980, I was 15 years old and a sophomore. Mom's friend Ginny came over for Easter with her four boys because her husband was at work. I thought Ginny was pretty cool because she treated me like her own daughter. She had always wanted a daughter. She loved arts and crafts and didn't have anyone to do them with. When our families got together, Ginny showed me how to make dolls. My favorite part was using the liquid embroidery to draw the dolls' faces and make them come alive. My mom didn't do that kind of stuff with me because she always worked.

Mom had made plans for Ginny and her two older boys to help her pick up a new bed. Dad wouldn't pay for delivery because he was too cheap. It should have been him picking it up, but he was drinking that day, as usual. Ginny started drinking, too, so Mom and the two older boys took Dad's truck to get the bed. The two younger boys went outside with my brother, sister, and me to play hide and seek. Those boys found places to hide that I didn't know we had. By the time I was finally found and had tagged everybody, I had worked up a thirst. I went into the house for some water.

As I stood in the kitchen gulping a glass of water, I realized the house was quiet. Ginny and Dad had been in the dining room talking and drinking when we kids went outside. As I headed toward the living room, I heard voices coming from my parents' bedroom. The door was slightly open, so I tiptoed quietly down the hall and peeked in. Ginny and my dad were rolling around the floor, laughing and kissing. I covered my mouth with my hand and made sure not to make a sound as I tiptoed backward all the way down the hall. I ran out of the house and tried to act like nothing had happened.

The other kids had started playing chase. I told them I was tired, but I was really so bothered by what I had seen that I just plopped down on the grass and closed my eyes. While I was lying there, my sister decided she wanted some of her Easter candy and went inside the house to find Dad. She knew if she didn't ask permission first, she would be in big trouble. She searched the house until she heard voices in Mom and Dad's bedroom. When she pushed the door open, she saw our father and Ginny naked on the floor.

I heard Dad yelling at her from all the way outside. He cussed at her and ordered her to go to her room. "I'll deal with you later," he yelled.

My heart was beating fast. I began to cry because I knew what was coming for her, but I didn't dare go into the house. The boys asked me why Dad was yelling, and I just shrugged and turned my face away so they wouldn't see the tears streaming down my cheeks.

Ten minutes later, a disheveled Ginny came running down the front steps. She'd been crying and seemed flustered. She told her two sons to get into the car. When they asked her why they weren't waiting for their brothers, she said she would send their dad for them after he got home from work.

I didn't say a word to Ginny. I had lost all respect and all feelings for her. She was a pig. I was convinced that the only reason she had been so nice to me was to get to my father. *How dare she use me and my mom and pretend to be our friend?* I thought.

As the traitor pulled out of our driveway, I ran into the house to find a horrible scene. My poor sister was standing in the corner of the living room with her face turned to the wall, whimpering like a hurt animal. I froze. I couldn't move.

Dad was screaming at her. "I'll teach you to stick your nose where it doesn't belong, you little bitch. You're all the same: your mother, your sister, and you! You're all good-for-nothing, stupid meatheads." Her cries hurt my heart.

With every word, he hit the back of her legs with his belt. Each time he struck, it left a mark on her and in me. The first few marks were already turning purple, and the new ones were bright red. My hate for him was rising, but my fear of him kept it in check.

Each time the belt struck her legs, she cried harder. She sobbed, "Please, Daddy. I'm sorry. I'm sorry. I won't do it again."

The poor thing didn't even understand what she was apologizing for. The more he beat her, the more he became disconnected from himself. He was out of control.

I stood still in the doorway, unable to move. I could feel every strike of the belt from the inside out, and I flinched with every one. I wanted to scream, "Stop!" but I was paralyzed with fear.

I finally understood how my mother felt when Dad beat me. Still, it wasn't right for her to let Dad abuse me—and it wasn't right for me to let it happen to my sister. I felt so sad for her. I loved my little sister, and she was breaking. I was overcome with guilt, hate, fear, sadness, and self-loathing.

Fifteen minutes went by before Dad realized I was standing there. It seemed like a lifetime that I had stood there and allowed him to hurt her over and over. Tears of helplessness and terror made tracks down my face. My fear made me powerless. Bonnie didn't know I was there until Dad spoke to me.

He told me to watch and learn. He forced me to stand there and watch him torture her for what seemed like hours, while Bonnie stood in the corner with her pants down around her ankles. Her legs were shaking, and her knees began to buckle. The marks turned to dark shades of purple, blue, and red. In some areas, her fragile, innocent skin was seeping blood. I felt sick to my stomach. It was more frightening to see Dad abusing my sister than it had been when I was on the receiving end. I couldn't wait for my mother to get home.

The rage he felt was for himself. Instead of having the courage to admit his wrongdoing, he forced my sister to wear his pain and guilt. Pain is inevitable in our lives. Choosing to end the suffering is a gift to be strung on our strand.

It was dusk before I heard the roar of Dad's truck coming up the driveway. I usually associated that noise with dread because it meant he was coming home, but that time I felt relief. Dad told Bonnie to pull her pants up and get her ass in her room. Relief was visible in my sister's bloodshot eyes as she pulled her pants over the wounds that would scar her psyche for life. When she ran to her room, I followed to make sure she was okay.

Bonnie had her face buried in a pillow to mask her sobbing. Her hair was stuck to her sweet face, and I could smell the sadness and hurt in her wet tears when I pulled her face against mine and hugged her tightly. I began crying myself, gently whispering over and over, "I'm sorry."

While Mom and the boys brought the bed inside, I sneaked into my room and stayed there. Mom didn't know what had gone on, and I prayed that she never would. I feared for my sister.

Mom found out about everything a couple of days later. My sister wasn't used to carrying that kind of pain. She was confused and terrified, and it was too much for her. She broke down and told Mom what she had seen in the bedroom and what Dad had done to her in the corner.

My sister's beating damaged me more severely than any abuse I'd received from my dad. Powerful emotions tried to rise to the surface. Because I didn't know how to handle them, I pushed them down deep, just the way Dad did.

105

I now know how to process profound emotions. I face them, acknowledge them, and let them go. I was not responsible for what happened to my sister any more than my mother was responsible for what happened to me. We were all victims of Dad's unprocessed life challenges. He didn't believe in the power of the Divine. He stood in the way of his own personal greatness.

Don't allow your strand to break. Instead, strengthen it and keep adding the luminous pearls that life so graciously offers us as lessons. Cultivate your pearls by choosing to turn negatives into positives.

I turned sixteen during my junior year of high school. I listened to songs by John Lennon, Olivia Newton John, and Rick Springfield. I watched with the rest of the world as Prince Charles and Lady Diana got married in a fairytale wedding. The world around us revolved while mine fell apart.

Mom had been in the hospital for 10 days, recovering from surgery to remove her gallbladder. Her absence left me to act as mother, daughter, sister, maid, gardener, student, and scapegoat. I should have been used to it since I had played most of those roles for years.

I had mixed emotions about my mother. I loved her, and I missed having her in the house. Her presence somehow helped me deal with life. But I resented her for being sick and leaving me to do everything. My young mind and body were overwhelmed.

Dad was acting even more strangely than usual. Whenever he tried to hit me in the head, I would duck and run away from him. He had taught me how to avoid a punch, and I used that newfound skill to my advantage. There was a part of me that was still afraid of Dad and the ways he could hurt me, so I usually kept my mouth shut and did what I was told. It was only the hope of one day experiencing life beyond Dad's control that gave me the motivation to move forward every day.

Dad had to go back to work while Mom recovered from surgery because someone had to be in charge at the station. On Mom's second night home from the hospital, Dad came right home from work. He seemed preoccupied. Instead of plopping into his chair and demanding I get him a beer, he freshened up in the bathroom and came out smelling of Old Spice. His hair had been combed into a perfect James Dean wave. He grabbed his keys and announced that he had to go back to work because he'd forgotten something. I was relieved and excited. When Dad was gone, it was like taking a vacation in my own home, a vacation from him. The idea of relaxing without the stress of his control made my heart dance the freedom dance.

Mom and I both knew that Dad would never have driven half an hour because he'd forgotten something at the station. He liked his beer too much. We knew he was lying. It was ridiculous for him to think he was pulling one over on us. I really didn't care where he went as long as it kept him away from me. Mom was visibly upset, but I didn't get concerned until she decided to follow him. I tried to stop her. She wasn't supposed to be driving so soon after surgery. She just told me to stay home with the kids and she would be right back.

Mom found his truck in the parking lot of a fried chicken restaurant in East Kingston. When she saw another familiar car, she drove slowly into the parking lot to get a better look. Her friend Carol was in the driver's seat, and Dad was in the car with her. Seeing her friend with her husband made Mom so angry that she did a donut in the middle of the parking lot and sped out onto the street.

As Mom drove home, some neighborhood troublemakers tied a piece of rope across the street to see what would happen. Mom's fury kept her from seeing the rope. She had no idea what she'd hit and slammed on her brakes, sliding off the road and into the ditch. Her stomach hit the steering wheel with enough force that it ripped her incision open, and she began to bleed.

The incision was sewn back together in the emergency room, but the doctor told Mom it was a temporary fix because she had sustained further injury. They sent her home and told her she would need another operation after the wound healed.

I'm not sure if Mom would have told Dad that she had caught him cheating on her again, but he made it home before she did. When she got home, he couldn't yell at her because she was in so much pain, both emotionally and physically. So he took it out on me.

"What did you do to your mother?" he demanded.

I made a huge mistake. I said, "What?" God help anyone who ever said "what" to my father. It was like waving a red blanket in front of a bull. He went crazy.

In that instant, I knew that I'd had enough of him. As he was screaming at me, I blocked what he was saying. He looked like a mime to me. I stood there staring at him, and everything he had done to me since the strand of pearls broke came flooding back.

I was done allowing him to control me. I would no longer tolerate his yelling, his beatings, the foul name-calling, the sexual abuse, or the belittlement. I was done with all of it. It was time to strengthen my strand.

I was shaking in my shoes, but I was the product of his creation. I made the choice to stick up for myself. I looked him in the eyes, and the words just came out. "I didn't do anything wrong!"

He lunged for me, and I ran for the door. He yelled, "Don't you dare leave this house, or you'll find out what's good for you, you stupid little bitch."

I didn't care what he said. He scared me, but I was finally old enough to stand up for myself. I took his challenge. It felt as if I were moving toward the door in slow motion. Tears began to roll down my face.

What was I doing? Where would I go? Would he catch me? I couldn't stop moving toward the door. I was on remote control. I was ready.

I got to the door before he did and dashed through it. He carried his rage outside the house. As I ran down the driveway, he bellowed, "I'll fix you for running away from me, you little bitch."

I cut through the woods to the next street and heard his truck start behind me. My adrenaline was fueling me, and I kept running. The sound of that truck made me panic. The fear of not knowing what was going to happen was so overwhelming that I ran as fast as my feet would carry me. The sound of my breathing competed with the sound of Dad's truck as I raced for my freedom.

My lungs had to work harder for me than they had ever worked for him. My heart needed to beat more rapidly than it ever beat when he abused me. My body shifted into flight mode, and I felt it as soon as it happened. Everything was working in perfect harmony. My breathing, my heart rate, and my feet all were in synch. They carried me down the side of the road away from the horrific sound of Dad's control to wherever I could live free.

I heard the engine as he revved it. He yelled, "Get your ass in this truck or you'll be grounded for the rest of your life."

I heard his words, but they didn't penetrate me as a threat anymore. They were just small words coming from a little man. We were neck and neck in the race for my freedom, and I realized that he had nothing to threaten me with anymore. I had already lived in the clutches of his control. There was nothing left that he could do to me. There was nothing I would allow him to do to me.

I kept running. He turned the truck's wheels toward me and came within inches of my legs. The second the truck was about to hit me, my legs became fueled by courage, and they escorted my body into the woods. I ran through sharp branches and wet, muddy leaves with no direction in mind. I was giddy with the realization that I had just overcome the power of fear by leaving my father and his truck behind.

I had never truly known what it was like to be free from my father before that moment. As I ran through the woods, I told myself that he would never again control me. I wouldn't let him hurt me anymore. I slowed down to get my bearings. I needed to think. Where was I going, what was my plan, and who would help me?

One thing was certain. I no longer had to accept a life lived in fear. That's all I knew at that moment, and it was good enough for me. It carried me forward. I had never been given an opportunity to fully explore and experience any of life's goodness. I had tasted moments of peace, trust, love, truth, and forgiveness, but I could never hang onto them. Breaking free from Dad's control was an amazing victory for me.

Today, I view that day as the beginning of the cultivation of my pearls. The lessons of bravery and courage helped me take charge of strengthening my own strand. My father gave me the gift of life. He created a foundation of pain on which I continue to build my strength as I claim a gift that was always just beyond his reach.

Chapter Seven

Rebel Without a Clue

The good man, even though overwhelmed by misfortune, loses never his inborn greatness of soul. Camphor-wood burnt in the fire becomes all the more fragrant.

~ Sataka ~

Alone and lost in the woods, I heard the crunch of last fall's leaves beneath my steps and remembered everything he had done to me. As I continued to dodge thickets and branches, I acknowledged my resentments and hatred for him. It was so fresh and raw in the forefront of my mind that I knew the direction I needed to head toward. I was, at last, on my way to success in escaping my father and his demons.

I know now that my poor dad was troubled. He couldn't find the pearls of courage and bravery to seek his freedom. He was hopeless and buried in fear. Hopeful energy keeps us going. Hoping for what you want is the first step toward freedom. Hope enables the source to work with you. Today, I hold the pearls of compassion, love, and forgiveness for my father.

I saw a bit of a clearing and recognized a familiar road. I could hear Dad's truck going up and down the street I'd left behind. He was still looking for me. Once I realized where I was, I decided to move away from the main road. I aimed for Pow-Wow pond, where some friends from school lived. It was getting dark, and I was afraid to stay in the woods, so I walked along the edge of the road in the dirt.

I was determined not to let anyone see me. Every time I heard a car coming, I ran behind the nearest shelter until the headlights and the sound of the motor were gone. It usually took me 20 minutes to walk to Pow-Wow pond, but with all of my hiding out, it seemed to take hours. I finally reached the winding road that led to the homes nestled around the shore of the large pond. I thought of stopping at Kim's house, but my gut told me to keep going until I reached the very last house on the street, which was my friend Val's.

I didn't know it at the time, but all I had to do was hope, believe, and trust. That night, my hope, belief, and trust were enough for the Divine to guide me on my path.

When I reached the door to Val's house, relief washed over me. I stood there ringing the doorbell for what seemed like an eternity. While I was waiting, I noticed what a gorgeous place it was, with views of nature all around the house. I had never noticed how pretty it was before because I was always too nervous. No one answered the door. I almost panicked until I remembered that they rarely used the front door. I ran around to the back and peeked in. Val's mom was in the kitchen. I tapped on the door.

She wore an apron and had a dish towel draped over her shoulder. "Hi, Deb," she said. "Come on in. Val's not back yet, but you can wait for her." The aromas of a delicious dinner, lovingly prepared, permeated the air.

I sat down at the table and wondered what to do next. I had planned to ask Val to help me. I wasn't prepared to tell an adult what I'd done. I knew that Val's mom could see that I was dirty and cut up. I think she knew a little bit about my situation at home, too, because Val probably told her.

While she stirred a pot on the stove, she said, "You're pretty scraped up there. Is everything okay? Can I get you something?"

I started to tremble and cry. Hanging my head, I mumbled, "I ran away from home. I got scraped up cutting through the woods. I was scared because my dad was chasing me. I think he was trying to hit me with his truck." It was embarrassing to tell her, but I also felt relieved.

She sat down across from me and said, "Oh, sweetie, it's okay. You're safe here. I don't want you to worry. We'll take care of you tonight."

"I appreciate your help, but I need help for more than just tonight. I'm never, ever going back there. What am I going to do?"

"Just relax and take some deep breaths. When Val gets here, we'll get you settled and then make some decisions."

She had compassion in her eyes and tenderly held my hand in hers as if I were a bird with an injured wing. Her comforting touch made me feel safe enough to tell her everything. I knew she would help me. She had seven daughters, and Val was her youngest. She was an incredibly strong woman with impeccable values, and she had raised her daughters the same way. She told me to wash my hands and gave me some water to drink.

When Val walked through the back door, she started excitedly telling her mother about her day. She stopped when she noticed me sitting there. "Hey, Deb, what are you doing here?" she asked.

I started to cry again. I used to pray that Val would be my best friend, but Kim already held that slot. I was the third wheel. Sometimes Val and Kim would go weeks without speaking to me. I really never knew why. Maybe they thought I was trying to break them apart so that I could move into the best friend position. It all seemed quite trivial at that moment.

As Val's mom explained my situation, I sat there with tears in my eyes. I looked back and forth at them and realized that I missed my mom. It was starting to become real in my mind that I had left home with just the clothes I was wearing and that I was never going back. With the adrenaline surge gone, I felt numb and very confused. I could hardly think about what might come next.

They assured me I could spend the night and that everything would be fine. Val's mother wanted me to call my mother, but I refused because I was afraid my dad would come and get me. She insisted that we call the police, and we did.

Val and I went outside for a cigarette before going upstairs to her room. I took a hot shower, and she gave me some warm clothes to wear. We were listening to a Rolling Stones record when Val's mom called us downstairs. Officer Neil Parker was in the kitchen, and he asked me to sit down so he could ask me some questions.

All I could think about was what my father would do if he got his hands on me after I'd reported him for abuse. A piece of me felt bad because I did love him. I don't know why—I just did. The rest of me hated him for the things he had done to me.

I told my story honestly but with shame and guilt. I was so nervous that I would somehow end up back home and my dad would really hurt me for running away. They assured me again that everything would be fine and told me I didn't have to go back home.

Chief Parker said he was going to my house to question my parents and tell them I was okay. He told me it was routine procedure. He also said he would issue a restraining order against my father. I was nervous about him going to my house, but at least Mom would know I was safe. Best of all, my dad would not be able to come near me. If he tried, he would be arrested.

A weight had been lifted from me, but I felt lonely. I don't know why feeling lonely bothered me so much. I had felt lonely from the moment I broke the strand of pearls. The vain hope I had carried for a normal home life with my family had ended, but knowing that I would never be under Dad's control again generated enough hope for me that night. Hope generates positive energy, and I needed energy to get through what would come next.

The following day, I was sitting in class and wondering how my mom and dad were feeling when I heard someone say my name. The principle came over and whispered, "Deborah, after school today Officer Bower will pick you up and escort you to your house to get some of your belongings. You'll be staying with his family for a while."

"I can't go…" Before I finished the sentence, he assured me Dad wouldn't be there.

I was shaking as I walked into my house behind Officer Bower. The negative energy was so thick it felt like someone was choking me. My memories of that afternoon are vague, but I remember that my mother was crying. I heard Officer Bower tell Mom she should start looking for a family member who would be willing to take custody of me. Otherwise, I would be placed with a foster family. I buried that thought as deep as I could because the idea of living with strangers was too much for me to handle.

Officer Bower took me to his house to stay until a court date could be set. I didn't mind too much because his daughter was a friend of mine. Her given name was Jean, but everyone called her Bunny. She was an only child, but she wasn't lonely, because she had loving parents and was very popular at school.

At first, staying at Bunny's house was great. Two weeks later, I just couldn't take it anymore. I felt like a poor little charity case. I knew they viewed me as the abused girl who had nothing. Pretty Bunny had everything—pretty hair, perfect teeth, beautiful clothes, and a gorgeous prom dress, which was prominently displayed in her bedroom. I envied her for all of it.

On the night of the prom, I was still at Bunny's house. My future was a mystery, but I forced a smile and told her she looked beautiful. I had never felt so abandoned, sad, and embarrassed all at once. My prom experience had been stolen from me. I felt like Cinderella with no mice to help me get to the ball.

When our hearts are heavy with the pain of loneliness and sadness, our hopes seem to be beyond our reach, and they stop whispering to us. It's just an illusion made of fog. The fog will lift, as it always does. And when it lifts, our hopes will whisper to us again. Listen.

I was kept in the dark about what would happen to me and where I would go. Finally, the court date arrived. I wasn't required to go, but Mom and whoever would be my new guardian had to be there. I couldn't wait for school to end that day. All the kids were staring at me with pity in their eyes. When I arrived at Bunny's after school, Mom and her brother Rick were waiting to tell me that the judge had allowed Uncle Rick to take custody of me.

It was a bittersweet moment. Dudley (my nickname for Uncle Rick) and I had enjoyed a special connection since I was little. Although I was happy for myself, I was filled with guilt for abandoning Mom, Bonnie, and Scott.

My own feelings of abandonment had shifted to gratefulness. I was thankful to Bunny and her parents for helping me. I hugged Mr. and Mrs. Bower and began to cry because I couldn't say goodbye to Bunny, too.

I put my unfinished oil painting of a rose in Dudley's van. When I hugged Mom, I held back my tears. I knew she would visit often, because my grandma and grandpa lived right next door to Dudley. As we drove away, I felt a rush of emotions. I was happy, thrilled, and sad, but I was also scared. Would Dudley's house feel like a real home? Would I be accepted by my aunt and cousins? Would the kids at my new school be nice to me or just stare at the new girl?

I was very comfortable with my uncle. His voice was deep and strong, yet understanding and calm. He knew what I had endured in my short life, and he assured me that everything would be great. He told me I could use their car whenever I wanted, and I would have my own room.

When we walked into the house, Aunt Linda was there with my younger cousin Eric. He was an incredibly cute boy, about seven years old. He called me Abraca-Debra. His little sister Lisa was three. She looked like a little angel with her platinum blonde hair and blue eyes. They all welcomed me with open arms. The kids showed off their toys while my aunt gave me a tour of the house. I had been there before, but I had never seen the bedroom they gave me.

My mouth fell open. It was breathtaking. Two walls had sliding glass doors. One led out to a deck that overlooked a field where two horses grazed peacefully. In the distance, the field descended into woods. I stood there in awe.

My aunt told me I could paint the walls any color I wanted to. I felt so lucky. The late afternoon sun was blazing through the glass doors, so I immediately decided to paint the walls a pale yellow. When I looked out the other glass door, my eyes grew wide with excitement as I took in the in-ground pool, the water glistening in the sun.

As I stood in my new room, thoughts of my dad's control issues evaporated. The ease of freedom moved into cells that had long been occupied by tension.

Completing my chores at my new home was a piece of cake compared to what I had to do in the old one. Most of the time, I offered to do more because I felt guilty. I didn't feel worthy to live there, so I needed to do more to earn my keep. I set the table for dinner, cleared the table, and washed the dishes.

I was always nervous and on edge as I did the chores. I expected to be yelled at or slapped in the head for doing them wrong. Instead, my aunt and uncle complimented me on my speed and efficiency. I didn't know how to accept compliments because I'd seldom gotten any. My uncle was floored when I helped out by cleaning the horses' stalls. He didn't know that working hard was the only life I'd known.

My new high school took one look at my transfer credits and granted me a complete for their junior year requirements. I wouldn't have to start school until the next fall. I was grateful that I didn't have to go to school right away. When I'd visited the school counselor's office, the students seemed so comfortable with their friends that they didn't even notice me. My fears of being the new kid were deferred to my senior year. I had the whole summer to get used my new home and meet people. It wasn't long before I met Rebecca (Becky), who became a lifelong friend.

Charlie, my uncle's black Newfoundland, loved having me take him to the beach to run free. We were buddies. We had instantly developed an unconditional love for each other. One day I loaded Charlie, my real-life teddy bear, into the car. On the way to the beach, I made my daily stop at the family pharmacy to buy a pack of cigarettes. Before I asked the girl behind the counter for anything, she handed me a pack of Marlboros.

I said, "That's my brand. How did you know?"

Peering at me through her huge glasses, she smirked as she rang me up. "You're new around here, right?"

I smirked back and said, "Yes, but how did you know?"

"York is a very small town. I grew up here, so I know everybody. I've never seen you before a couple of weeks ago when you started coming in here for cigarettes every day. That's how I knew your brand."

I felt my face redden. She told me her name was Rebecca and I told her my name. At first I thought she was older than me, but it was the glasses. I was excited when she said she was going to be a senior. We exchanged phone numbers, and from that moment on we became very good friends.

The two of us can be apart for years, and when we reconnect, it is as good as ever. We have both shifted our energy over the years, each finding our life purpose, but the loving energy of our friendship stays strong.

Becky and I spent the rest of the summer cruising the beach in her brown Cordoba or my Aunt's white station wagon while we smoked cigarettes. We thought we were being cool. Suddenly, summer was over.

On my first day of school as a senior, I was shaking in my shoes. I walked into my first class praying to meet some friends. I didn't want to be left out any more. I took a seat in the back of the room so I wouldn't draw attention to myself. Immediately, a girl named Lisa leaned over and introduced herself.

Every morning Lisa, Chris, and Chris's twin sister picked me up for school. Lisa had a standard four-speed Pinto. It had a distinct sound as it headed down our driveway, and cigarette smoke bellowed out the windows even when it was 30 degrees outside.

I would start smiling as soon as I heard Lisa's stereo, accompanied by the putt putt of the Pinto's muffler. I'd run out, open the car door, and wave the smoke away so I could see Chris's smiling face. As soon as my door shut, he would light up a joint.

The first time they gave me a ride, I got quite an eyeful. I didn't know what a joint was. When Chris lit one, he sucked on it so hard I thought he was going to pop. He held his breath and started making snorting noises. It was pretty gross. He handed the joint to me, and I said, "No, thank you." I think he was insulted. The smoke stunk, and I definitely got high off the fumes. It made me paranoid to go to school. What if the teachers smelled it?

It was wonderful to have friends. They didn't really know me, and I was willing to do anything to keep them as friends. I wasn't sure who I was at that point. I hadn't found my soul, my truths, or my voice, and I remained under the control of my ego. When Chris offered me a joint the second morning, I accepted. I didn't like it, but I did it anyway. I was trying to be someone I wasn't in order to be accepted.

Rebecca and I graduated from high school in January at the age of 17. We spent a lot of our free time partying. The first time I got drunk should have taught me a lesson, but it didn't. Becky and I bought a bottle of Jack Daniels with her sister's old ID. We drove the Cordoba up to Nubble Light House. The first sip of Jack and Coke tasted harsh and kind of putrid. I hated it. But as the bubbles from the Coke rolled down my throat and fizzled into my tummy, I loved how it made me feel. I felt the warmth of the whiskey in every cell. Complete relaxation moved through my body and mind. It made me happy.

Later, I remember someone picking up my limp body. I was awake, but I couldn't move or talk. I became aware of someone laying me down in a shower stall fully clothed and turning the water on. I wanted to say no, but I couldn't. Cold droplets of water pelted me in the face and soaked my clothes.

The cold water worked, because I regained the power of speech long enough to yell for Becky. I was scared and embarrassed, and I didn't know where I was. I was mortified when she came into the bathroom and laughed at me. A bunch of people that she was partying with followed her, and they all had a good laugh. From that night on, they called me the Blonde Betty Bomber. I hated that name, and I hated what happened to me that night. Unfortunately, it didn't make me hate alcohol, although I never drank whiskey again.

I had been raised like a caged animal, and I was finally free. I was going to live it up. That was the energy I put out, and it was the energy that came back. Deep inside, my soul was crying. I refused to listen.

Graduating from York High School half a year early filled me with pride. It was my first major milestone, and I was so excited. Rebecca and I attended the graduation ceremony with the other students in the spring. That night the entire graduating class had a huge party to celebrate. We pitched tents down by the river. Out front, by the street, there was a live band and a bonfire. My Uncle Dudley set up his huge tent for me and my friends to use. He was so cool; he even had a beer with us.

Most of our graduating class left after the band stopped playing. Some older party animals that Becky and I knew convinced us that the night was still young, so we took the party to my tent. The last thing I remember was picking up the wrong beer can. I took a huge chug and swallowed a mouthful of ashes, butts, and beer backwash. I puked immediately and then passed out.

When I woke the next morning, I was shocked at what I saw. My uncle's poor tent had been trashed. It was ripped, burned, and soaked with spilled beer. I sat there dumbfounded. How was I going to explain it to Dudley? The truth was that I didn't know what had happened, and that's exactly what I told him.

I had no clue that drinking was controlling me. All that mattered was fitting in somewhere. I was still running and getting lost. I was unaware that my pearls were rolling away from me. My ego controlled my life and allowed the protective layers to become thicker, while my strand grew thinner. The whispers of my injured heart and soul were buried deep.

My aunt and uncle were willing to help me go to college, but the thought terrified me. I was living in a normal house with a normal family, but I still felt like an outcast. I pretended to be happy and always wore a smile on the outside, but inside I was filled with fear and sadness. Their house was more of a convenience than a home. It was my truck stop just off Party Avenue. I wasn't willing to give up my party life or my new friends to get an education.

That's what I projected, and that's what I attracted. It was my only direction. The rest of the world made me feel lost and completely alone, so I surrounded myself with people who partied the way I needed to party.

As a compromise, one that would take as little effort as possible, I enrolled in Barbizon modeling school. I had to be in Boston every Saturday for all-day classes. I took the bus from Portsmouth, New Hampshire, into the city. It was exciting at first. I felt exhilarated when

I stepped off the bus from the boonies and entered the energy of the city. The energy shifted again when I entered the school.

The other students were mean bitches who were stuck up and wore too much makeup. They had zero personality and were more than willing to stab me in the back to get ahead. There was nothing real about them. I knew I didn't belong there. I had made a mistake, but I couldn't let my dad be right about me, and I couldn't let my uncle down. I had to prove that I was somebody, so I sucked it up and kept going.

After I turned 18, Becky and I made road trips to Brattleboro, Vermont, every Friday afternoon to pick up our booze. We had plenty of friends who were old enough to buy anything we wanted, but it was more fun taking road trips to Vermont where I could buy legally.

One Friday night Becky introduced me to her favorite cousin Todd. The three of us got dressed up and went out for a fancy dinner in Portsmouth. When I met Todd, I thought I'd fallen in love. Now I know it was just infatuation with an older boy who partied like me.

The three of us had a blast. The waitress served both Becky and me even though we were underage. Drinking erased my nervousness about eating dinner in front of a guy I had just met. I remember leaving the restaurant, but that's about all I remember about that night.

The next morning I had to get up early to catch the bus for Boston. I panicked because I woke up at Becky's house. She saved my butt. She had already chosen a gorgeous white dress for me to wear to Barbizon that day. I hurried to get ready, and she drove me to catch the bus. I felt green and ready to hurl at any moment. Having a hangover and dealing with those prissy bitches was too much for me to handle. I quit and walked out.

Dudley and Aunt Linda were not happy that I hadn't come home the night before, and they were pissed when I told them Barbizon school was out and so was the nonrefundable tuition. I was scared about getting in trouble, but the loss of their money didn't faze me. My ego made me selfish.

I got a job at a sub shop in Kittery, but I soon ditched it because the owner's son had a crush on me, and he made me uncomfortable. My next job was at an ice cream shop. After making swirlies all day, I should have gone home and stayed there. But if there was a party, I had to be there. My uncle's car was available, so I always offered to drive. My ego liked to show off by making a statement, and after I had a couple of drinks, I felt invincible.

Most of Todd's friends had their own places because they were in their twenties. Someone always had a place to party. We would all meet up and have a few while we decided what we wanted to do. We drank, told jokes, and laughed a lot. It was the perfect diversion to keep me from facing myself.

Skeeter was a good friend who became the big brother I never had. That particular night I'd had enough to drink that Skeeter expressed concern about my driving home. "Be careful driving, sis," he said.

"I will. I'm fine," I said. I believed it, but I should have known better.

I was one block from my aunt's and uncle's house when I saw the cat. I swerved to miss it and drove off the road, shot over a hill on someone's front lawn, and crashed into a tree. I hit my head and passed out. I woke to a flashlight shining in my eyes, but then it moved away. When I lifted my head off the steering wheel, blood poured from my nose into my lap. I panicked because I realized I'd had an accident. I stumbled out of the car and saw that I was close enough to walk home.

The house was dark when I got there. I was desperate for help, but I couldn't see. I dragged my hands along the walls, staining them with blood as I searched for a light switch all the way to Dudley's and Linda's bedroom. I woke them and mumbled about seeing a cat in the road and crashing the car. Dudley jumped out of bed and flipped on the light. He saw the blood all over the walls and all over me. I wanted him to hug me and tell me everything was okay. He did more than that. He protected me.

My uncle didn't ask any questions. He just put me in his van to drive me to the hospital. As we drove down the street, we saw flashing red and blue lights at the scene of the accident. My uncle stopped to speak with the police. I heard everything. He stuck up for me. He told them about the cat and said that I must have hit my head on impact. He explained that when I came to, someone was there with a flashlight. When I saw all the blood, I got scared and ran home. The officer threatened to give me a citation for leaving the scene, but he said he would let it slide, given the circumstances. The police had no idea I had been drinking. My uncle knew because he could smell it. Before the police could check on me, he told them he was taking me to the hospital.

The emergency room doctor told Dudley I was very lucky. I could have been seriously injured. The fact that I was drunk may have saved my life, but the doctor said there probably wouldn't have been an accident at all if I had been sober.

Dudley was so saddened and distressed that he cried. The car was totaled, and Aunt Linda wasn't happy. The next night after dinner, Dudley had a serious talk with me. With tears rolling down his face, he said, "I never want to have to tell my sister that her daughter died in a car accident from drinking while living under my responsibility. Promise me you'll never do that again."

"I'm sorry, Dudley. I won't." I said.

I had been shaken up by the accident, but I minimized the trauma. Still, it made me sad to see my uncle cry. Although I promised I'd never drink and drive again, I didn't mean it. My ego told me I was invincible.

On the inside, I was broken. That accident should have scared me into unveiling my truths, but all the tragic things that had happened to me were absorbed and stored instead of embraced and faced.

Dudley and the family spent the summer in Nova Scotia. I stayed home because I had to work at the ice cream shop. One weekend, I allowed Todd to talk me into having a party at my aunt's and uncle's house. I knew it was wrong, but I said yes because I wanted to keep up my tough rebel image for him and our friends. I wanted to show off a house that I pretended was mine. I wanted to be seen as a kid who lived in a nice home with an in-ground pool and a cabinet full of booze. I wanted to throw the best party in town.

I pushed the fact that I was really a girl from an abusive environment—a girl who had lived in a trailer—deep inside where it could never be reached.

The party got so loud that it woke my poor grandparents. Grandma came over, gracefully walked into the living room, shut off the music, threw everyone out, poured my drink down the sink, and told me I should be ashamed of myself after what my uncle had done for me. On her way out, she said she loved me and recommended that I go to bed.

I pretended to be furious with her for embarrassing me, but it was all an act. I really loved my grandmother, and I had never wanted her to see me in action. Deep inside that wasn't really who I was, and she knew it. The Divine power flowed in Grandma, and when I was in her company I felt a tiny flow of her influence. I humbly carry that pearl today.

I didn't know that Todd had hidden in my room while my grandmother dismantled the party. He insisted on staying over and suggested that we christen my aunt's and uncle's bed. I didn't want to, but I was afraid he wouldn't be my boyfriend unless I did as he said. It makes me feel sick now to think about the control I gave him over me back then. That night I lost my virginity. It was not what I wanted, but I was buzzed enough to go along with it.

I was trying to sleep off my regret and a hangover when I heard Dudley's voice. Dudley and Linda had come home early. I shook Todd awake and scrambled to get out of their room. It was too late. The door opened, and we were caught in their room. They threw Todd out of the house. My aunt said she'd had enough and demanded that I move out. She gave me a week.

I went to work that day, but I couldn't stop crying. I had blown the wonderful opportunity that my uncle had given me. My bosses finally got it out of me that I had been kicked out of my house. They were extremely sympathetic and valued me as an employee. They gave me the day off to gather myself and offered to help me move. I was self-destructing and didn't even know it.

I called Becky and told her what had happened. Her parents had fostered kids in the past, and she didn't think it would be a problem for me to move in there. I can't help but think that if finding a place to live had been more difficult, I might have strengthened my strand. But that's not what the universe had in store for me. Becky told me that I would be living in her bedroom as her friend and that Todd, who also lived there, was off limits. I was thankful and agreed.

I was not really a girlfriend to Todd, so I didn't care. What kind of boyfriend was willing to steal his girlfriend's virginity and risk getting her into the kind of trouble I was in? The following Saturday after work, my bosses helped me move my stuff from Dudley's to Becky's house. It was very uncomfortable. My aunt watched over us like a hawk protecting her young as we loaded up my belongings. She made me feel unworthy and made it clear that she didn't trust us. I don't blame her.

I regretfully quit the job at the ice cream shop because I had no way to get there without the use of my uncle's car. I was thankful that they had been so kind to me. They knew I was troubled and helped me anyway.

Becky's dad was a safety engineer on construction job sites, and he heard about two flag girl positions available on Route 1 right around the corner in York. The project was just days from beginning, and the construction trailer had arrived the day before. We were two giddy girls after we were told we could start work a week later. It gave us a whole week to celebrate.

We flagged cars on Route 1 between York and Ogunquit for the summer and into the winter months. It was perfect. We went to work together every day. It was a full-time job and paid great wages. Having a fun job shifted my energy partway into self-control and self-worth instead of self-destruction.

We worked with the hot sun beating down on our hardhats, and we wore orange vests over our tank tops. The smell of freshly laid hot top permeated our noses. Becky and I worked at opposite ends of the Route 1 shutdown. With the help of walkie talkies, we directed the flow of traffic one side at a time. It was tricky when traffic was heavy on both bounds, and the loud roar of the heavy equipment around us made it difficult to hear one another.

We laughed and joked and commented about everybody who drove by, deciding who was cute, who was handsome, and who wasn't. We met lots of people and became extremely popular. We drank gallons of Coke and got great tans. We were praised by the people who drove by, and our boss said we were doing a great job. We received gifts and flowers every day from admirers and had smiles pasted on our faces all day long. It made me feel good to finally receive recognition for doing a good job, but it also fed my ego, which kept my true self-identity locked away.

Becky was able to buy her own car with the money she saved and a little help from her dad. I was a bit jealous, but I benefited because we were always together. With Becky driving her own car, we had the freedom to go to Ogunquit every weekend. That's where our new best pals lived.

Frank and Marco had become really good friends who accepted us for who we were. They didn't make up silly nicknames or make fun of us. They treated us with respect and as equals. We weren't the little sisters that we felt to Todd, Skeeter, and the rest of the crew. On weekends, we did what the classier people did. We dressed up and went to clubs. Of course, we weren't old enough. But Frank and Marco knew the bouncers, so we got in.

One night, our hair was done, we'd put on makeup, and we were all dressed up. We were just about to leave for Ogunquit when Todd pulled out his charm and conned Becky and me into going to a party at Skeeter's new place. The only reason Todd invited us was because he didn't have a ride.

Becky and I did not want to go because we knew it would be the same old stuff. Everyone would be sitting around and getting as drunk as possible. But Todd talked us into going. When we arrived at Skeeter's new pad, we were really bummed. There was almost no furniture. All we saw was a keg of beer. We looked at each other and rolled our eyes, and Todd started calling us his favorite insulting names. "Look," he said, "it's bonehead and idiot."

He no longer felt a need to be cordial; he'd gotten his ride. We went upstairs and sat on the dirty floor of an empty, dark bedroom and smoked a joint, contemplating whether we should leave and go to Ogunquit or stay there and drink with the guys.

We could hear how loud the voices were getting downstairs, and we knew things would only go south from there. We decided to make a break for it. We took our shoes off so we could sneak out, and Becky went first. We tiptoed down the stairs and slipped through the front door. Becky had made it down the porch stairs to the sidewalk when I heard a voice behind me say, "Where do you think you're going, idiot?"

Lying out of fear, I said, "Nowhere. We're just going for a ride around the beach."

As I put one foot on the first step, Todd grabbed my other foot and ripped it out from under me. I pitched forward, and my head bounced off the first step. He told me I wasn't going anywhere. Still gripping my ankle, he twisted it viciously. I heard a crunch and felt an explosion of pain. As I screamed, I looked into his eyes. He looked possessed. He held onto my foot for a few minutes; then he dropped it to the floor and walked away.

Becky was watching from the car, but she was afraid to help me. Terrified that he would come back, I pulled myself up and hopped on one foot to the car. We didn't go to Ogunquit that night, because Todd had purposely sprained my ankle. I couldn't walk on it at all. The next day I got an X-ray to make sure it wasn't broken, and the doctor told me that a sprain can be worse than a break.

I hated Todd for overpowering me, hurting me, and trying to control my life. How had I gotten involved with another abusive, controlling, troubled man? I was right back where I'd started, in pain physically, emotionally, and mentally.

Today I know who I am. I am able to embrace, process, and overcome pain, retaining the energetic blessings of positive pearls. Our pearls project and reflect the miracles within us and others.

After hopping around on one leg for a few weeks, I realized that I my period might be late. I wasn't sure, because I was never regular. I didn't know what to do, and I was afraid to tell anyone. I was living at my best friend's house, and Todd lived there, too. Even though Becky's parents were very kind to me, I certainly couldn't tell them. Deep inside, I wasn't comfortable telling anyone I was a screw-up. I didn't want to be perceived that way.

I asked an acquaintance I trusted to give me a ride to the free clinic. I found out the worst possible outcome for me. I was pregnant. I didn't even need to think about it. A little voice inside me took over and set up an appointment for an abortion. I felt trapped and more alone than ever. I was positive I was in no position to have a child. I was only nineteen years old.

I held the sadness and fear deep inside. An immense sense of desperation was eating away at me. I thought it was easier to ignore my feelings, because I was sure showing my vulnerability would hurt me more. I felt plagued. Life kept throwing bouts of physical and mental anguish at me. They seemed to hit me one after another.

As I lay there on the cold table after the procedure, I cried myself into pieces from the pain of what I had just endured and the pain of what I was missing. I craved love, trust, acceptance, and forgiveness. As I got up, I felt numb. I left my emotions on that cold table, sure that I would never have to think about it again. The physical pain went with me, because I knew it would eventually heal.

What I didn't know was that the damaging energy of holding on and resisting had layered on another coat of armor, and it was affecting my posture. My shoulders rolled inward and down to protect my heart.

In December, our boss held an open house for the holidays. Food and cheer were spread all through the construction trailer. I was feeling depressed and didn't want to go. Becky said that we should at least stop by the trailer for a little while and say goodbye to our boss. I knew she was right, so we hopped in her car and went over to make an appearance. We stayed most of the afternoon, reminiscing about the summer. I had two drinks while we were there, just enough to distract me from myself. I refused the whiskey shots that my boss was handing out.

The snow was really coming down, and the streets were covered. It was a winter wonderland snow globe. Becky was smiling from ear to ear and sputtering about another party down by the beach. While she gathered some leftover booze to take with us, I realized she couldn't drive, because she was more than a little drunk.

"Becky, where are your keys? I'll drive," I said.

Our boss asked me several times whether or not I was okay to drive. He even gave me a little sobriety test and deemed me sober enough. I normally would have been nervous to drive Becky's new car, but two drinks had taken me to my invincible place. I didn't realize how bad the roads were.

Becky's car was a four speed, which I had no problem driving. But getting used to her clutch and gear shifter on slippery roads wasn't a great idea. I was inching my way along when I pressed the brakes a teeny bit to make it around a gradual bend in the road. We began to slide, and I lost control of the car. As we rolled down an embankment, I was a witness to my fate as I watched the snow-covered world turn upside down again and again. I heard the car being crushed like a can as it landed on its roof. The finale was the sound of glass shattering as a giant rock smashed through the sun roof right between our heads. We were both spared, but it scared the shit out of us. I was stunned and couldn't move.

How did I not have a scratch? I would never have dreamed that I would one day say that the accident was a synchronistic event, one which helped shape my destiny to create an infinite strand of pearls.

Becky seemed to sober up instantly. She got out of the car, screaming, "What have you done to my car?"

"I'm sorry!" I cried. "The road was slippery."

She started tossing bottles of booze away from the car into the snow, but it was too late. Only seconds seemed to have passed, and the police were there. Someone must have seen the accident and called. We were in trouble. They separated us and searched the car. I had to take a breathalyzer test, which I failed by a couple of points. The officer didn't put cuffs on me, but he drove me to the police station. I sat in the back of the cruiser with a barrier between me and the officer. I was alone again. That time I was in the kind of trouble I couldn't hide from. I was charged with drunk driving, and the whole town knew about it.

The exact energy I was hiding from was already hidden deep inside me. It was projecting its energy to everyone around me and attracting the same energy back to me.

Becky's car was totaled. She didn't speak to me for months. When she moved my belongings into the upstairs hallway, my heart sank. I knocked on her door. When she answered, I told her how sorry I was and begged her to forgive me. She just looked at me and slammed the door in my face. I wanted to crawl into a hole. I was humiliated, guilt stricken, embarrassed, depressed, and alone again. If I could have crawled out of my skin, I would have. My best friend had invited me to live with her, and she had kicked me out.

Todd took advantage of the situation by inviting me to stay in his room. I couldn't see any other option. I felt like a fly entangled in his web. After I moved in, my days were long and repetitive. He barely spoke to me unless he wanted sex. He never told me he loved me. He didn't even seem to like me. Neither of us had a driver's license. We were both losers who, deep down, wanted nothing to do with each other. He had no use for me other than to keep one side of his bed warm. I did what I needed to do to have a roof over my head.

I never felt at ease living in that house after the accident. I was always nervous. I experienced the same emotions that had poisoned me when I lived with my dad, but I couldn't fathom a way out.

I had no money and no job. I couldn't contribute any rent to Becky's parents. I felt trapped and confined again. I was no longer in control. I was back in survival mode, and I was deeply depressed. I felt withered and undernourished, but I didn't even know what was missing.

Becky was gone most of the time. Her father had gotten her another job in construction, but there was only one position available. I finally got a job walking door to door, selling solar panels for rooftops. It was a joke. I was promised a salary, and they never paid me. At least it kept me busy and out of that house until spring came.

Todd got a job as a merchant marine in Texas. When he left, it was a huge relief. Becky finally got over the fact that I had wrecked her car and forgave me. I moved back into her room, and we became friends again. But the nature of the friendship had shifted for me. I couldn't relax. I didn't know how to act. I was always trying to project an image that I thought Becky and our friends wanted to see.

I was falling apart inside. I was a broken girl who was afraid to trust. My self-esteem was nonexistent, and I felt like a lower-class person. I was sure everyone saw me as Becky's needy friend who lived at her house and rode around in her car. I felt inferior and pitied by the world. I kept to myself except when I could escape from myself by partying.

I was desperate to be perceived as a girl who was perfectly fine. I projected the idea that I was just in the midst of a stream of bad luck. It was an illusion that I came to believe as fact. The miraculous gift of all the illusions of being lost was discovering I never was. Our power to heal our strand of life lies within.

Chapter Eight

Tragedy Strikes

The mark of your ignorance is the depth of your belief in injustice and tragedy. What the caterpillar calls the end of the world, the master calls the butterfly.

~ Richard Bach ~

The spring of 1983 brought a new beginning for my family. Mom and Dad were divorced. Dad had moved back to Nova Scotia and bought a house on a lake in the boonies where he was most comfortable. Mom moved to an apartment in York with my brother and sister and worked for my grandpa.

I had a new job painting for a contractor. The owner gave me a ride to the locations of various small projects around town. One day, as I stood on a ladder watching my hand stroke a house with a paint brush, I realized I was interested in buildings and how they were designed and constructed. It was quiet, and I heard my soul speak to me. In that moment, I had a revelation. I wanted to go back to school.

I secretly began to look into colleges that offered engineering degrees. I'd always had a passion for school. It had been one of my only escapes, and I'd earned good grades. I really wanted to have my plans nailed down for fall. I didn't know how to pay for school or how to make it happen, but I really wanted to go to the University of New Hampshire. I was also desperately searching for a way to get out of Becky's house, because she would be leaving in the fall to attend a two-year program in travel and tourism.

Becky and I had returned to cruising the beach in her parent's brown Cordoba. That summer I did it with a real smile because I had a secret plan. I kept my plan to myself, because I didn't trust anyone. One day, as we took our typical loop around Long Sands beach, we noticed a black Toyota pickup in the parking lot of the Anchorage restaurant. It wasn't from around town, and it was still too early for tourists. We were curious. The truck was shiny and new, and it had a Massachusetts license plate.

With the black truck facing the ocean, we had to look over our shoulders as we drove by to see who was in the driver's seat. We were so obvious. A very good-looking blond guy with dark sunglasses sat behind the steering wheel with one foot propped on the window opening. His work boot was unlaced. As we gawked, he nodded and smiled.

Becky and I looked at each other and whispered, "Who is that?"

We drove by a dozen times before we worked up the courage to pull in.

We must have amused him. Becky parked right next to his truck. I did the talking because I was closest to him.

Trying to appear casual, I said, "Hi there."

His beautiful white smile hit me hard in the chest as he said hello.

As we chatted, I went on autopilot to take in the view. His smile was gorgeous. He had a Bon Jovi look to him, but better. Becky told me to ask him to take off his sunglasses. I was already smitten, but when our eyes met, I got butterflies in my stomach. It was an instant crush.

I felt absolutely alive. I could feel my eyes sparkle with adoration. Every cell in my body seemed to be smiling. The sun looked brighter, and the water was bluer. Even the air coming into my lungs felt happy. I was flying on a first-crush high.

We asked him all kinds of questions, and he asked us just as many. His name was Rob, and he had just moved from Hull, Massachusetts. He was our age, and he was perfect. Becky and I were both head over heels for him.

When he asked if we had boyfriends, Becky immediately said, "She's my cousin's girlfriend, but I'm single!"

I was so mad at her. I wasn't officially Todd's girlfriend anymore, but I didn't want to embarrass myself by arguing. I just wanted to slide down into the seat and disappear. After that, Becky did all the talking, leaning over me to see him. It felt as if she was doing and saying whatever she could to make me look unavailable and unworthy of him.

Rob quickly became part of our group of friends. He was a perfect fit. He was witty and easygoing, and he liked to party as much as we did. His character was as laidback as his attire. He wore button-down shirts with a tank top underneath, blue jeans, and work boots that were always untied.

Rob had blue eyes and beautiful blonde hair that wasn't too short. He was so easy to get along with that it felt like we'd grown up with him. Everyone loved Rob. He wasn't loud and obnoxious like Todd. He treated everyone, especially women, with respect.

All the girls had a crush on him and, of course, he quickly landed a girlfriend. It was fine with me. He ended up becoming a great friend, but that didn't stop me from flirting with him. It became a game to tease him. We all did it, even the guys.

I can still picture Rob resting his forearms on the back of his truck, holding an icy cold beer. He was never in a bad mood, and he always had a smile on his face. His calm, happy energy was what made him so attractive.

He adored his mother. Rob had moved to York with her, leaving his sister and brother in Hull with their father. He left his mom by herself a lot that summer to party with us.

One of our gang's favorite summer pastimes was hopping on 4WD vehicles and driving through extremely rough terrain just to go swimming at Folly Pond. It was against the law to swim there because it was a reservoir that supplied water for another town. Of course, that's part of what made it so much fun. We loved challenges, as long as we didn't get caught. I loved going there because it took me to a place where I didn't have to deal with myself. I could continue to hide and ignore everything outside of Folly Pond and everything inside of myself.

Once, Becky and I rode to Folly with Rob by ourselves. She was a bit buzzed, and the ride was crazy fast and very bumpy. Becky had decided to wear a motorcycle helmet that belonged to our friend Hubba. It was hysterical. I could not stop laughing at her. We laughed all the way to Folly Pond. I didn't want it to end. When I was pleasantly occupied with laughter and beer, nothing else mattered. We spent the entire day drinking, swinging on ropes, and splashing into folly Pond.

The Folly Pond ritual enabled me to keep my true self hidden every weekend that summer. Now that I've strengthened my strand, it's hard for me to imagine that I ever had to live like that. No one should have to. No one should need to.

I went to a party across the street from Becky's house one night toward the end of the summer. A friend of Becky's sister came over and sat down next to me. I was skeptical about Kerrie wanting to talk to me because Becky's sister Lori didn't seem to like me much.

Kerrie surprised me. She told me she could tell that I needed to get out of Becky's house. Kerrie lived in a boarding house just off Short Sands beach that had a room opening up. She told me that if I had a job and three weeks rent up front, she would put in a good word for me to Mrs. Norton. I felt my face shine with delight. I hugged and thanked her. I was so excited I couldn't contain myself.

I will forever be thankful to Becky's parents for taking care of me, but I needed to move on for many reasons. I wanted to stand on my own two feet. I didn't want to be controlled by anyone. I would always be Becky's friend, but I needed to be free and independent and find my self-respect, which is what I was always striving for. Little did I know all those things were always accessible to me no matter where I was.

I will never forget Mrs. Norton. As soon as I arrived at her home, I knew that I belonged there. She was one of the loveliest, sweetest, kindest women I've ever met. Her home reflected her personality. She was definitely one of my role models. Mrs. Norton had a sweet, soft, tender voice and was as huggable as a teddy bear. I felt a deep sense of comfort in her company.

She took me upstairs and showed me my new room. It was gorgeous. It had a half-round sitting nook surrounded by windows that looked out to the ocean. There was a double bed with a spread and matching curtains in a shade of cotton candy pink, complete with lace trim. I felt at home there, as if the room had been waiting for me to arrive.

Mrs. Norton cleared a shelf in the refrigerator for my food and said I could use the phone any time. I had to do my laundry at the laundromat, but it was a very short walk down the street. It was all perfect! I told her immediately that I would take it. At last, I would be free to walk my path my way!

The only way to be truly free to walk your path is to express pure honesty. No amount of ocean views and pretty pink rooms can do it for us.

I still hung around with the gang, but I did it on my terms. Living on the other side of town made it easy to meet and hang out with different people. Sometimes I even enjoyed spending time alone. I started running on the beaches every day.

I was finally starting to enjoy living. During moments of solitude at the places that spoke to me, I began to feel that there was something else to life. I didn't know what or where it was. When I had those thoughts, I usually came to the conclusion that I was daydreaming and snapped out of it.

Were those whispers from the universe? It was all part of my series of synchronistic events. I just didn't know it at the time.

While Becky was away at school, I developed a short-term friendship with a girl named Kim. She was preppy and helped ground me a little bit. We often hung out at her house because her mom was never home. Kim loved to cook and taught me her culinary secrets while we laughed and drank wine.

Kim was part of my old group of friends, along with Todd and Skeeter, but she was more a part of the new group. People in the new group were older than I was and not too receptive to newbies. I bounced between the two groups just as I had in high school.

The weather was turning cold, and the tourists were long gone. One weekend I stopped at Butch's house during a run on Long Sands beach. It was a central meeting spot for the new group. As I approached Butch's place, I noticed Rob was parked in front of the house. He was watching the ocean, as he often did. My friend Kim was dating Butch at the time, and the two of them were deep in conversation.

I walked up to Rob and said, "What's up with them?"

He rolled his eyes. "I don't know, but I'm bored waiting for Butch. What are you doing?"

"I'm just finishing up with a run. Why?"

"You want to hang out?"

"Where's your girlfriend?"

"Working."

Smiling, I said, "Sure!"

I finished my chilly run and went home to get ready. He picked me up about an hour later, and we went right to the liquor store and bought a lot of beer. We were only nineteen, but we each had a fake ID. We cruised the beach, listening to music and talking. Then we headed out of town to visit all the other beaches in the area. At each beach, we drank beer, talked, and laughed. We took turns driving. It turned into a marathon drinking game, as we hopped out to smoke and play on one beach before driving to the next.

When it got dark, we decided to head back up north. We returned to Butch's on York Beach, but he wasn't there. He had beer in his refrigerator, so we laughed and said, "Why not?"

We had no intention of leaving, because we were both too drunk to drive. At some point, Rob announced that we were out of cigarettes. We searched Butch's room, both of us laughing hysterically. When our search came up empty, we decided that we could make it to the store before it closed.

To this day, I can't remember who drove. I don't even remember leaving Butch's house.

My first memory is running down a dark, quiet street, whimpering from fear. Something wet, warm, and sticky covered my body. I remember wondering if it was blood. I couldn't see anything in front of me, but there was a faint blinking behind me. I had to get away. I wasn't sure what I was getting away from, but I couldn't look back, because I knew whatever was back there was bad.

What I really needed was a luminous light to guide me onto a path of self-realization, but I wasn't ready for that kind of healing. The only healing I wanted that night came from a purely physical need. I wanted someone—anyone—to wash me up and put me to bed so I could wake up in the morning and be relieved that it was only a dream.

An endless path of darkness loomed ahead as I ran down the pitch black road. With every sprint, my purse bounced off my side, causing pain as sharp as a knife. Each time I went from walking to running, cold air penetrated my body and sliced through my lungs.

My blood roared through my body. It was like the rapids of a river reacting to my fright, flight, fight response from whatever I'd left behind me. I could feel my heartbeat pulsating in every vein and pounding in my ears, but I couldn't understand why. I did understand that I needed help, and I needed it right away. I felt alone, hurt, very cold, and confused.

I knew it was late because no lights were on in any of the homes I passed. I finally saw the flickering light of a TV in a window, and a sense of relief flooded through me. I ran to the house and frantically banged on the door. When the outside light flashed on, I squinted against the sudden brightness. I was confused when I realized that the woman who answered the door was the mother of a friend of mine named Rob.

As she rushed to help me up the front steps, she gasped and said, "Oh, my God! Debbie, is that you? What happened to you?"

I couldn't answer. She sat me down and asked me again what had happened. In the light, I could see that I was definitely covered in blood. I began to shake. I'd seen that type of injury on TV, but I never thought anything like it would happen to me.

"I don't know," I finally said as tears rolled down my face.

"I'm calling the police," she said.

Suddenly, I remembered that I had been with Rob. "Rob and I were going to get cigarettes," I sobbed. "Where is he?"

Her eyes grew wide as she realized that her son might have been in whatever accident had left me bleeding and injured. "You were with Rob?"

As she ran to the phone, I screamed, "Yes! Where is he? Where is he? I think he's hurt! Oh, my goodness. I think we were in a car accident! Why is this happening?" My heart raced with fear for Rob's safety. "We need help! Get help! Where is he? Is he hurt?"

As she dialed 911, my mind was racing. Why is this happening? Where is Rob? What just happened? From there, my mind goes blank. I don't remember the ambulance coming or riding in one.

That night, I could not have imagined that something as simple as my willingness to accept pain and suffering would one day enable me to discover the granular seed of my soul. The strand of peace that now holds the pearls of my lessons enables my soul to continue to grow. When acceptance, forgiveness, and love are present in your heart, the gifts of life's treasures are infinite.

The next thing I remember were the lights at the hospital. They were blinding, and I was freezing cold. I started screaming, "Where is Rob? Where is Rob? Why aren't you answering me?"

They had to strap me down so I wouldn't further injure myself. The doctor leaned over and whispered, "Your friend Rob didn't make it."

I refused to believe him. "You're lying. Where is he? You liar, where is he?"

My screaming and crying were disrupting the entire ER, so they took me to another room and gave me something to make me sleep.

I woke early the next morning. I could feel the energy of my world collapsing around me. My body felt as if a cement mixer had rolled over it. I knew deep inside that there had been a horrific accident, but I couldn't remember being in it or leaving it.

Through the years, I've had dreams where I see flashes of the yellow line on a winding road, and I hear U2's "Sunday Bloody Sunday" playing on a radio. I don't know which one of us was driving. I will never know.

As I lay there trying to remember, a nurse came in and told me the police were waiting to talk to me. The State Police officers didn't sugarcoat it. They told me I was in big trouble. They said I should start talking, and fast. Rob's truck had flipped upside down before impacting a tree 10 feet in the air. It had landed on its roof, crushing everything inside.

As one of the officers described the scene of the accident, my body quivered. Rob was gone. Why wasn't I gone? Was it my fault? Had I killed my friend? *Oh, my God*, I thought. *Why did this happen? It should have been me, not him.*

I just looked at them and said, "I don't remember." I wanted to die. They told me there would be a thorough investigation. They were going to fingerprint every inch of Rob's truck. If they determined that I was the driver, I would go to jail for the rest of my life. Every time I told them that I couldn't remember leaving Butch's house, they called me a liar. I later learned that they had questioned me illegally and against doctor's orders.

Mom showed up right after the officers left. All I could do was sob. I was in the worst turmoil of my life. My body was broken and bruised. My heart and soul were broken and bruised. The loss and shock weighed me down until all I could feel was immense sadness.

Mom hugged and kissed me and asked me what I needed. I told her to call Dad. I needed her to get him there. He was the person who had hurt me the most, and I thought he could fix everything.

Looking back on that decision to have Mom contact my dad, I realize there was a hidden love that lived deep inside. I did love him because he was my dad. I also loved the Dad I wanted him to be.

I was scared, weak, and vulnerable, like an injured bird that couldn't fly. I needed my dad's control to fix my situation, fix me, and make everything all better. But it was Mom who always tried to fix everything. She called Dad and told him to come. She took me to my grandparent's house to recover, because they were in Florida for the winter. She contacted a lawyer after the nurses told her about the visit from the police. It was Mom who tried to mend my broken wing, not Dad.

My father showed up, but he didn't know how to support me, because he couldn't fly himself. My wing didn't heal, and I was unable to fly for years. Instead, I used it to protect my heart and soul. I stuffed the tragedy deep inside where it couldn't hurt me anymore. I carried it in every cell of my body for years.

I begged my mother to take me to see the truck, but she refused. She didn't understand that I needed to see it. I thought it might help me remember. My friend Keith offered to take me. He knew where the truck had been towed.

Mom was right again. When Keith pulled in, I saw the horror of the night that took Rob. I trembled with fear and couldn't get out of the car. It was too real for me. The truck looked as broken as I felt. There was crushed, jagged metal everywhere, and the seats were mangled. There was a lot of dried blood.

I never imagined at that moment that I would ever smile again, let alone spread my wings and fly free in peace. The truck was a reflection of who I was at the time, and I had to get out of there and never look back.

The accident with Rob was a horrible tragedy. While I will never forget about it, I'm no longer running from it. I have accepted the pain and loss even though I lost my friend. I have learned many lessons and gathered them as luminous pearls since that tragedy. The most important pearl of wisdom is my gratitude for the gift of life. I am free to fly, with my wings holding my infinite strand of life.

The wake for Rob was my worst nightmare. Mom purchased a new outfit for me because I had no money and nothing appropriate to wear. The idea of attending the wake intimidated me, but I had to be there to honor Rob. I recall the day vividly. I have never felt more rejected and isolated by a group of people.

Getting to the funeral home was painful. I had several broken ribs and a broken arm that still needed to be set by an orthopedic surgeon. My face was severely cut and bruised. My mental and emotional states were extremely fragile. I remember trying to focus my mind on the weather.

As soon as I got out of Mom's car, people started whispering and glaring at me. A few pointed at me. It was clear that they all thought I should have died in the accident, and I wished again that I had. I felt humiliated and guilty for surviving.

Rob's friends and family from Hull were inside, along with the people from York that I'd considered friends. I looked through the doorway and saw them all sheathed in black. I pulled back and shut my eyes tightly, rejecting the tears that were building. Mom asked me if I was sure I still wanted to be there. I looked at her with tears in my eyes and then turned to walk inside.

Rob's mother couldn't look at me. I felt such remorse and fear that I was terrified to approach her and extend my condolences. Instead, I went up to his sister and said, "Laura, I am so very sorry." I started crying then, and those were the only words that would come out. She hugged me and said, "Thank you." It meant the world to me that she accepted me. We remain friends today.

My eyes locked on Rob in his casket at the front of the room. My heart was in my throat. I was petrified to approach him because I had no answers for anyone who might have stopped me on the way. I sat in a chair in the back and cried until Mom grabbed me by the arm and insisted we leave.

Thinking back to that challenging time in my life, I feel deep compassion for everyone involved, including the poor girl who had to endure surviving. I have a passionate respect for all the pearls on the strand of life that I have

discovered. Those pearls came from embracing a peace that can be found within us all and accepting the synchronistic events in the Divine quest of life.

The funeral was held the next day in a Catholic Church down the street from the funeral home. I went with Becky and Todd. I was shaking with anxiety. When the funeral began, Todd's inappropriate behavior made me feel worse. As Rob's family entered the church behind Rob's casket, Todd made insulting sexual comments about Rob's sister.

I don't remember anything else from the funeral. I was there in my physical body only. The rest of me zoned out until the end of the funeral procession. I regretfully and silently said goodbye to my friend Rob as his casket rolled past the end of our pew.

After several visits to the surgeon, my young and resilient body healed. The time it took for my body to heal was extremely short in comparison to the mental and emotional healing I had to do. I pushed my mental and emotional injuries deep into the hole where I always stored challenging experiences. My mantra then was out of sight, out of mind. Once my physical injuries were no longer visible to me or anyone else, I was sure I would be fine.

I was wrong. Difficult times are invitations from the universe to learn, grow, and open to love and light. They are not invitations to poison your mind or hide in the dark. Whenever we confront difficulties, they become opportunities for us to learn.

Trauma of any kind, such as an accident, loss, abuse, sadness, or abandonment can sometimes make us close our hearts for protection. We hide from ourselves, from others, and from the Divine. We are certain we can never get over such misfortunes.

It is possible to transition from self-torture and the destruction that comes from dwelling on the past and discover the gifts within you. There are hidden treasures that will allow you to discover the true you. They are the tools that will open your heart and allow you to forgive, accept, and experience life on life's terms.

I never dreamed it could be so easy to just let go and give myself permission to search for my true self when I was running from everything. All it takes is giving yourself permission to search inside your heart for the bright, sparkling pearls of love and light, which allow your soul to shine.

My purpose in sharing my life experiences is not to persuade or convince, but to demonstrate the healing through transformation that can happen any time you set your intention. I'm here to tell you that arriving on the other side of the journey is wonderful. Yes, it will take some work. Whether you are midway through the journey or haven't yet begun, you will be okay!

The tools to help you acknowledge, heal, and let go come from within. Your buried treasure is already inside you! Bring yourself from feeling like a victim into survival. The only initial requirement is the desire to do so. With the deepest sincerity, I can say that it is as easy as this quote from Luke 1:19: "Ask and it shall be given to you. Seek and you shall find." Spiritual awakening and transformation will follow.

Once I was physically healed and living back at Mrs. Norton's, I needed a real job, and one came to me. Lynn, my friend Claudia's sister, was applying for a position with the IRS as a tax examiner. I asked her if I could tag along. She said it would be great if we both got the job because the commute to Andover, Massachusetts, was long, and we could split the gas and keep each other company.

We were so excited when we walked in. And then we saw the application and the test. The first line on the application read "no college degree, no job." I panicked as I wrote that I had a degree in business, and I was a nervous wreck while taking the test because I had lied on the application.

We laughed all the way back to York. We both got a job because we had passed the exam. After a two-week training period, we became tax examiners for the U.S. government. I had done what my father said I could never do. I had accomplished something. I wasn't stupid. Even though I was not a college graduate, I had passed the test, and I was a tax examiner for the IRS!

I worked very hard at that job. Lynn and I were up at 3:00 a.m. and at work by 6:00 a.m. My ego was so proud of me during tax season for rising early and working hard that it told me I deserved to play hard, too. Between the job and partying, there was no room left over for soul searching. It was the last thing that would have ever entered my mind.

By the spring of 1985, I had started dating Kim's old boyfriend Steve. My mom had been remarried for almost a year, and her husband cosigned a loan for me to get a car. I needed a car to get to my new waitressing job at the Weathervane restaurant in Kittery.

One afternoon, I headed to an outdoor party at Butch's house. My life was going just the way I wanted it to go. I had friends, a job, a car, and a new boyfriend. It all started going south again when I turned around and saw Todd.

He had pulled into the driveway in his blue jeep with the music blaring. His ego was huge, and he made his usual grand entrance. Todd parked his jeep right next to where I was standing. I turned my back and tried to ignore him, but he started using what he considered to be charm on me. I was very uncomfortable. Steve noticed, and he came over to get me out of the situation. While Steve talked guy stuff with Todd, I went to talk with Becky. I asked her why her cousin was back.

"Todd had a lot of time to think while he was in Texas. He says he's come back for his girlfriend." I thought she was referring to Laura, Rob's sister, but Becky cleared that up. Todd had come back for me.

I must have had rocks for brains or been a glutton for more abuse. For whatever reason, Todd broke me down after a few days, and I got back together with him. I told myself a lie. I told myself he had changed.

Everything did seem okay between us at first. But Todd was still Todd. One day, I had finished a run and was heading toward the ocean too cool off. I heard Todd yelling at me to hop in his truck. He had a nice, shiny red truck that he bought with his money from working in Texas as a merchant marine. As the daughter of a mechanic, I had an eye for a cool vehicle. I ran over and hopped in.

As he peeled out of the parking lot, I realized I should have had an eye for how drunk he was. After the accident with Rob, I was frightened to be a passenger in any car. With a drunk driver at the wheel, I feared that my life was about to end. Todd either peeled out from stop signs or blazed through them without stopping. He repeatedly stopped and started in the middle of the road just to lay rubber.

As Todd drove like a crazy person, I gripped the sides of the seat so tightly that I broke off several fingernails. I screamed for him to stop and let me out, but he ignored me. It was the joy ride from hell. I thought I was going to die. I screamed and cried and begged him to stop, but he was so crazed by whatever he had taken that he didn't even hear me.

Something caught his eye, and he slowed down for a minute. I didn't even think about it. I just opened the door and jumped out onto the side of the road and started running.

Egos attract and run from pain. An open heart and soul radiate and attract happiness, not allowing others to project their pain onto us. Have compassion for them, but don't absorb their energy.

Todd was remorseful for his actions even though he couldn't remember what he had done. I caved in and accepted his apology. If I had known what was coming next, I would have walked away from Todd and never looked back.

Beaterman, a friend of ours in Portsmouth, was having a dinner party at his apartment. It sounded on the up and up to me, and it was better than going somewhere just to get drunk. I never wanted to do that with Todd again. I didn't trust him. I respected Beaterman, though. After all, he had a real job, an apartment, and a girlfriend.

It started out very well. We had dinner at the table with real plates, silverware, and wine. My skepticism shifted to thinking that it was going to be a nice evening. That didn't last long, because when I came out of the bathroom, the guys were snorting cocaine for dessert.

Waldo and Skeeter were there, too, and they must have said at least 10 times, "Come on, sis, It's time to go home."

Each time, I said, "I think I'm gonna stay for a while."

They practically begged me to leave with them. It was as if they knew what I was in for. They knew Todd's history and what he was capable of all too well. They finally left without me.

By 2:00 a.m., I was wishing that I had gone with them. I was exhausted and needed sleep. I asked Beaterman if I could lie down somewhere. He showed me to the guest room, and I collapsed in bed with my clothes on. I fell asleep with a sense of relief, knowing I had a place to put my head down.

I had fallen into a sound sleep, but I awoke suddenly to find Todd sitting on me. There was evil in his eyes as he put his hands around my neck and started blubbering words I couldn't understand. At first I thought he was playing a not-so-funny game. It was clear he wasn't himself. I panicked and tried to get up, but I couldn't move. I was completely powerless.

He tightened his grip on my neck, trying to choke me. It was one of the worst feelings of my life. Terror overcame me because I couldn't breathe. I wet my pants in fear. My heart was racing, but I tried to concentrate on taking air in slowly through my nose. Todd's breath smelled sour, his hair was disheveled, and his eyes were bloodshot and heartless. It was fortunate that he was so out of it that he couldn't maintain a tight grip.

My inner voice told me to get out. I immediately grabbed his fingers and tried to tear them away, all the time feeling pain and terror race through my veins. The adrenalin surge gave me the strength to kick him as hard as I could. He was so drunk, he let go. As I tried to catch my breath, he hit me in the face. I fell back onto the bed, and he pinned my arms. I kicked and screamed for help, but he covered my mouth with his hand. Every time I thought I was gaining an edge, Todd used more strength to hold me down.

I knew that my advantage was being sober, while he was wasted. That was my only defense. I played his game, conserving my energy as I waited for him to wear himself out. He finally got sloppy, and I was able to scream again for Beaterman to help me. That time Todd got mad and grabbed the pillow. As he pushed it against my face, I was able to slide sideways. I rolled onto the floor, knocking him down.

I ran into the living room and screamed, "Beaterman!" I was frantic and out of breath. I was sweaty and drooling, and my eyes were cloudy with tears.

My soul had been severely scarred. I am now proud to bear that scar because of the growth it gave me. I was hurt and angry then. Today, the pearl of compassion surrounds my heart for those who resort to controlling others.

Todd must have exhausted himself and passed out from abusing his body and mine. He slept it off, not even knowing that he had terrorized me.

Hysterically, I yelled, "Your crazy-ass friend just tried to strangle me!"

As he tried to peel his eyes open, Beaterman said, "Sorry, Deb. What do you want me to do?"

"Just let me use your phone."

He sat with me while I used his phone to call my other friend named Rob. He was one of the good ones. He never got into trouble, and he was dependable and trustworthy. It was to his mom's house that I had run after the accident. The phone rang and rang before he finally answered. I told him what had happened, and he told me to get out of the apartment and wait outside by the road.

The wait seemed like an eternity. It was chilly outside, I had no coat, and my pants were wet with urine. I was shivering from cold and anguish after having been assaulted. I was dizzy with hate and disgust for Todd. I went from feeling alone and hurt to deeply angry.

Twenty minutes later, Rob pulled up. Skeeter was with him for backup. Rolling the window down, Skeeter said, "Get in the car, sis. Are you okay? I told you to ride home with us last night!"

Relieved, I said, "I'm fine now."

Skeeter was with Rob because they weren't sure if they were going to need force. They knew battling Todd was like fighting an army. They couldn't believe I'd gotten away from him.

I was on a mission. Todd was going to pay for what he'd done to me. My ego was in protective mode, and it turned me into Miss Tough Girl instead of helping me let go and feel.

I had them drop me off at Becky's house. I told her parents that their nephew had gone too far this time. I told them he had tried to kill me, and I wasn't going to be meek-mouse Debbie any more. I was done with Todd's bullshit abuse. I told them I respected them, but I would be filing charges and getting a restraining order against their nephew.

Todd's uncle offered me a ride to the police station, and I accepted. I walked in there holding my head high with independence and confidence. I was never, ever going to allow another man to abuse me. I had given Todd too many chances. Living the torture of letting someone hurt me was over.

I had the courage to set myself free from Todd, but I was never really free from anything until I found and opened my heart and soul. A French proverb says that hope is the dream of a soul awake. I had finally begun to wake up.

Chapter Nine

The Identity Bud That Couldn't Bloom

You cannot help but learn more as you take the world into your hands. Take it up reverently, for it is an old piece of clay, with millions of thumbprints on it.

~ John Updike ~

In the 1980s, most of my actions came from my damaged spirit, which had diminished my soul and allowed ego and will to take over in an effort to protect me. The universe knew that my whole was not yet healthy enough to allow the true me to be awakened.

The calamities and life challenges I had experienced did nothing more than allow my coat of armor to grow thicker, clouding and overshadowing the windows to my soul. I was strong enough to continue enduring the grains of sand, so I stored them and allowed them to slowly develop into pearls. My strand had to become strong enough to embrace them, learn from them, and let them go.

My ego once trusted only my will, but my heart and soul have now bloomed into flowers of love, faith, and trust in life and others.

I worked evening shifts at the Weathervane. After serving the last of the summer lobster-eating crowd, we cleaned up and closed. Those of us who were single with no children or other responsibilities often went to the bar at the Quarterdeck restaurant for shots and beers. I usually got bored after one drink and went back to York to make the rounds with the partygoers. It wasn't really boredom; it was an inability to stay present. Sometimes I just headed home and went to bed, but that didn't happen very often. I thought I was happy wherever I could find great music and alcohol.

I was spending all my tips on booze and partying. I didn't use my earnings to buy groceries. I did my laundry only when I ran out of clothes. I drove drunk almost every night. I would arrive at Mrs. Norton's at all hours of the night and wake her up by flicking on the lights all the way from the front door to the kitchen. After raiding the refrigerator for everyone else's food and leaving a mess in the kitchen, I went to sleep. I slept half the next day, got up, and walked to the beach to sleep some more. When evening came, I dragged myself back to work and started the cycle all over again.

I was selfish and inconsiderate. Although I was aware of everything I did, and I felt remorse for my actions, I quickly stuffed those feelings down deep and ignored them. I pretended I was fine and acted kind and considerate when I ran into my housemates. I avoided them as much as I could, because it eased my conscience.

Everyone who lived in the boarding house heard me when I stumbled in late at night, but Kerri was the only one who ever said anything to me about it. She always stood up to me because she knew I had potential and was concerned that I was blowing my life. I was a selfish, self-seeking thief, and my actions were planting weeds around the seeds of my soul.

Even though my grandparents lived in the same town, I was too humiliated and ashamed to visit them. Grandma always had me figured out, and she never had a problem telling me what she thought. I clearly didn't want anyone pointing out how horribly I was spinning out of control. I was in denial. I loved Grandma so much, but I had to stay away because she always made me feel bad by pointing out my flaws. She didn't give up on me, though. Grandma often mailed me cards from across town with money in them. She really cared about me and loved me. I adored her too much to expose her pearl-white roses of joy to the shadow of my broken strand of life. Grandma's garden reflected the light like a field of luminous pearls. *Love kills the weeds of the ego in the garden of the soul.*

I fit in with the people from the Weathervane. We all worked hard and played hard, and they didn't judge me. I became friendly with young woman named Pam. She was married and had a baby girl. Pam partied once in a while after work, but she was very responsible. I could have learned something from her if I had been paying attention. We looked like sisters, and she was very nice to me.

Pam had a great sense of humor. She was always smiling, and her energy was delightful. I admired her grace and poise. She was the first person I allowed in my company who didn't party like I did. She had the perfect balance of nourishment, and her internal garden was growing.

One night, we started our partying at the Quarterdeck. Exhausted and reeking of fried seafood, we all piled around the bar and toasted the night with a few shots and chasers. One of the cooks told us that he knew where a huge party was being held. We all headed for the parking lot at the same time.

I didn't make it out of the parking lot because I backed into someone else's car, and the police showed up. They didn't arrest me, but I lost my license for driving to endanger.

I had set no boundaries for myself. I still thought I was invincible. I just did what my ego needed and suffered the consequences as they arrived. I left my fate in the hands of whoever might jump to my rescue. I never thought anything bad could happen to me.

Of course, it wasn't logical. I had been in an accident when I was driving my aunt's car and another when I was driving Becky's car. I had been seriously injured in the accident that killed my friend Rob. Those experiences should have taught me many lessons, but I was so closed down that I wasn't processing any lessons. The abuse I had suffered as a child had left me unable to take in traumatic events and process them.

I was not living from my true self or from my heart and soul. I didn't have love, faith, or trust in myself or anyone else. I was alive, but I wasn't awake. It didn't show on the outside, but I was afraid of everything. My body, mind, and soul functioned like a hard drive, storing my life challenges for the day when I would be willing to look inside for truth, answers, and lessons.

The lawyer Mom retained for me was able to negotiate a 90-day loss of my license. That presented a problem for me because I had no way to get to my waitressing job in Kittery. My awesome friend Pam offered to give me a ride.

Shortly after I lost my license, I found out that Mrs. Norton had lymphoma. Learning that such a wonderful woman had cancer broke my heart. But she had more bad news. Hanging her head, Mrs. Norton said, "Debbie, I don't want to do this, but I need you to move out. I need rent money, and you haven't been paying it. I love you, but you have too many problems for me to deal with right now."

It was not a surprise. I was quite aware of what a tyrant I had been. Mrs. Norton needed money, and I hadn't been paying her. She and I shared a deep connection on a soul level. I can honestly say I loved that woman, and I know she loved me. Otherwise, she wouldn't have put up with my shenanigans for as long as she did.

Even though I knew it was what I deserved, I was devastated. I loved Mrs. Norton, and I loved living in her house, but I had abused the privilege and taken advantage of her. I felt so guilty for hurting her that I couldn't look her in the eye.

My intention was never to cause pain, but my ego was bigger than my love. I begged her to let me stay. She said no. However, she did say she would hold my room. If I could get myself straightened out, she would allow me to come back. I could also leave my car parked in her yard until my license was returned. I ran to her and hugged her squishy, giving body and dripped mascara-laden tears all over her.

Pam came to my rescue again. She and her husband Steve lived in Cape Neddick, and they offered to let me stay with them. I took them up on their offer. It was only a temporary solution, but it was perfect. Pam and Steve had a lovely post-and-beam home and a beautiful little girl named Camille. She had blonde hair and ocean-blue eyes just like her parents.

Pam and Steve were wonderful role models who showed me what a normal home life could be. Because they didn't have any authority over me, I was more open to their influence than I had been when I lived with my aunt and uncle. Pam and Steve were my age. Sometimes I thought they were boring, but it was only because I was so wild. They didn't smoke, and they were both runners. They included me in their family meals.

Pam and I became close, and her extended family accepted me, too. It was a joke in her family that I looked more like Pam than her sister did. Although I was grateful for being included, I had to wear a mask around them. I acted like the person I thought they wanted me to be.

Every day, Pam and I would go to work and then go right home after our shift. I stayed out of trouble that summer, but my 21st birthday was approaching. Pam and Steve told me we could have a huge bash at their house. They lived in a wooded area and had plenty of room. It was an awesome feeling to know that someone accepted me for who I was. They gave me the structure of a normal family life. I was so comfortable with them that the bud of my true identity started to open a little.

August 10, 1985, came quickly. I was 21, legal, and happy as a petunia. A few days earlier, I had gotten my license back. Mrs. Norton, as sick as she was, agreed to let me move back into my room. I had saved enough money to pay her, and I did.

I picked Pam up, and we went to a liquor store in Portsmouth to purchase a keg of beer for my party. I walked in with a huge sense of confidence and an even bigger grin. I handed the clerk the paperwork for the keg, and he said, "ID, please."

With a big smile, I handed it to him and said, "Here ya go." It was a magnificent moment for me.

I invited everyone I had met since moving to York, with the exception of Todd. He was still not allowed to come within 500 feet of me or he would be arrested. Steve hung tiki lights and had reggae music playing. He even wore his Hawaiian shirt. Both Pam and Steve were amazing cooks, and they had prepared all kinds of food.

It was one of the best nights I'd had for a very long time. I didn't get too drunk, because I had wonderful role models with budding pearls on their interwoven strands of married life.

A few weeks after turning 21, I decided I needed a job that had more to offer me. I drove to the Villeroy and Bach outlets and noticed that the newest store, a Totes outlet, wasn't open yet. The manager, assistant manager, and district manager were having a meeting when I walked in. I filled out an application, and the district manager hired me on the spot. I was so happy that I jumped up and down while saying thank you.

My ego was firmly in control, and it was about to drown the seedlings of my soul. Would the pearls be revealed when my blooms opened up or would my ego suffocate them?

I gave notice to the Weathervane and started working at Totes before it opened. Barbara, a friend from York, was hired a couple of weeks after I started. The assistant manager was a fun, sassy woman with an infectious smile. She was very kind to me.

We all got acquainted as we unpacked stock, set up the store, and opened the doors for business. Kittery is an outlet town, and business continues year round. About a week later, we were selling rain gear and umbrellas, but the sun was always shining on us in the store.

I knew the products by heart because I had unpacked them. We were very busy, and I was working full time. I was proud to be part of an effective and happy team. Our team became great buddies in and out of work. We worked hard and rewarded ourselves at the end of the day. I enjoyed the reward too much and never knew when to quit. I was drowning my seeds in alcohol.

My car had begun to act up. Sometimes it wouldn't start, and it became completely unreliable and unpredictable. As the daughter of a mechanic, I knew it was the alternator, but I couldn't afford to fix it.

I was becoming unpredictable, as well, even to myself. Deep inside, I was seeking approval and acceptance from anybody. I began to do things that revealed a complete lack of self-esteem. One particular incident stands out in my memory.

After-work drinks usually led me to find a party. I needed the alcohol and the noise to keep my mind from focusing. Most late nights, a bunch of us would go to Portsmouth to have breakfast at Denny's or to Gilly's, which served the best chili dogs ever.

As I stood in the long line at Gilly's one night, the aroma of the hotdogs made my mouth water with anticipation. The guy behind me struck up a conversation. I recognized him from the Portsmouth bars. Once we got to the front of the line, he leaned in and said, "Hey, wanna come over and have a beer with those dogs?" I never said no to an invitation for a drink.

"Sure! I'll follow you."

I followed him in my unreliable car. We ate our food and had a beer before engaging in a one-night stand. I knew I'd made a terrible mistake, and I sobered up fast. How could I allow myself to become so desperate for attention that I would humiliate myself? I was horrified by my actions, and I hated myself for degrading my values.

I waited for the guy to pass out before tiptoeing to the door. I prayed that my car would start. I ran outside and gulped in some clean, fresh air. It was so cold that I could see my breath. "Please start. Please start," I whispered as my key shakily entered the ignition. I was so relieved when it started right up.

I never drove as cautiously as I did that night. I told myself that the random act of filth I had just committed never happened. I marched myself up Mrs. Norton's stairs and went to bed as quickly and quietly as possible. I had trouble falling asleep because I realized I had crossed a line. I cried myself to sleep in the fetal position.

I had never in my life done anything like that. I was troubled, and I subconsciously sought what I had seldom experienced in my life: love, approval, and acceptance.

It was the dead of winter when the universe delivered a synchronistic event that changed my life. I was driving home from having a couple of drinks with the girls from work when the car lights became dim. "Please, car, don't fail me now!" I said as I made a right-hand turn onto the beach.

By then, the lights were so dim they weren't even lighting my path. My car began to choke. I was able to pull over before it completely died. I put the car in neutral and tried to start it. Nothing happened.

I didn't know what to do, but I wasn't given any time to think, because York's finest pulled in behind me with their flashing blues. I hung my head with regret. I knew I was as done for as my alternator. I wasn't drunk, but I was sure I was over the legal limit. The flashing blue lights flashed my mind back to the accident, and my heart beat erratically. *Would my strand of life ever have pearls in full bloom?*

The officer tapped on my window. My heart was pounding as I rolled it down. I was a nervous wreck. With tears in my eyes, I said, "Officer, my car has died."

He just said, "License and registration."

While I nervously fumbled through my glove box, he leaned in and sniffed. "You been drinking tonight?"

I didn't have a chance to answer. As I handed him my paperwork, the officer said, "Step out of the car, please, Ms. Adams."

He asked me to walk the yellow line as he wrote me up. One foot fell just outside of it. He didn't handcuff me, but he took me to the police station and charged me with drunk driving. Usually, an arrest for drunk driving meant spending the night in jail, but an officer drove me around the corner to Mrs. Norton's. I wanted to wither and blow away like the petals of a rose after it has fully opened, except that I had never opened.

Mom and her lawyer could not get me out of a third drunk driving charge. There was no surprise there. I knew it was my fault, and I had to suffer the consequences. It was part of all the lessons that would build into an awakening.

I didn't tell Donna, my manager, about the drunk driving charge because I was embarrassed. She knew my car was not running, and I let her think just that. Scheduling was difficult because she usually put Barbara and me on opposite shifts. Barbara was giving me a ride, so we had to work the same shift. I also had to make an excuse to get out of work to go to court.

My court appearance went much worse than I expected. My lawyer was deeply sorry, but there was nothing the courts could do for me. The judge sentenced me to 30 days in an addiction rehab facility plus two days in a women's jail. My heart fell to my feet. I had a huge lump in my throat when the lawyer told me. I knew my days at Totes were numbered.

I didn't have to serve either of my sentences directly after court, which gave me some time to put my affairs in order. I just wanted to run away and start over. *Isn't that what we all want to do when life gets too tough for us to handle, even though it was our own doing?*

When I arrived at work the next day, Donna asked to see me in her office. Our assistant manager was getting her own store in North Conway, and I was next in line for her job at the store in Kittery. We had a staff of about 10. It would have been an honor, but I knew I had to be honest with her.

Before I could say a word, however, Donna said, "I have to give the job to Barbara. I'm sorry. You don't have the flexibility to do the job." I hung my head in shame and despair.

It was like my dad had shoved the sword into my heart himself. He was right. I was a stupid, good-for-nothing girl. I sat there and cried while I told her about my pathetic drunk-driving problem. Donna said my job would be waiting for me after rehab. We hugged and cried, but I felt sick to my stomach for allowing myself to screw up the opportunity. I had been rejected again, and that time it really hurt, because the promotion to assistant manager should have been mine. I had worked hard, but I had made terrible choices due to self-seeking.

But I had to face stringent consequences for my actions—consequences that would allow me to open all my petals to receive shiny pearls of wisdom later in my life.

There isn't a whole lot I can say about jail or rehab, because I shut myself down completely. All I remember is feeling abandoned and alone. It was if I was a flower bulb waiting for winter to end. I existed, but I was covered in dirt.

Mom drove me to the women's jail and dropped me off. I know she was worried about me, but she couldn't stay. I was scared to be alone, but my tough shell protected me. It wasn't like they show on TV. I was allowed to wear my own comfy clothes. They kept me separate from hardened criminals, and the guards were really very kind to me.

I served those two days in jail over a weekend. I had my own room, and I was allowed to go out onto my fire escape to smoke cigarettes. I passed the time reading magazines, smoking, and eating the food they served me. I did not use the time to reflect on how I actually got there. I didn't think about what had gone wrong in my life that I was so willfully controlling. I didn't look inside to search for the seed of my soul. I didn't feel or search at all. I just did my time, and that was that.

The court-ordered addiction rehab was a bit different, but not much. The biggest difference was that I was surrounded by lost souls in rehab. I learned one thing and remember two. I taught myself how shoot a basketball backward and upside down. Every day, I practiced my basketball trick during free time and learned the words to John Fogarty's song "Center Field."

I thought the only reason I was there was because I had gotten caught, and that was my punishment. It was a conditioned reaction, because that was what I had learned as a child. In my mind, I didn't belong there. My perception was validated when I saw a woman in her forties being brought in. My curiosity got the best of me, so I dropped the basketball and snooped around a little. We had a common area where everyone mingled. On the other side was the place they took people who came in under the influence.

The woman was dirty, and her hair was a rat's nest. I didn't know what detox was, but that's where they had taken her. I asked a member of the staff what the detox place was. Once I found out, I was positive that I didn't belong there. I didn't have an addiction problem. The court just wanted to make an example of me.

Every time I saw that woman sitting in the common area, I caught myself staring at her. I remember thinking how glad I was it wasn't me sitting there looking that sad and weak. I was sure it never would be. My mind was so muddy that I truly believed drinking was something that all young people did. I just got caught. What was her excuse? I kept my distance from that sad woman.

Looking back, I now realize that my fear of her was really a fear of her reflection. It was the reflection of a withered garden. I knew deep down that it could be me.

During my stay in rehab, we went on field trips to different halls where all these weird people smoked their brains out and drank coffee and told stories about their drinking days. It was quite entertaining, and the stories were funny. I found out it was called Alcoholics Anonymous. I had no clue what that meant, and I didn't care. I didn't belong there. I was only serving a sentence for getting caught.

My very first night home from that horrible hotel called rehab, I had Laura pick me up, and we went down to the beach. As we sat in her car, she opened a beer for herself. She didn't even ask me if I wanted one.

I was confused and annoyed. "Where's mine?" I asked.

"I thought you were supposed to quit drinking."

I was furious. I felt the blood rise to my face. *She can't sit there and drink in front of me*, I thought.

"The only reason I was at that place was because the court made me go," I said. "I didn't belong there, and I don't need to quit drinking."

She looked at me strangely and handed me a beer. At first, grasping that beer felt awkward. But it was cold, and the aroma was calling my name. My first sip was heavenly. Such a warm feeling circulated through my entire body.

Today I don't need to escape from myself. As Rumi said, "Whatever was said to the rose to make it open was said to me here in my chest."

I didn't learn anything from my punishments. It would be a few months before I could afford the fine, but it didn't matter, because the State of Maine had revoked my license. As a result, my options for nightlife were limited. That was perfectly fine with me. I had no desire to hang out with the old party crew. I stayed connected with Laura, though. She was Rob's sister, and I felt close to her.

It was spring again, and three of the four places I liked to go were getting busier. They were only half a mile from Mrs. Norton's, so walking there was easy. I also started dating a friend from the beach. We had known each other for years, but we hung in different circles. He was also my neighbor, which was convenient. His name was Mike. We got along well because he accepted me for who I was.

Being a Leo, I sometimes needed my space. He was a very easygoing person, and he allowed me my space with no questions asked. I know that Mike really cared for me, because he took me to his hometown in New Hampshire to meet his family.

When I wasn't working at Totes, I spent the spring and early summer at the beach, either lying in the sun or running. I tried to stay out of trouble, but the desire to cleanse my ego and collect pearls of pure light wasn't even a thought.

Chapter Ten

A Teddy Bear of a Remission

*You are
in the Right Place
at the Right Time
doing the Right Thing
with the Right People
for the Right Reason.
Everything is perfect.
You can have the Right Results!
All you need is a Right Heart and Mind,
an Open Heart and Mind.
And remember to keep your eyes open, too!*

~ Author Unknown ~

I left Totes in the summer of 1986 and started working at Shelton's Café, right across from Short Sands Beach. When I applied, they hired me on the spot. I worked various shifts, which was ideal for me. When I worked the breakfast shift, I could go to the beach in the afternoon. If I had an evening shift, I spent the day at the beach. I had it all figured out.

My intention was to make money, be happy, and stay away from anyone who reminded me of my weaknesses. With three party bars near my workplace, my plan to behave was short-lived.

Avoiding people, places, and things that remind us of our weaknesses seems easy, but it doesn't work. The weaknesses are within us. As soon as we look in the mirror, there they are. We are our own obstacles, and we can't avoid ourselves. Using our intention to dig deep and face our weaknesses will bless us with happiness, which is one of the many miraculous pearls we receive from the Divine.

The universe presented life to me in simple terms back then because it knew that was all I could handle. I had a very easygoing boyfriend who adored me. He supported me when I needed support, and he made himself scarce when I needed my space. It was exactly what I needed in a relationship at that point.

Walking was my only transportation, and it was certainly all I could handle. Everything I needed was within walking distance of Mrs. Norton's. Shelton's was a three-minute walk. Bogarts and two other bars were located on the same block as Shelton's. The laundromat and a small food store were another block away.

I was ever so gently being guided onto a path that would lighten my temptation to get into trouble. Of course, I didn't know it at the time. I was functioning purely from the control of my own will and ego. In fact, if anyone had tried to tell me otherwise, I would have laughed in her face and told her to talk to the hand. I was living at a low-level state of consciousness, one that tried to protect me. There was a tiny piece of me that was content, but I was carrying too much armor around my heart to really be free and happy.

Shelton's was a beautiful, classy place with views of the serene ocean. It offered a delicious gourmet brunch, along with menus for breakfast, lunch, and dinner. At first, working there made me feel as light and elegant as a princess, with not a care in the world. But I was filled with heaviness from my past.

In the evening, Shelton's featured live entertainment. The piano music and subdued lighting combined with the sights and smells of a warm evening at the beach to create a delightfully relaxing atmosphere for the patrons. Not long after starting work there, I began to feel that I was below the class of the people I was serving. I felt like a version of Cinderella, the one who scrubbed floors in rags. I was jealous of the hostess. She dressed in gorgeous clothes, wore her hair down, and greeted the customers. She was on their level, while I was Cinderella before the ball.

The truth was that I felt insecure. I didn't love myself. I tried to smile and pretend I enjoyed my customers, but I wanted more from life. It was working at Shelton's that made me realize that. I wasn't aware of some of the hurdles I would have to overcome before I could feel that I was as good as everyone else. I needed to prove it to my dad. I had to prove that I was smart. I had to show him that I was somebody.

I got downright disgusted with my attitude when my friends came in to support me by having me wait on them. Today, I see my job at Shelton's as an honor. I should have been able to hold my head high, smile, and enjoy myself and my friends. I couldn't see it that way then. I thought they were taunting me because I had to work. They would come in and order dinner and tons of drinks and then leave for a night on the town, knowing that I had to stay and work. I was so jealous of them, but I was also grateful for the awesome tips they left me.

I had to keep that job and push my low esteem and insecure feelings down with the rest of my dark emotions. I know today that the reason I partied all the time was to numb the pain of those stuffed emotions. Parties, bars, and sleep were my best friends and my medications of choice. They helped me escape from myself.

I became a regular at Bogarts, and the tips I earned at Shelton's became regular tips for Bogart's bartenders. I spent more time there than home at Mrs. Norton's. I became friendly with everyone who worked at Bogart's, including the bands, the bartenders, and the DJs. The summer DJs were twins from Massachusetts. Dean and David were on summer break from college and staying at York Beach. I knew Dean better than David because he had been attending Plymouth State College.

One night, Laura and I were partying at Bogart's. Dean's friends from college were there to support him while he was spinning records. He had the volume cranked up high that night. We girls were bellied up to the bar on our favorite stools. After a quick chat with the bartender, we spun around to watch the people. I loved it when the bar was packed. It was easier for me to hide from myself in a crowd, and it was a great opportunity to meet new people.

On Dean's break, he came over to say hi. "Hey, ladies," he said, "How we doin' tonight? Did you meet my friends from school yet?"

"In harmony, Laura and I said, "Hey, Dean." We all laughed. I looked over at the table of new guys and said, "No we haven't met yet. I think they want to meet us, though. They keep winking at us."

The guys at the table reminded me of roosters. They were all leaning back in their chairs, pushing out their chests and widening their necks. They cocked their heads and watched us as we walked to their table. I could feel their macho energies competing for our approval. I kept my cool, but inside I was laughing at them. After Dean made the introductions, Laura and I returned to our familiar barstools.

Even though I'd forgotten most of their names before the evening was over, meeting Dean's friends distracted me from myself for a short time. There was a part of me that was genuinely uncomfortable meeting people because I didn't feel adequate. I was very self-conscious. My clothes, hair, makeup, and jewelry weren't as nice as Laura's.

I didn't know then that I would someday have a strand of life so strong that it could hold an infinite number of pearls, all of them acquired by empowering myself to seek peace from within.

The next day I was walking a huge male golden retriever that belonged to the owner of the Bluff. He never had time to exercise the poor dog. Animal lover that I am, I felt compelled to walk that big dog every day. We both benefited from it. I soaked up his unconditional love, and he got a taste of freedom from his life in captivity. I think I saw a piece of myself in him. His owner kept him on a short leash in the hot sun all day long and often forgot to give him water. I made it my business to give the dog fresh, cold water after every walk.

That particular day, he saw something interesting and took off running, dragging me across Short Sands beach. As I was being dragged through the sand, I saw the group of college boys I had met the previous evening. At first, I couldn't remember any of their names. Then one popped into my mind. I screamed, "Help! Joel, please help me!"

Joel came running over with a smile. As he grabbed the leash and got the dog under control, he said, "Wow, he's strong."

Joel finished the walk with me, and we made small talk. I think he wanted to ask me out on a date, but I just said, "Thank you for your help. It was nice to see you again."

We had a blast walking the dog that afternoon, and I am grateful to the universe for allowing me to remember his name. It was definitely part of a Divine plan.

Evenings at Shelton's went by very slow because all I could think about was getting off work so I could go to Bogarts. When my shift finally ended, I marched myself next door. Joel and his friends were usually there. He and I became really good friends and started to hang out a lot. He was consistent and trustworthy, and there was no competition between us because he was a guy.

When I worked the brunch shift on weekend mornings, Joel would walk by in his funny little mismatched outfits and yell hello. His plaid shorts and patterned shirts with clashing colors cracked me up. It made my morning as bright and cheery as the sun itself.

One night after work, I went to Bogarts, but I was tired and didn't stay long. I was standing outside, saying goodnight to Joel. We were around the corner from the entrance when Mike walked by and saw us together. It was clear that he was surprised to see me with another guy. Instinctively, I braced myself. I expected Mike to get jealous and yell or hit me. Instead, he handled it pretty calmly.

"What's going on?" he asked. "Are you coming or going? Who's this?"

"Hi," I said. "I thought you were working. This is my friend Joel. Joel, this is Mike." They said hi to each other, but it was an awkward exchange. Then Mike asked if he could talk to me.

Mike was older than I was, but he was nothing like Todd. Mike was mature. He had already graduated from college and had a job. He was in a good place in his life and didn't need to escape from himself the way I did.

I hadn't been cheating on Mike. Joel and I were just friends. We had never even kissed goodnight. Mike was a gentleman about the situation, but during that conversation, we agreed that it was best for us to stop dating. Mike sensed that I was more interested in hanging out with my friends than having a boyfriend.

Joel had always treated me with respect and kindness. He either walked me home or gave me a ride. It mattered to him that I arrived home safely. It made me feel good to have someone care about me, but I was not ready for another boyfriend, so I kept my distance.

I assumed that Joel was okay with just being friends until one night when he walked me home and tried to give me a goodnight kiss. When I pulled away, he said, "I want to kiss you. Why won't you kiss me?"

Stupidly, I said, "I thought we were just friends."

After Joel's attempt to kiss me, I felt confused. I loved being in his company, but I wasn't sure how I felt about going together.

There was something about him that made me happy. He had a very different and fresh energy. His college boy ways, his taste in music, and just about everything else made him the complete opposite of me. While I have blonde hair and blue eyes, Joel's are dark. His interests and experiences were different from mine. Even his birthday was on the opposite side of the year from mine. We always had things to talk about, so hanging out was never boring. Because we were opposites, we made great friends, but I didn't know if we would be great as boyfriend and girlfriend.

One evening Joel became frustrated when I again refused to allow him to kiss me goodnight. I felt bad, but I told him that I didn't really want a boyfriend. A few days later, he said he was heading home to Marblehead to visit his family. He asked me if I could go, but I had to work. Laura volunteered to drive him down in her new black Mustang. When they swung by Mrs. Norton's to say goodbye, I thought they were rubbing it in my face.

"Bye, Deb," Joel said. "Have a good time at work. See you tomorrow." They were laughing as they drove away.

I was very upset that I couldn't go with them. I knew that I had given up any right to claim him as my boyfriend since I wouldn't even kiss him. I had told him more than once that I wasn't looking for a boyfriend, so I had no reason to be jealous. Nevertheless, I got furious when I found out Joel and Laura had partied and spent the night in the same room. They even shared the bed.

I was so pissed that I pulled a fast one on Joel. I had invited him to a Jimmy Buffet concert, and Becky had gotten the tickets for me. To get back at Joel, I told Becky to give them to Todd. I didn't even tell Joel.

I just blew him off. Later, I felt horrible, but I'd been so mad that I couldn't help myself.

I should have realized then that I really did want Joel to be my boyfriend. But it wasn't until the day I stopped by a party at his apartment that I admitted I felt more than friendship for him. I think he was drunk, and I didn't like what I saw. I was sober, and he and his friends had been drinking down the keg for a while. I decided to leave. As I was walking down the stairs, he got mad that I was leaving and smashed his beer mug against the wall, slicing his hand open.

I didn't realize he'd hurt himself until the next day, because I had just kept going. He had to have a plastic surgeon sew him back together. His entire hand was bandaged. I felt so much sympathy for him that I went to visit, taking him a teddy bear to hug. From that day on, we called each other Teddy.

He would go by Shelton's on his way to get a newspaper and yell, "Hey, Teddy, how are you today?"

I'd answer, "Great, Teddy. How are you?"

It was our daily flirting game. I knew he really cared about me, and I obviously cared for him, too. We became an item. But having Joel in my life didn't keep me from doing something really stupid.

We must love ourselves completely in order to give the best of ourselves. If we do that, the best will come back to us.

Joel was working one day when I wanted to escape from myself, so I turned to the old gang for something to distract me. We had been drinking, and I noticed that most of them were eating little bits of paper. They looked like miniature mailing stamps. I was curious, but I didn't say anything. Everyone else was doing it, so I figured it was okay. Blindly swallowing that little piece of paper was one of the dumbest things I've ever done.

After laughing our asses off at anything and everything for hours and snorting cocaine between fits of giggling, I finally asked what the little stamp was.

Someone yelled out, "It was a blot of acid, you idiot."

That made me laugh so hard I almost wet my pants. My face and jaw were hurting from all the laughing.

Todd and Waldo took turns living on the edge. All of us headed to the Picataqua River Bridge so they could climb the ladder to the top and grab the blinking lights that warn airplanes. After that, we went to the Portsmouth circle and drove around it 18 times, laughing like hyenas the entire time. It was like riding on a roller coaster. We were lucky we survived that night.

The farthest thing from our minds when we are altered by drugs is our safety. When we live through our ego, life can become a punishment. Blockages obstruct our positive flow of energy. Living from our hearts brings a life of love that heals.

We didn't come down from our high until daybreak. We went back to Hubba's house, which was right around the corner from Joel's beach house. I started to feel weird, so I sneaked out of Hubba's after everyone else fell asleep. I didn't want them to how weak I was.

I went to Joel's and tapped on his bedroom window. I had been up all night long, and I was supposed to work the morning and lunch shift at Shelton's. I started to cry because the reality of what I had done hit me hard in the chest. It felt as if a boulder was holding me down.

Joel woke up and let me in. "Where were you last night?" he asked. "I waited for you. What is wrong with you? Why are you shaking?"

Crying, I said, "I did something stupid last night, and now I'm scared. I ate a piece of paper because everyone else did. They told me what it was after I ate it. It was acid. I'll never do that again. I feel sick. I've been up all night, and I have to go to work!"

Joel was sympathetic to my needs and tried to calm me. He told me to lie down, close my eyes, and try to relax. It was a delightful idea, but my mind would have none of it. My body was numb with exhaustion, but my emotions and mind were not in harmony with my body. What kept running through my mind was that I had screwed up again.

How had I gotten to such a place of self-destruction? In the darkness of that moment, I would never have believed that someday I would see life as my guru. Life delivers what we need, over and over and over, until we learn.

My desire to numb myself on a regular basis gave me much more than the headache I was sporting that morning. I gave up on sleep and trudged home to take a shower. As soon as I walked in the door, Mrs. Norton said that Shelton's had called, looking for me. She wanted to know why I didn't go to work, and she reminded me that I was three weeks late with my rent again. I couldn't look her in the eye. I mumbled that something had come up, and then I ran upstairs.

Disappointing her again made me feel lower than ever. I was so disgusted with myself that I could feel it squeezing my heart into the size of a pea. I loved and respected Mrs. Norton so much, and she had gone way above the expected call of duty as my landlady and dear friend. She had given me way too many chances.

I showered and dressed for work as quickly as I could before running all the way to Shelton's. I wanted to throw up from nerves, embarrassment, and an accumulation of toxins. I had started to work my station when one of the owners called me into the kitchen. I shut my eyes tight and tried to transport myself ahead in time because I knew what was about to happen. I was terribly embarrassed and remorseful.

He said, "Debbie, you don't need to work your shift. We have you covered now. Unfortunately, you're fired. You left us high and dry this morning and didn't even call. This isn't the first time this has happened. We love you, but we need a responsible and reliable staff. When you are here, you work hard and have a great heart. But today you smell like a brewery. You should have just called in sick."

He stood there staring at me, and I was mortified. I wanted to crawl in a hole. He asked me to leave immediately and gave me my final check. As I handed him my apron, I cried and said, "I am so very sorry." Then I turned and left.

The check wasn't enough to satisfy my tab with Mrs. Norton, and I was nervous about going back there and telling her. When I walked into the house, she knew that I had been fired. She told me I had to be out of my room by the end of the week and that it was for good that time. I started to cry and told her I was sorry. I was ashamed to be in her presence. Hurting her humiliated me, but I was also angry that she was kicking me out.

I had nowhere to turn and nowhere to go. I ran upstairs to think for a minute or two. That's about all the time I ever gave myself in serious situations. It was a way of protecting myself. Pretending everything was fine when I was in the midst of disaster kept me from falling apart.

Mom and Skip were already upset with me because of the car payments I had been negligent in paying. My sister was a new mother, and my mom and stepdad had their hands full helping her with my new nephew Christopher. I absolutely could not ask them for help. I had no right to even ask.

My attempts to avoid the world in order to forget my weaknesses had failed. That time I was in trouble in every area of my life. I had to figure out how to bail myself out of the consequences of my own poor choices. I changed my clothes and sat on my bed and cried. It was a moment of despair and hopelessness.

Become aware of your own hope. Turn your thoughts inward and ask your soul to unveil truths. Believe in yourself and receive a positive, energetic flow of crystal clear answers in the form of bright, shiny, shimmering pearls.

I felt dreadfully alone, desolate, and depressed. I was experiencing regret, shame, humiliation, worthlessness, and extremely low self-esteem. I was vibrating on a very low level. I had created the position I was in. It was a very dark place. I needed to figure out how to take care of myself. I needed love for myself to radiate within me.

I wiped off the tears and told myself that I was tough. I was indestructible and invincible. My problems would pass any minute. I got up and walked downtown. I went into every summer shop I knew of until I got myself a job.

I set my intention to fix my life. If I'd only known then that it was that simple to heal.

I landed a job at the T-shirt shop on the same block as Joel's house. It was also across the street from Shelton's. I was reminded of my loss every day while folding T-shirts.

Later that day, I ran into Joel and told him that my entire life had changed in two hours. He had a brilliant idea, and I accepted immediately. He invited me to move into the summer house with him and Pablo.

Joel helped me move my belongings into their apartment the next day. My best friend had become my savior. Not only were we dating, but he had saved me from having to worry about where I would live. It was the best solution for me. I could work at the T-shirt shop and live half a block away. The problem was that it was a temporary situation. Joel and Pablo would be going back to school soon. I put that thought out of my head and focused on work. I told myself I would be fine.

I didn't know it then, but my higher self stepped in to take a primary role in my journey. Synchronistic events soon played yet another role in my life's path.

One of Pablo's friends had a grandmother who was looking for someone young to live with her and keep her company. Her family owned the new IGA, and it was also possible that I could get a job there. I thought it was a great idea, but I was afraid Mrs. Pape would reject me once she met me. I had no referrals to give her. I had burned all of my bridges.

Joel went with me when I met Mrs. Pape. She seemed to be fond of us right away, and she agreed to have me move in. It was a good situation for her and for me. She was a darling woman who reminded me of my grandma, and I loved her immediately.

My self-esteem was partially restored. My intention of believing I would be okay sent out a shift of positive energy, and the Oneness in which we all live sent me what I needed.

There were only a couple of weeks left before Joel had to go back to Plymouth State College, so we spent the time together. I wanted to wait until he was gone to apply at the IGA. Those 14 days went by fast. As Joel's last day in York approached, feelings of loneliness, abandonment, and sadness overcame me.

I was conditioned to feel that way every time someone left me. I became tentative about moving into Mrs. Pape's home because I wasn't feeling it at all. The time came, however, to move my things into a complete stranger's house and prepare for Joel to return to Plymouth.

It was a very sad day when Joel packed up his car to head back to school. Crying, I said, "I wish you could stay. I'm going to be lonely here."

He gave me a hug and said, "Don't worry. I'll call you every day. I promise. Don't cry; you'll make me cry."

That made me laugh a little. Joel squeezed me tight and then got into his car. My heart hurt. "I miss you already," I said.

"Miss you too, Teddy."

As Joel drove away, I cried harder than I had ever cried before. It felt as though a piece of me had left with him. I didn't feel as whole as I did when we were together.

Ours was a connection that helped me believe. The feeling that I might lose it created a wound that eventually became a treasured pearl from my heart.

My room at Mrs. Pape's was dated, but I didn't mind because it reminded me of my grandmother. There were lots of little floral prints, lace, antique furniture, and pretty glass lamps. The first few nights were very rough because I literally felt sick, from my belly to every pore of my skin, because Joel was gone.

After I established a little routine for myself, I felt a bit more at home.

Joel called every night, just as he'd promised. The sound of his voice and the fact that he cared enough to call strengthened the connected strand between us.

Mrs. Pape was an absolute doll. Somehow she knew how I was feeling, and she put her maternal instincts to work to make me feel better. She cooked for me and had caring talks with me. A couple of days after settling in, I walked to the IGA. I was hired to work in the deli and bakery, making my living slicing meat and cheeses.

For once, I decided not to let my ego degrade me. Something inside me consciously guided me into self-discipline. I walked to work in the cold all through the fall and winter. After work, I walked home to Mrs. Pape's house, where she usually had a hot meal waiting for me. After speaking with Joel, who called like clockwork each night, I looked forward to my simple evenings, because I was always smiling when I hung up. Mrs. Pape and I watched TV and turned in early. The next morning, I got up and got ready for work, and off to the IGA I went.

When love exists, life comes alive. Life wasn't perfect. Sometimes, I really didn't know what my problem was. I know now that my ego was challenging my heart. It was a battle I wasn't aware of for years.

There were days when I felt jealous of the gals who were the bakers. They came in at 5:00 a.m. and got to leave at 2:00 p.m. They had the cushy job of making delicious goodies for the bakery. They made it look so elegant. I went in at 9:00 a.m. and stayed until 5:00 p.m. I waited on arrogant customers who bossed me around and complained. I was sure they were looking down on me and seeing me as their servant.

I hated having to scoop smelly tuna fish, chicken salad, olives, and coleslaw. The boss was kind of snarly, but I'm sure I acted the same way to her, too. She was one of the bakers, and I wanted her job. I became friends with Pam, another girl in the same department. She and I got along great. It was nice to be able to talk to and relate with a girlfriend at work, even though she was the other baker.

After a few weeks, I fell into a comfortable routine. I became more at ease with my living arrangements and my job.

～

The ego can become a hindrance to the heart when it suspects threats in life, big or small. Then it creates illusions we don't recognize as such.

Erika Harris wrote on LifeBlazing.com: "It is good to feel lost...because it proves you have a navigational sense of where 'Home' is. You know that a place that feels like being found exists. And maybe your current location isn't that place but, Hallelujah, that unsettled, uneasy feeling of lostness just brought you closer to it."

I was far from home, but the seeds had been planted in my soul. The definition of home in this instance was my heart, not the physical place where I resided. I was beginning to gradually open my heart and let go of resisting my true self. As Albert Einstein once said, "You cannot solve a problem from the same consciousness that created it. You must learn to see the world anew."

～

Joel's character, values, ethics, positive outlook, childlike finesse, and soulful affection had a genuinely fresh and positive influence on me that came at a critical time. He was a human angel placed to join me on my path. I looked forward to Fridays, when Joel would sometimes come for a visit. Without any notice, he would pick me up at the IGA. It was a surprise that I always loved.

He spent most weekends at his college. I had only experienced Plymouth State College and the students on weekends. I'd seen parties galore. Those kids were crazy drinkers. The entire town was one giant party. One year, they made the top three party schools for *Playboy Magazine*.

With Joel in college, my interest in getting a degree returned. I applied to a couple of colleges, but one in particular spoke to me. It is a magnificent campus, nestled into the beautiful, scenic New England coastline. Gorgeous architecture is dispersed across the beautifully landscaped grounds. My favorite architectural structures on the campus are the historical buildings. College hall was a castle built in 1915, which was influenced by gothic revival architecture. Tupper Manor, built in early 1905, was influenced by the Greek and Italian revival styles. Reynolds Hall was built in an 1870 Tudor style.

At the time, Endicott College was an all-girl school. It offered architectural and design majors, which was what I was looking for. Although I had originally planned to go into engineering, it was a reminder of where I had been in life. I needed a new path.

My mother and I visited the campus late in the spring of 1987. It was breathtaking. The staff was delightful and so pleasant that they made me feel extremely welcome. The institution itself possessed a charming, honorable tradition of female independence. I could feel the ancient energy of respect and propriety, especially in the older buildings. With the ocean as my neighbor, I would feel right at home there. I felt in my bones that Endicott College was the place for me.

I applied that day and was accepted in a couple of weeks. Mom and I went back for orientation during the summer. I met my roommate and some of the other girls who were working toward a design degree. I was so excited that I couldn't stop smiling.

It was a very happy time in my life. The cells in my body felt alive and rejuvenated. I was finally on a road that would expand my mind with knowledge instead of pollution, and I was traveling it with great intention.

Mom and I went on a mother/daughter evening boat cruise with the other incoming students. It was a great event. The sunset was gorgeous, with a color spectrum ranging from violet and blues to oranges and reds. Feathers of clouds left their silhouettes. Unfortunately, I became very ill with a respiratory infection and had to be rushed to the hospital when the boat docked. I regretfully missed the welcome dinner at Endicott, but it was okay because I knew I would become acquainted with everyone very soon. Pearls of self-esteem were being cultivated. My life was taking an altered direction, and I was enthusiastic about it.

When I turned 23 that summer, Joel gave me the most beautiful, loving gift. It made me feel giddy and special. I also felt as though I didn't deserve to receive something so wonderful. I wasn't there yet. My wiring still told me I had to work hard for everything in life. My father had always said that nothing should be handed to me and that anything in life worth having is worth working hard for. There was great value in what he said, but the way he delivered the message had made the lesson painful.

The gift was an amethyst ring. Joel's sweet mother worked at the jewelry counter at Sears, and she had helped him select it. I was so very touched that the two of them had chosen it specifically for me.

After that special birthday, it was time to give my notice to IGA and almost time say goodbye to Mrs. Pape. My journey in York Beach, as tragic as it had been, was coming to a close.

I would return to York from time to time because my adoring grandparents lived there. I loved them unconditionally, and they loved me. They were impeccable role models for love. They were married forever! My soul is grateful for yesterdays' misfortunes.

In the fall of 1987, I became a freshman at Endicott College at the age of 23. I felt so privileged, honored, and proud to be able to attend there. My very first class was a design class. Professor McAllister became one of my role models, but it didn't start out that way. At first, I thought he was crazy. After roll call, he muttered the words "bubble gum" and then wrote "10 pages next class" on the board.

I looked around and said out loud, "What does that mean?" Nobody answered me. They were busy taking notes. *What are they writing down...the words "bubble gum"?* I thought.

I freaked out! I had no idea what he was talking about. I looked at my schedule and saw that I had the man for three other classes. I ran to the guidance office and begged them to change my class assignments. They said there was nothing that could be done. At that time, there were four professors in design, and he taught most of the classes.

Professor McAllister was an engineer by trade, and he was so intelligent that he was almost impossible to read. I went back to my dorm room and contemplated what he was talking about. The class was about space planning. What did bubble gum have to do with that? After hours of thinking, I had an ah-ha moment. When a bubble is blown, it makes a space. I had figured out his quirky philosophical way of teaching!

At that moment, I came to adore him. He showed me how to think outside the box. A pearl made it onto the strand.

I had to motivate myself to get a job on campus in order to buy books and pay for some fun during free time. The tuition was too much for me to manage alone, and I had to apply for grants and loans to put myself through school.

During the summers, I worked up to four waitressing jobs in Joel's college town to make enough money for the upcoming year. I really wasn't fond of Plymouth. I felt claustrophobic there. I didn't know that a secret place existed in Plymouth, a place that would one day save my life and set me on the path to happiness.

When I wasn't waitressing, Joel and I fixed up the college houses that his dad owned. We worked hard and played very little. When we had a day off, we went to Weirs Beach to relax.

During the school year, I spent many weekends at the house Joel and his roommates rented near campus because it was the only time we could spend together. I have many happy memories of those times, but one memory wasn't as joyous as the rest.

One weekend night, I was awakened by an extremely vivid, terrifying, and alarming dream. I dreamt that my father had died. I sat up in a cold sweat, gasping for air.

Shaking Joel, I said, "Joel, wake up. Wake up. I'm scared."

"What? What? What's wrong?"

"I just had a nightmare that my dad died."

Lying back down and rolling over, he muttered, "It's just a dream. Go back to sleep."

Needless to say, I didn't sleep much the rest of the night. The next morning, I was finally dozing off when the phone rang. My heart sank. Mom was on the other end, and she gingerly told me Dad had died. I already knew it. The Divine had prepared me through my keen intuition.

My father died on January 29, 1988, at the age of 59. On February 1, I laid my father to rest in the cemetery for his home town of Upper Port Latour, Nova Scotia. The 2:00 p.m. service was performed by Rev. Sidney Snow. It was a bittersweet day for me.

They performed Dad's favorite songs, "In the Sweet Bye and Bye" and "Where Is My Boy Tonight." I wept through both, picturing my dad singing them with Aunt Faye. I remembered the way he smiled as he sang, a smile that came from his soul. I also remembered that his smile never lasted, because the darkness of his life always overcame him.

I will forever remember the feelings I experienced as I walked down the long driveway of Parkdale Cemetery behind my father's casket. I remember the sound of my boots as they squished into the mud. My face was covered in an ocean of salty tears. My heart had a hole in it. I muttered all the way down that driveway, "Why did you leave me?" Over and over again, my mind kept asking. I was angry with him for leaving the world and abandoning me once more.

Even though the effects of his abuse prowled in my every cell, there was a sense that as long as he was alive, I would have his strength. It was backward, I know. A piece of me expected him to always be available to exercise that strength and protect me from the world's hardships instead of inflicting them on me. I needed his acceptance and unconditional love.

I was living on the delusional strength of a man I considered undefeatable and immortal because he had had such control over me. I was sure he must have been able to take on the world with invincible strength from within, much like Superman. But that man didn't exist in reality.

My healed higher self knows he wasn't strong at all. His ego was trying to hide his weaknesses. It was a protective mechanism, a mask he wore to display an identity he wanted others to see. He was really a pressure cooker, which would build up until it exploded all over me. His ego wouldn't allow his heart to view surrender as strength. The strength from which I was living really came from my own desire to prove myself to him in order to receive his unconditional approval and fatherly love. It was a demonstration of love that I was never able to truly receive from him.

I would never feel his physical, human arms deliver that loving hug of approval, because he was gone. I would never get to admire and witness him in his true smiling moments, which happened only when he was at home in Nova Scotia.

I still get emotional today over the loss of my father. It's no longer grief but forgiveness and gratefulness for the abundance of challenges he gave me. Those challenges have since transformed into pearls of wisdom.

I was, however, devastated to hear how he died. He was found in his car. He had frozen to death. The ignition key was still in the on position. He had gotten his car stuck in the snow in an attempt to get help. Because he was having an asthma attack, he didn't have the strength to walk back to his warm home. He sat in his car, slowly drifting to sleep, while it ran out of fuel. They found a suitcase in the back seat. He was probably trying to get to the hospital because of his breathing problem.

There was so much unfinished business between us, and I was left to work through it on my own. I loved my father because he was my father. His death changed my life forever. At first, the wounds were extremely raw. Later, a healed strand of life opened to receive an infinite number of lessons in the form of pearls to string.

I would never get to show him my hard work at school. He wouldn't walk me down the aisle. He would never meet his grandchildren, with the exception of my nephew Chris. I knew he wouldn't be there for any of the milestones in my life. It tore and scarred my heart, closing it down like a flower at night.

I felt that a loving piece of conscious acknowledgement and fatherly love would be missing from every momentous occasion to come. I needed him there with me. Every time I thought of him, I cried uncontrollably.

For years, my ego continued to build a suit of armor with many layers. Little did I know he was there in spirit, cheering me on.

The rest of that school year was tremendously challenging for me. The first semester, I had received straight A's. In the second semester, I didn't even make honors, and I barely accomplished a D in Art History. I managed to pick my grades back up in the third and fourth semester. My focus returned, but I had a difficult time finding a way to turn up the corners of my mouth. Joel stuck with me through that trying time. His light kept my path lit when I was unable to see.

The following summer, I worked grueling hours, waitressing at a diner, an Italian restaurant, and a Bahamian restaurant to earn as much cash as I could. It helped numb my pain to stay excessively busy.

Joel and I adopted a German shepherd puppy at the shelter in Lynn and took him to New Hampshire with us. He was awesomely crazy, and I loved him. Animals have always brought my innermost compassion and love to the surface from a place nothing else could touch. Joel and I named the dog Bogart. We thought it was fitting because it was the name of the bar where we met. It definitely suited him.

In the fall, Bogart became a party dog. He drank beer and played stick. He would stumble home with tired, hungover eyes, collapse on the porch, and sleep all day. He eventually got hit by a car after we gave him to a friend. He had lived his life to the fullest, always lovingly present in the moment.

That was something I had no idea how to do. It's the most simple, natural form of healing, and it is born within all of us. We all have the One inside. All that's needed is to have the faith to look inward and open the heart that God gave us so that we can manifest love for ourselves and others. *Break into the seed of your soul.*

One afternoon, Joel and I went to Weirs Beach with a cooler filled with Purple Passions. They tasted like grape soda, but with grain alcohol. We were having a great time enjoying our day off. The day was perfectly sunny, and the lake water was cool and refreshing. We were sitting in the sand, relaxing and talking about life. We reminisced about how we met and talked about being best friends. Then Joel asked me to marry him. I said yes.

We were so giddy that we just sat there and laughed with life. After we told our families, we went into Boston, and Joel bought me an engagement ring. We chose a one-carat pear-shaped diamond. Its facets were polished to a highly reflective shine.

I was beginning to create space in my heart for someone I loved. The diamond of my soul was entrapped in my heart. It had one facet wiped clean, which allowed a small sliver of light to shine through.

Chapter Eleven

Unconscious Milestones and
Physical Manifestations

If you are centered, nothing can be destroyed. No fire can destroy your centering. Not even death is capable of distracting you. And this centering is possible only if you start living each moment meditatively, fully alert, aware.

Don't move like an automaton. Don't react like a mechanism. Become conscious. Collect yourself more and more so that a crystallized consciousness continuously illuminates your inner being, a flame goes on burning there and it lights wherever you move. The path, the way, whatsoever you do, it lights it.

Heaven is not somewhere else: it is a way of living. So is hell—a style of life. Hell is living unconsciously; heaven is living consciously. Hell is your own creation; so is heaven. If you go on living unconsciously, through your unconscious desires, instincts, motives—of which you are not the master but only the victim—then you create hell around yourself. But if you start living a conscious life, a life of bringing more and more light to the deep, dark corners of your being, if you start living full of light, your life is moment-to-moment ecstasy.

~ Osho ~

I'll start this chapter with a quote that was delivered to me two mornings in a row by the website for the Sri Aurobindo Society, which provides quotes for guidance in life. The answers/quotes depend upon your question and your needs for guidance. It is simple, yet powerful.

Never forget that the greater the difficulties,
the greater also our possibilities.
It is only those who have great capacities and a big future
who meet with the great obstacles and hardships.

~ The Mother ~
(White Roses, Sixth Edition, 1999, pg 150)

I was attending a prestigious all-girl school and planning my wedding. I was on top of the world. I had come full circle, and my life was falling into place. My best self still wasn't shining through, however. Some of my biggest obstacles and hardships were still to come.

I'm solid in my belief today that the universe distributes lessons to us during our lives' transcending experiences only when we ourselves have evolved and are fully equipped to learn and grow from them.

In June of 1989, I earned an Associate's degree in design and graduated with honors. I was proud to have my mom, my little brother, and Joel's parents watch me receive the diploma I had worked so hard for. I wasn't going to stop there. For the first time, Endicott was offering a Bachelor's degree in design, and I was already signed up to begin the rest of my education that fall. I was so excited.

After the graduation ceremony, the celebration continued with Joel and his parents at Woodman's, where we dined on lobster. The one person who mattered the most was not there to witness my success, however. Even though I pasted a smile on my face that day, I felt melancholy.

Why was Dad's physical presence still so important to me? It was important because I wanted him to know that I had become all the things he said I couldn't be. We all need some loving recognition from our parents. It fuels our light so that it can burn brighter. My ego was still calling the shots, so I needed my father to acknowledge my accomplishment. I longed to hear him apologize and tell me how passionately proud he was of me.

I knew it was an impossible dream, and it made me deeply sad. I couldn't accept that I had no control, that I couldn't change how my father had felt about me. I couldn't see that the perfect sequence of events was materializing.

Trusting life and having faith that everything and everyone are exactly where they are supposed to be is a state of peace and presence. They are two miraculous pearls that are cultivated after your soul awakens to allow your best self to shine.

Joel and I found an apartment in Marblehead, where his family lived. We had also adopted a Doberman puppy named Amber. We decided to have a summer wedding and chose the date of August 19. We had been struggling with the location for our wedding because my mom and stepfather weren't blessed with enough money to contribute. I was still in college, and Joel had just started his first job. We, too, had very little money. We looked at places in York, but everything in Massachusetts was too expensive.

Joel's parents ever-so-graciously offered to help us. They lived on the water in Marblehead, and they offered their back deck for the wedding ceremony. We thought it was a perfect solution and accepted their offer. I was both honored and grateful.

I am the luckiest woman ever to have Joan and Bob as my second mother and father. I have adored them ever since we met twenty-five years ago. Their hearts are always open to give and receive. They are the ultimate role models and an example of the universal law of attraction.

Joel and I went to dinner with Joan and Bob one evening to discuss the wedding and tie up loose ends. We were enjoying a glass of wine and eating appetizers when my almost-father-in-law asked, "Who are you going to have give you away, Debbie?" He had no idea the question would have such a profound effect on me.

I felt a lump appear in my throat as tears welled up in the corners of my eyes. I looked at him and began to cry. I couldn't answer. Bob saw how upset I was and said, "I'll give you away." I was touched by his gracious and kind offer, but I had to decline. I couldn't have him give me away when I would be joining their family. It needed to be someone from my family.

I went to the ladies room to compose myself. I couldn't stop wishing that my dad could be there to give me away on my wedding day. I needed him to tell me how proud he was of me and support me on such an important day. I was angry, but I also felt such an intense sadness creep through my entire body that my limbs went numb.

I managed to stop crying and washed my face. When I returned to the table, I downed my glass of red wine.

My mother in law, Joan, is so sweet. "Debbie, we are sorry," she said. "Bob and I didn't mean to upset you. We want you to have the perfect wedding and not be sad. If there is anything we can do to help you, we will. You know that we love you."

"I love you too," I replied. "I think I'll ask my Uncle Clayton to give me away because he is the closest I can get to my dad. He even looks like Dad, and he never had any children. He was always fond of all his nieces and nephews. I hope he can make the trip from Nova Scotia. I don't know what I'm going to do if he can't."

I got in touch with Uncle Clayton by phone. He wasn't feeling well at the time, so he turned me down. When Mom found out I had asked my uncle instead of asking my stepfather, Skip, to walk me down the aisle, she became very angry with me. I liked Skip, but I didn't know him very well. I had a feeling in my gut that asking him wasn't right for me.

My soul wanted my father to be there for me on my wedding day. I yearned for his approval. I was overcome with sadness because I needed a father, and I couldn't control or accept my dad's fate.

The whole situation was draining my energy. In the end, I decided to ask my brother. He was Dad's only son, and he had meant everything to my father. My brother saved me by saying yes. Mom resented my decision so deeply that she refused to speak to me. On top of my dad being gone, my mother was abandoning me, too, just when I needed her the most.

Today, I understand her feelings. She had found love again. In her mind, the man who had married her was the right person to give me away. Back then, she couldn't understand why I had so much trouble getting over my father's death. She asked me more than once, "Why do you worship him so much?" At the time, I couldn't tell her. I can tell her now. I missed the man who was my father, and I missed the father I never had.

Mom was so disappointed that she didn't show up for my wedding shower. I had to wear a mask of happiness at my own shower to hide my disappointment and sense of betrayal. I was embarrassed and deeply hurt. Although I was happy to be getting married, the feeling that my mother had abandoned me, too, weakened my strand.

Grandma Hart was there for me with a hug and a loving smile. It was at the shower that she saw the toll my past emotions were beginning to take. That was the first of many times she wondered why I wasn't smiling when I should have been happy. "Why are you so sad, my dear?" she asked.

I thought I was hiding my sorrows well, so it surprised me that she saw through my mask. I was genuinely happy to be marrying my best friend, a man I loved. But my grandma saw the underlying sadness through the windows of my soul.

When we find our highest self and live from it, we let go of control and move into acceptance. Judgments dissipate and love illuminates. I definitely did not experience my milestones in a state of consciousness that kept me fully present. However, it's living through the hardships and coming out on the other side as a survivor that counts. What happened in my life was supposed to happen. The universe knows what's best for us. We just have to believe that the affirmations of our soul are waiting for us to discover them.

On August 19, 1989, my brother nervously walked me down the aisle. My sister Bonnie, my new sister Andrea, and a couple of girlfriends stood up with me. My cute little nephew was the ring bearer. Joel and I said our vows at sundown in the perfect celebration of love!

A gorgeous sunset of deep oranges and reds reflected off the ocean as they faded into dusk. I soaked up the warm smiles as I walked past our guests to join Joel. My heart was beating deep and strong, but not from fear. It was the heartbeat of anticipation, and it escorted me toward a life of love and happiness.

Our life together began with simple, yet gorgeous, words spoken by the Justice of the Peace. As I stood facing Joel, he and I smiled at one another. I took in the glorious aroma of the white gardenias in my beautiful bouquet and heard the JP say, "Deborah, do take this man, Joel K. Livingston, to be your lawful husband?"

With a smile that extended from ear to ear, I replied, "I do."

When Joel broke the glass and said mazel tov, we became Mr. and Mrs. Livingston. The JP introduced us as husband and wife for the first time, and the party moved into the front yard.

I wish I could have frozen that moment in time. It was one of only two times that I was fully present prior to my soul's awakening—the other was the day my daughter came into the world.

We had a fabulous reception dinner, followed by dancing and cake. I barely remember the details because it whizzed by so fast. We left before the festivities were over because we were flying to Florida early the next morning.

My memories of our honeymoon are much clearer than those of our reception. We spent our honeymoon on a Carnival cruise and had a blast. I felt as if I were living in a fairytale. My favorite day was in St. Martin. The ship sponsored a booze cruise, so we signed up for it. The cruise boat looked like a pirate ship. When we boarded, the smell of 151 rum and puke was overwhelming. I soon found out why. The crew made rum punch drinks from the moment people boarded until the moment they stumbled off. The drinks were already potent, but they left a bottle of rum on the bar for the serious drinkers.

After a few nautical miles of drinking, our pirate schooner reached its destination, a sunken ship. That's where the party really started.

The best part was watching people swing off the upper deck and into the ocean. I was too frightened to try that. For me, drinking and water activities don't mix. I did, however, put on a life jacket and snorkel my way to the sunken ship to check it out. Once everyone had had enough exercise and adventure, we proceeded to get extremely drunk. By then, everyone was adding extra rum to their drinks. One lady balanced her drink on her head, took her bra top off, and started to dance on top of a bench. That certainly raised the energy of the crowd, many of whom began chanting, "More rum, mon" and "No bikini top, mon."

The next evening at dinner, we asked the woman's husband about his wife's performance. He claimed he didn't know anything about it. Since he had been standing right there, cheering her on, we weren't sure how he'd missed it. Maybe he was so drunk that he didn't recognize his own wife.

The next two years were a piece of cake. I loved being at Endicott. I was used to studying, and I had passion for what I was learning. Amber became an important part of our little family, and we decided to breed her. She gave birth to eight beautiful puppies. It was an amazing experience to watch Amber go through the process of pregnancy and give birth to her babies. I will never forget how her maternal instincts took over immediately after the puppies arrived.

It was the most gorgeous example of unconditional and natural love. It reached the center of my core, dispersing the effects of love throughout my being. The energy of animals is sacred, and their hearts and souls are completely open. We can all learn from them.

The best part of the experience was watching Joel try to build the whelping box. I told him he should stick to his day job, as I gently removed the hammer from his hands to finish it myself.

Once the puppies were old enough to travel, we moved to Chelsea into a triple-decker that Joel's mom and cousin owned. The second-floor apartment was bigger than most homes. The rent was extremely affordable for a young couple, and it enabled us to save some money. We sold all the puppies except one. We named him Cortez. We had our hands full with that dog. He was a maniac.

One day in the late fall of 1990, I drove home from school in the rain. As I approached our home, I saw Joel running toward my jeep. I thought it was peculiar. He appeared to be laughing, but it was raining so hard that I couldn't tell. When Joel reached my car, I asked him why he was outside in the rain. Then I noticed the dog chains in his hand and saw that he was crying.

He could barely speak. "Amber and Cortez were just hit by a car, and they are dead!"

I freaked out and yelled, "Joel, where are the dogs?" He just pointed up the hill. I left him standing there and slammed the accelerator to the floor. As I sped to the park where Joel exercised the dogs, I kept screaming, "Oh, my God, no!"

I hopped out of my jeep and ran out into the rain. A dump truck from the town was parked on the side of the road, and some guy was shoveling my dogs into the truck as if they were trash! That vision lives with me today. How dare he treat my family that way? Most people would say they were just dogs, but they were much more to me!

I was devastated. Those dogs were beloved family members. They slept in our room on their own beds, and Cortez was only eight months old. He was just a baby. I was depressed, sad, and angry. I couldn't accept that they had left me, and I needed someone to blame.

Why did God keep taking from me? Why did the universe keep testing my strength by giving and taking, leaving me abandoned over and over? There was a lesson there that I was failing to learn. Incomplete lessons require life challenges to be presented until the soul has cultivated a pearl by embracing and learning from them.

Because there was no one else to blame, I got mad at Joel. What had he been thinking to take them to a place with no fence to protect them? I couldn't get over it, and I couldn't hide my anger. I resented Joel for my loss for years.

After finding the power and peace within my heart, I realized that it wasn't Joel's fault. The unfolding of outer life situations is not ours to control. It is the nature of a progressive life. Only our inner reactions to life are within our control. Whatever we encounter on the journey of life, good or bad, happy or sad, acceptance transforms us. We need to let go of the rest.

Joel's father, being the generous, kind soul that he is, gave us the funds to buy another dog. I searched the Boston Globe and was excited to find an ad for Dobie pups in Westfield, Massachusetts. The thought of a new baby with unconditional love to give and receive warmed my heart and soul, which blossomed into a huge smile as we drove to meet our new puppy.

We picked the cutest little girl. When I looked at the pedigree for the mother of the pups, I nearly fell off my chair. Our new puppy's mother was Amber's sister. She was already family. We named her Brisa.

The universe had gently whispered to me on the day I read the pedigree. Today, I'm positive I heard it. I have faith that the universal energies work with us.

We were amazed at what a well-behaved little darling Brisa was ... until one night when we came home from dinner to find that she had climbed over the kitchen gate and escaped into the living room. She had torn into a pillow, and there was stuffing everywhere. She had also discovered a roll of toilet paper and dragged that all through the house until the roll emptied. Once Brisa had tuckered herself out, she curled up in a tiny ball in the corner of the couch and fell into a sound sleep.

Her inquisitive zest for life had left the apartment looking like a cocoon of cotton, which I spent hours cleaning. Years later, after cleaning off and uncovering the protective cocoon around my heart, my zest for life was born.

The following spring, I graduated from Endicott with a Bachelor's degree. Our country was in a mild recession, and I was unable to find work in my field. I ended up getting a job liquidating office furniture. I worked with a gay man who I came to adore, but we fought like sisters.

That job fed my ego, and it kicked into high gear. My secret mission was to make so much money that my dad would rise up from the grave and shake my hand. I was soon making $10,000 a month in commission checks. While the rest of the country was in a recession, Steve and I were liquidating skyscrapers full of furniture in Boston.

It was exhilarating to make so much money. I had finally proved Dad wrong. I was rich on my own. Whoa, baby! I bought myself a white Corvette right off the showroom floor. "I wish my dad could see me now," I said as I drove it out of the dealership.

Joel was doing well, too. While working for Ideal Tape, he had proven his loyalty and work ethics to his father. He moved to his father's company and learned the business. We were yuppies living in Chelsea. I should have been completely happy, but I felt that something was missing from my life. I could never put my finger on what that something was.

What was missing was my strand. I was lonely for me. The real me was the hidden treasure I had been seeking all my life. At times I became downright irritable for no reason. Joel would ask me what was wrong, but I never had an answer because I honestly didn't know.

Joel and I talked about having a child, which surprised Mom. I had always vowed never to bring a child into the world because I didn't like kids. I didn't want any child to grow up the way I did.

As a mother today, I easily wear the pearl of parenting, with gratitude for the lessons I learned from my dad.

I wondered if it was my job that kept me from having the life I was supposed to be living. I was 27, and I decided that maybe a family was what I was missing. I got pregnant on our first try. I was very excited, but the whole idea had become real too fast. I was terrified because I couldn't control the outcome.

My daughter was breach, so the doctor scheduled a C-section for March 6, 1993. On February 25, my daughter decided to take charge of her own birth date. I was taking a bathroom break during "Seinfeld." The sudden flood of fluid scared me to death. I screamed for Joel.

"Joel, come quick! I think my bladder just burst as I was rocking bath and forth to get all my pee out."

As he ran down the hallway, listening to my nutty explanation, he started to laugh. When he reached the bathroom, he said, "Your water just broke, you silly. I'll go call the hospital." As he dialed, I started to panic because I realized he was right. I was about to become a mother!

Brigham and Women's told us to come right down. Thank goodness we weren't living in Rowley yet. I would have delivered the baby in the car. The ride from Chelsea to Boston took just a few minutes. By the time I arrived at the hospital, my water was flowing like a stream. I locked myself in the ladies' room to change my mouse mattress because I was very embarrassed. The nurses banged on the door, but I refused to come out. The only reason I finally left the bathroom was because the contractions were excruciating.

As they rushed me into an OR, I became terrified. What was happening to my innocent little baby? What would happen to both of us if she was breach? I had no control. My ego turned up the fear factor.

We need to keep the faith and believe during trying moments in our life that the power of the cosmos will take care of us.

There were 20 people in the room, a different person for every part of the procedure. They strapped me down and gave me a shot. I witnessed the entire thing through the glasses of the anesthesiologist, who was standing over my head. I was scared because I didn't understand what I was seeing.

Shortly after midnight on February 26, 1993, our daughter, Cassandra Rae Livingston, came into this world. Joel and I were so happy. She was perfect in my eyes, but her poor little feet had been up by her ears from being in the breach position.

Deep inside, I again felt the pain of missing my dad. I was experiencing another milestone moment that I couldn't share with him. My truest self tells me today that the feelings I had for my dad at each milestone were really due to his spirit speaking to me.

Most people would be grateful to have the people I had in my life to share such a special moment, but my heart ached to have my dad see his granddaughter. Fyodor Dostoyevsky wrote: "There are ... things which a man is afraid to tell even to himself, and every decent man has a number of such things stored away in his mind." Milestones without Dad were piling up and pushing deep, crushing my buried treasures.

When Cassie was three or four months old, we moved into a new house in Rowley, Massachusetts. About a month later, I began to feel tremendously sick. I woke up exhausted every day. I felt as if I hadn't slept at all, even though I was sleeping 10 hours a night. The doctor ran a lot of blood tests because I had no reflexes, my heartbeat was very slow, and I was ice cold in the middle of the summer.

I was diagnosed with severe thyroid disease. My TSH level was in the 300s, and a normal reading is between 5 and 7. It was perplexing to the doctors because a level that high indicated that my thyroid was extremely slow, but I remained at a normal weight. I should have weighed 250 pounds. They started me on medication, and I wasn't the same for many years.

My illness signaled the beginning of many physical manifestations that resulted from holding onto my traumatic emotions. When we don't let go of life's events, the cells in our bodies can eventually manifest the pain as disease.

The familiar sense that something was missing crept back in. Selling office furniture made me feel inadequate because I wasn't using my degree, so I began to look for another job. I came across a construction management position with the City of Boston for the building of the new Boston Police headquarters. It was perfect. I sent my resume and waited. They called me two weeks later for an interview.

The entire process was exciting and stimulating. I loved challenges that utilized my motivation and got my blood moving. I felt alive and had new ambition. My interview was a bit scary, though. When I walked into the room, there were at least 8 to 10 people with a vested interest. The other project managers were there. The police, fire, and EMS departments were represented. At first, I thought I had walked into the wrong conference room. All those people were seated on one side of the table. I quickly realized it was the right room, and my future bosses were sitting across from me.

I smiled, took a deep breath, and swallowed down my nerves as I greeted them. They asked me many questions. My heart was beating so hard that I thought it would escape from my chest and land on the conference table. I must have answered correctly, and to their liking, because they awarded the job to me.

I had the drive to keep searching for better and better professional experiences, and my job as construction manager was the best one I'd ever had. It suited me for the phase of life I was in. I was not yet ready to strengthen my strand of life and string it with lessons of pearls.

At the time, being part of the management team for such a prestigious construction project was important to my ego. As a team, we had power and were in charge of millions and millions of dollars. I worked hard at that job. I got up every morning with a smile on my face because I had the cutest baby girl ever, the best husband, and the greatest job in the whole world. The project was so interesting that it temporarily filled the void.

Michel de Montaigne said, "I know well what I am fleeing from but not what I am in search of." At some point on our journeys, we have all felt this. The feeling of always needing something else was in slight remission, but not for long.

The prominent job with the city, which had put me into a slight remission from self-destruction, brought dormant emotions from the past to the surface. Those emotions eventually allowed me to be born. The hard work I was doing to satisfy my ego provided the right conditions over the next four years for the onset.

In Flight to Arras (1942), Antoine de Saint-Exupery wrote, "No single event can awaken within us a stranger totally unknown to us. To live is to be slowly born."

Trying to balance everything during the first four years of Cassie's life took a toll on me. The job was stressful. So was the stress of trying to stay on top of everything at home. I had been conditioned and groomed by my dad to aim for perfection. My need to be perfect and in complete control became my enemies.

I began to have chest pains, and it was often difficult to breathe. I would have to get off the train at random stations on my way to work just to catch my breath. The doctors told me that I was experiencing panic attacks. I was relieved, because I'd thought I was having a heart attack. They put me on Prozac to calm me down. The medicine took forever to work. I would be watching TV at night, relaxing with Joel, and suddenly my heart would race. I always ran outside to get some relief, gulping in the night air as I gripped the porch rail until the dizziness subsided. At times, I really thought I was dying.

It is so clear to me today that I was experiencing the physical effects of old, traumatic events manifesting in my body. Because I had never dealt with them, they were coming to the surface.

I was relieved when the increased dose of Prozac started to work. It didn't mix well with my drinking habit, though. Every time I drank, the pills intensified the effects of the alcohol, and I passed out.

As K.T. Jong said, "It is only when we silence the blaring sounds of our daily existence that we can finally hear the whispers of truth that life reveals to us, as it stands knocking on the doorsteps of our hearts." It was when I wasn't working or running the household that I most needed to silence the knocks on my doorstep, because I wasn't ready to answer the door.

As I sought relief for my physical pain on top of my usual need to escape, I filled my weekends with drinking. I was losing the battle. Because the prescription medication amplified the effects of the alcohol, I often passed out after a couple of drinks. I couldn't judge my intake anymore.

By the time insomnia set in, I was working more than full time in Boston and taking care of my daughter, my husband, and our home, along with a macaw, a cat, and a dog. Not sleeping wasn't an option, so the doctor gave me a prescription for that, too. The physical manifestations were having a domino effect. My poor quality of health made me reliant on drugs to get me through normal life tasks.

I wasn't aware that I was resisting myself. At that point in my life, surrender was a sign of weakness. Life, as I live my path today, has proven to me that surrender is a lovely form of strength that comes from within.

Physical manifestations continued to unfold. I started to lose my hair. My doctor blamed it on the thyroid disease, but I knew in my heart it was more than that. After tremendous hair loss and three years of asking the doctor to send me to a specialist, I was diagnosed with endogenetic alopecia. On top of the psychological trauma that losing my hair inflicted, my joints were hurting so bad that I could hardly move. I went to every doctor under the sun and moon, and nobody could help me.

My gut told me there was a root cause, but I couldn't figure out what it could be. Everything we think enters our cells. Happiness makes our cells smile. Long-held negative thoughts damage them.

The doctors finally diagnosed me with fibromyalgia, which I didn't believe. My primary care physician restricted me from white flour and white sugar because she suspected I was developing food allergies. Digestion issues had been a problem for me since childhood.

All of these manifestations were opportunities and whispers to change my life. I wasn't ready to hear that, but I continued to sense there was something missing. I was positive there was a root cause, and I wasn't giving up until I discovered what it was.

Today I'm healed. I have recovered from all of the pain symptoms. They were manifestations of many years of stuffing my emotions instead of embracing them. Hope for our healing comes from inside. It is there for the taking. When we generate it and embrace it, miracles of pearls appear.

Chapter Twelve

Highway to Hell

The grace and protection are always with you. When in any inner or outer difficulty or trouble do not allow it to oppress you; take refuge with the Divine force that protects. If you do that always with faith and sincerity you'll always remain calm and peaceful in spite of all superficial disturbances.

~ Sri Aurobindo (SABCL, 24:17) ~

Swampscott, Massachusetts, is a quaint little ocean town where most homes sit on lots of 10,000 square feet. We found the perfect house on Sampson Avenue. It had an open-plan layout, which was important to me for entertaining. Wooded conservation land backed all of the homes on our street. We put in an offer, and it was accepted, contingent on the sale of our house.

It was the perfect time for us to relocate closer to Boston. Cassie was five and had just started kindergarten. Our house sold in two days. Because the couple that sold the house to us were getting a divorce, they were anxious to close. We moved very quickly, and it was quite exciting. It was meant to be.

The house was gorgeous. There were lots of windows, and French doors opened from the step-down living room to a full-length deck, with a pool below. A spiral staircase descended into a half-finished basement, which made the perfect playroom for Cassie.

It was the ultimate house for entertaining, and that is exactly what we did during every free minute from work. My ego was loving life. I worked hard during the week at a job that was extremely fulfilling, and we partied at our house on the weekends. It was the perfect, predictable life for hiding pain.

In *Animal Dreams,* Barbara Kingsolver writes: "Pain reaches the heart with electrical speed, but truth moves to the heart as slowly as a glacier." During my twenties and early thirties, I was in a remission of sorts from the pain, which my ego directed to lie dormant. I was operating my life like a mechanical robot, with little feeling coming from my heart. When my mind wasn't totally occupied, I needed a way to numb the pain. The mental and emotional pain manifested as physical pain and chronic illnesses, for which the doctors had no answers.

I continued to live my life with a certain lack of awareness of what was happening to me and around me. I lived as if I were in a play, with my ego as the starring actress. I allowed people to see only what I wanted them to see. When I needed assistance in displaying the image of a happy career woman with the best husband, daughter, and house, I called on my makeup artists to apply my mask. Those artists were usually the friends who partied like I did, and alcohol was my favorite makeup tool.

Those were my wild and crazy days, when I escaped from my cage, unleashed again. Whenever achieving stimulation through the perfect life and career became less effective, I had to sedate my ego in order to cope. To paraphrase Brian Johnson, lead singer of ACDC, I was on a highway to hell.

Today, I feel sorry for the woman I was. I am not trapped inside anymore because I found me. I found peace by discovering my soul. It was buried for years as an unnourished seed within my heart. Today, my heart smiles.

By 1998, my adrenaline-charged project management position was coming to a close. The mayor was up for reelection, and the funding for my position had run out. My self-esteem and confidence levels were still soaring high. I felt grateful to have been part of a once-in-a-lifetime project, but I was sad that I had to leave.

Fortunately, I had reputable contacts in the industry, and one of them told me about a position that was available. I applied and had two interviews right away. Just as my ego had expected, I was hired for the Construction and Repair division of Tufts University Medical and Dental Schools in Boston. They had lured me to the position by telling me they were on the brink of constructing a new building for their medical school. Once I was on staff, I realized that they didn't have the funds to break ground. I was soon bored stiff working on tiny little projects.

One day I came out of my office and found a guy the size of a sumo wrestler holding onto the front bumper of my car as he passed a bowel movement right in front of me. I immediately decided it was time to look for another job.

My ego wasn't satisfied. I needed to keep busy so I could feel great about myself. The darkness of my ego was constantly wanting and needing more of everything. When we live through the light of our souls and our heart, the Divine in us is constant in providing.

Live quietly in the moment and see the beauty of all before you. The future will take care of itself.

~ Paramahansa Yogananda ~

Shortly after I decided to find a different job, my sweet grandmother, Dorothea Hart, died. I didn't handle it well at all. She was the one person who had me all figured out long before I did. I needed her, and she had left me. I missed her loving, supportive wisdom so much after she was gone. She always made me feel warm and fuzzy, and she accepted me with all of my flaws.

Sometimes I can hear her tender voice whispering the inspiring words that I received from her from the day I was born. I told my grandfather that if I had just one slice of her elegance, I would be a better person.

The loss was so overwhelming that I threw up several times at the wake, and I ended up getting a respiratory sickness after her funeral. As always, I plunged full force ahead to occupy my mind and push my grief away.

The City of Boston heard that I was looking for a job. The rapport I had built in my first position with them enabled me to land another contract position. That time I was in charge of the initiative for the electrical and technology upgrades for the Boston schools. I felt distinguished and secure once again. I returned to working hard during the week and partying when work was over.

I lived the next three years like a rock star. Joel and I and our partygoing friends found any and every reason to get together. During the summers, we had at least three families and their children at our house every weekend, because we were the only ones with a pool.

People started showing up in the morning, and soon the quiet backyard echoed with the sound of icy cold cans of beer being popped open. The men played ping pong, and their competitive voices could be heard each time they scored on each other. We women basked in the sun while we drank beer and joked and gossiped. The kids ran around the pool, laughing and playing. The sounds of splashing water with loud music in the background went on all day.

More and more often, I would wander off by myself to have a cigarette. What I was really doing was escaping the entire scene. That summer, another physical manifestation had set in. I was becoming depressed. The worst times came when several of us vacationed together. I still wanted to escape, but the depression made me want to escape by myself instead of with a bunch of people.

If only I could have known that there was no escape from my pain. I should have been diving into myself instead of into a bottle or a lake. Our thoughts and preconceived notions about life are just conditioned ideas. If we are willing to be open-minded and let go of old perceptions, our minds will quiet enough for us to listen to the truths of our inner voice.

Our group swarmed to Squam Lake like bees on honey. It was a quaint location with 17 miniature cabins. We filled them all. Some of the partygoers referred to it as "The Compound" because we didn't leave unless it was necessary to go on an alcohol run.

I was already fighting depression, and I hated it there. The lake was the only source of entertainment. How many times can a person go tubing while shitfaced? The drinking started in the morning with Bloody Marys. We usually switched to beer after lunch, and by evening we had moved on to mixed drinks and shots of Goldschlager.

Almost every morning, I woke with a sense of dread. I felt like a prisoner of my own free will. I didn't want to be there. By afternoon, my true feelings were veiled by alcohol, so I thought I felt better. I was never truly happy anywhere until I was numb enough for my spirit to be set free.

My drinking habits in the fall and winter usually centered around football. The Patriots were, of course, the best team on the league. When they won, it gave us a good reason to celebrate with vodka drinks all day long. The whole neighborhood could probably hear us chanting, "Go Patriots!" or "Defense!"

Going out to dinner was a favorite activity, as it was a guaranteed drink fest. I usually started with wine at home, downing at least one glass even before taking a shower. Joel started to realize that maybe I had a problem. He would tell me not to drink before we went out, but I didn't care what he said. I did it anyway. I was great at hiding it. I just waited until he was in the shower.

When I opened a bottle of wine, just hearing the sound of the cork popping gave me the sense that relief was coming. Savoring the flavor was not an option. I grabbed the first fishbowl-sized wine glass and filled it to the top. As the first sip slid warmly into my stomach, it delivered a calming relief like nothing else. Well, that's not completely true. Dirty martinis were better.

I had already knocked back a couple of glasses to take the edge off by the time Joel was ready to leave. By then, I was ready, too. My nerves were soothed, and I was happy. I also no longer had to worry about passing out, because I had talked my doctor into taking me off the stupid Prozac. That stuff was ruining my drinking skills. When I didn't drink, I was a bear because alcohol had become my primary medication. *I needed alcohol to reduce my stress, quiet my mind, warm my body, and boost my mood.*

We would meet our friends at the restaurant and order drinks. I usually started with vodka dirty martinis, which were followed by wine with dinner. Joel was often furious with me, because our friends had begun to notice how much I was drinking.

He would lean in and whisper, "Deb, you've had enough. Please don't drink any more." I heard him, but I didn't care. I thought I had everything under control. Who the hell was he to try and control me?

Smiling so no one would suspect, I would whisper, "I'm fine. Leave me alone."

We all were heavy drinkers, but I drank to get drunk. It was the only time I was happy. We were typically the first to arrive and the last to leave. Halfway through the evening, we girls would sneak up to the bar for shots, and the guys always wondered why we were drunker than they were.

Joel would get mad because he had to be the designated driver. He got so frustrated. "Why do you always do this to me? Why am I the one who always has to be the designated driver? Just once I'd like to have a good time!"

I was so selfish. I didn't care about his feelings at all. It was all about how I could feel better. When I think about what I put Joel through during that time, it breaks my heart. But I have forgiven myself, because I hadn't yet found my true self.

When we awaken the seed of our soul, the nourishment of love and caring compassion are released to us and dispersed outward to others.

In 2001, the mayor of Boston was up for election for a new term, and he took a look at employment ordinances. City workers were required by ordinance to be residents of Boston. I had gotten around it by always working under contract. When he realized that I had been there for several years, he asked me to leave because my working there created the potential for negative publicity.

Once more, I had no qualms about finding a job. I had developed so many contacts that it was a piece of cake. I sent my resume to a private construction management company, and they called me in less than 24 hours. It was quite an ego boost!

I was invited to KV Associates for an interview the next day. The position was the ultimate. The person they hired would join a team of project managers that were in charge of construction for new and renovated schools for Salem, Massachusetts. My interview with the owner went well, and I also hit it off with Tony, the project manager at the site. I was hired immediately. My daily commute took only five minutes. I gave the City of Boston my two-week notice. They weren't prepared for me to leave so quickly, but KVA wanted me yesterday.

My immune system was already fried from all the partying it had been forced to endure, and I often struggled with my other health issues. The two-week frenzy before I could leave the city job was already taking its toll when I learned that my grandfather, Fredrick Hart, Sr., had passed away.

I dropped into a severe state of depression because I had loved him dearly. With Grandpa gone, I had no more ties to the grandparents who always made me feel loved. I came down with pneumonia, so I had to fulfill the last week of my two-week notice while feeling terribly ill.

The old sense of abandonment overcame me again, even though my adult mind knew that death and dying are a part of life. My grandparents' presence had been the most consistent part of my life since the day I was born. While my own husband and daughter had become new constants, the hurt still ran deep.

When we allow it, the consistency of love shines eternal strands of light, like rays of sunshine from inside our heart. When we have faith, we experience an eternal love that never dies.

The new job was great at first, but it didn't entail the scope I'd grown used to. I was very bored until the renovation project for the Witchcraft Heights Elementary School commenced. That project was chock full of challenges. It started with the civil work.

A gigantic tree on the site had been scheduled for removal in order to build a new access road in the neighborhood. The tree-removal contractor took one look at that tree and ran to his truck. "I'm not touching that tree!" he said. "That's the very tree where they used to hang the witches of Salem." He nervously fumbled for his keys and said, "You'll have to get someone else to cut that thing down!" I just stood there in awe. He was gone before I had a chance to respond.

The second challenge involved a multimillion-dollar change order due to site contamination. When excavation got underway, the crew noticed a strange smell. When another project manager and I climbed into the pit to investigate, we found very old glass medication bottles, perfume bottles, and other debris. We learned that it was an old dump site for Peabody Tannery, and the soil was contaminated with arsenic. I had to go to the hospital and have seven vials of blood drawn and tested to make sure I hadn't been poisoned.

The situation was so scary that I decided to have a four-margarita lunch with my coworkers. Thank goodness it was Friday, and thank heaven I was pronounced toxin free by the hospital. On Monday, we were told we had to remove all of the soil from the entire site. Hundreds of dump trucks drove in and out all day long. The project was way over budget and very hectic.

On September 11, we heard on the radio that two planes had crashed into the twin towers in New York City. Along with the rest of the world, we were stunned into silence. It was dreadful, and the entire nation mourned, all of us with it.

The following summer, I got some really bad and unexpected news. My boss said the economy was killing his business, and he had to make cuts across the board. He laid me off. I was devastated. Only my father had made me feel more rejected than I did that day.

I held back the tears and kept my composure as I cleared my stuff from the site trailer, but my ego had been bruised. I was angry and fearful about getting another job. I was jealous of the workers who would get to remain with the company. It made me angry to realize that I wasn't the last one in the door, and I was the only female project manager. I felt discriminated against.

My sense of outrage and hurt were soothed only after I got home and made myself a dirty martini. I downed several before deciding to go next door and jump on the neighbor's trampoline.

Descending into a childish state with a buzz helped remove the feelings of rejection I thought I had overcome. That moment was the beginning of my highway to hell.

A week before, Joel and I had met a couple named Phil and Tara at Cassie's dance recital. The four of us hit it off right away. We had stopped hanging around with our other friends because they accused me of drinking too much. *How dare they?* I thought. *They all drank too much, too!*

Phil and Tara loved to kick back and have a few, just like I did. They also had a boat. We had been down to the marina to see it a couple of times, but we never dreamed they'd invite us to go on a 10-day boat trip with them. We politely declined the invitation because we had to work, but I was disappointed. The weekend after I lost my job, we were invited to have drinks on their boat.

Joel said, "Hey, if that invitation is still open, we can go now." I was shocked and embarrassed all at once.

Tara said, "Of course. We'll have a blast."

I felt like a kid in a candy store, but I put on my cool-and-collected mask and shrugged my shoulders. "Sure," I said. "Let's go. It's not like I have a job."

We had never been on a boating trip before, and we were very excited. Cassie was nine, and it was just as thrilling for her. Phil and Tara had two kids about her age, and a girl named Chelsea from Cassie's school would be going, too. We packed and left midweek.

It was so breathtaking to see the coast of Massachusetts and go through the Cape Cod Canal on the first day. Every afternoon, Tara and I would fire up the blender and have several cocktails. We always had something to talk about over drinks and cigarettes, as we took in a variety of spectacular views. We were both avid drinkers, and we became the best of friends. We ignored the rest of the boaters, but we had lots of fun. Every day was sunny, and the waters were calm and beautiful. We visited Oaks Bluff, Menempsia, Block Island, and Newport. We had a ball.

Joel and I enjoyed the trip so much that we bought our first boat the following season. Boaters know how to party! I had found a new hobby that suited my selfish needs perfectly. However, boating trips weren't as much fun when the responsibilities were all ours and we had no clue what we were doing. Two dangerous situations got our feet wet right away, so to speak.

The first incident occurred as we were approaching the entrance to the channel for Block Island and hit heavy fog. Joel hadn't yet learned how to read charts or his GPS. We were following Phil, but we lost sight of his boat. The fog was so thick that we felt isolated even though Phil was a few yards ahead of us. We called Phil on the radio, and he told us to take a hard turn portside when we hit the red buoy at the beginning of the channel. He said to watch for it on the GPS. Joel froze because he didn't know what to do. Phil called back and asked where we were, because the ferry boat was on its way out of the channel.

I saw the buoy on the GPS and screamed, "Turn the wheel!" He didn't. Joel stood frozen in place, so I grabbed the wheel and turned the boat as quickly as possible. Just then, the fog lifted a little, and I could see the buoy and the ferry boat. My trust in our ability to boat safely vanished with the fog. My heart was beating so hard that I could feel the electricity it generated in my fingers, which were still locked around the steering wheel.

I shook like a leaf the rest of the way through the channel because I knew we had to dock, and we sucked at that, too! The second we were docked, I downed several drinks.

My boating skills ran parallel to my life skills at that point. Both were unsafe and kept me on the edge. Today I have a compass and am able to navigate my life through rough seas, storms, and fog, knowing that smooth water is always ahead. We all get off course once in a while, because we are human. The compass of our Divine self always points us in the direction we need to go.

We stayed in Block Island for two days, and then we were off to Oaks Bluff for three days. On the evening before we were to depart for Newport, we heard that the weather was going to be pretty hairy, with high seas and wind. You couldn't pay me to boat in that weather today.

Everyone decided we should leave at dawn. There were five boats, one following the other. We were a boat convoy that looked like toys in a bathtub. We were buffeted by high winds, it was pouring rain, and the waves were five to seven feet high. At one point, a huge wave pushed the bow and the whole boat went sideways. Thank goodness we didn't capsize; we certainly came close. It was one of the scariest moments I'd experienced since the day Todd took me on the joy ride from hell.

I felt like I was going to throw up and wet my pants at the same time. My stomach rocked and rolled along with the boat. Every six seconds, waves crashed over the bow. Each time the bow dropped, I prayed it would come back up before another wave came crashing upon us. I was terrified of drowning.

The ocean is a powerful force, and it's to be respected and never underestimated. Our 34-foot Sea Ray carried us to safety. I had never been so thankful to reach land as I was that day.

The second we docked, Tara ran over and showed me her shaking hands. I was shaking from head to toe. My adrenaline had been pumping for five hours, and my nerves were shot. After we hugged, she said, "Where's the beer? Let's have one."

As I walked to our cooler, Joel rolled his eyes at me. I ignored him and grabbed two cold ones. I didn't care if it was 10:30 in the morning. I needed a beer. It took a lot of beers before my nerves leveled out.

Drinking was becoming my safe haven while boating. I was drinking more heavily than ever. Because everyone partied on their boats, I thought no one would notice that I was drowning my sorrows. I thought I could blend in. After all, drinking and boating went hand in hand with that group.

We continued to party in our 34-foot boat for another two seasons. Joel had gotten better at driving, docking, and navigating, so we decided to upgrade to a 39-foot Trojan. It was our fourth year of boating, but my nerves were still bad. However, boating was the perfect cover for me to drink.

Little by little every one of our friends from the boating group decided they had had enough of my drinking sprees. It was the second set of friends that drinking had cost me. Tara remained my friend for a little while longer.

After dinner and drinks, we usually went to Governor Bradfords. One night, Tara and I decided to sing karaoke. It wasn't my shining moment, that's for sure. We sang "Hit Me with Your Best Shot" by Pat Benatar. I got into a fight over the microphone with the hostess, who was a man dressed as a woman. I tried to tell him that his purple lipstick was on crooked, and he yelled at me to back off because I was getting garlic breath on the microphone. His parting shot was, "What did you have for dinner, bitch, Caesar salad?" While the remark was funny, my singing was not. Then I proceeded to trip and fall on the dance floor on the way back to my seat. It was quite embarrassing, but not until I remembered it the next day.

What sealed my fate with my friends was an evening out gone bad. I had excused myself to go to the restroom, and I got a little sidetracked on my way back to the table. Tara's sister-in-law saw me in the bar doing shots of something called Oatmeal Cookie. I shouldn't have been drinking at all, as I had recently been diagnosed with celiac disease. She told on me, and Joel was absolutely furious.

That was our last night out with everyone. I knew the group made dinner plans most weekends, but we were no longer included. I spoke up and asked what was going on, and Julie said she just couldn't associate with me anymore. My feelings were crushed. I cried hard, but it didn't slow my path to self-destruction a bit. In fact, things got worse from there.

I was losing control of the ebb and flow of my life. Actually I had never had control. My ego did.

We were known in the community for our awesome Christmas parties. Every year we invited 80 people and served tons of food and even more booze. The year after my dog Brisa passed, we adopted two more Doberman puppies. They were in the basement during the party. Another animal lover wanted to see them. I was excited to show her, so we headed down the basement stairs. I was wearing spiked heels and carrying a glass of wine. There were no handrails, and I was a little tipsy. My long wide-legged pants caught on the heel of my shoe. I tripped and fell down the last three steps, smashing my head on the concrete floor.

I knew it was bad, but I refused to go back upstairs. I was too embarrassed. I was in terrible pain physically, from the fall, and emotionally, from a lifetime of unexpressed emotions. Everyone took turns coming down to see me. They probably made fun of me once they were back upstairs.

By the next morning, I looked like a cartoon character. I had a huge Easter egg on my forehead and two black eyes, but the craziness of the situation didn't send any message to me at all. I blamed my accident on the lack of railings, not on my drinking.

We always put blame and judgment on someone or something else when the healing truths are buried inside but are too painful to release. The more pain we experience and release, the more we change.

One Friday night the following spring, Cassie, her friend, and Joel ordered pizza. After they all went to bed, I stayed up to drink wine because it was taking more and more to get the relief I needed. Around 2:00 a.m., I decided to take the pizza boxes outside to the trash barrels. It was dark, and I was having trouble walking straight. I lost my balance and fell down our stone steps to the driveway. As before, there were no railings.

That time was worse than the basement fall. I sliced my head open on one of the rock steps. I remember feeling myself lose control as my ragdoll body fell to the cold pavement below in slow motion. The fall knocked me out. I lay there bleeding for a long time. When I finally came to, I didn't know where I was. Once I managed to pick myself up, the light from the front porch showed me that I was soaked in blood. I felt dizzy, so I crawled up the stairs and into the house.

I yelled, "Joel, I need you to get up."

"What do you need, Deb?"

I knew he would be mad, but I had no choice. I was scared. "I fell in the driveway and hit my head."

He took one look at me and said, "Are you fucking kidding me? You have a serious problem! Get in the car. You need stitches."

He drove me to the hospital and told them I fell because I was a drunk. I sat there and hung my head. I didn't respond. In the cold ER, I received 10 stitches in my forehead.

I remember telling the doctor that Joel was angry and that he was going to leave me because I drank too much. I told him that I had been upset about something and that had motivated me to start drinking. He ordered a CT scan on my head to make sure there was no swelling on the brain.

The next morning when I woke up, my blonde hair was covered in blood. I was in tremendous pain because I had a concussion.

Today the scar on my forehead is a reminder of the person I used to be when I lived in the dark and my heart and soul were asleep. I knew down deep inside that there was something wrong with me, but I was too terrified to address it. I was afraid of what would happen to me. I should have been more afraid of what was happening to me because of my self-destruction. Why do we beat ourselves up when we are in pain? All that's needed for healing is to allow our hearts to peel open, revealing love in harmony with its own beat.

One evening we took some friends for a ride to Boston on our boat for dinner. It was dusk when we pulled into the marina in Boston Harbor. I tossed a stern line and, as I ran to the front of the boat, I caught my Croc on a cleat and lost my balance because I had been drinking. I fell into the ocean and literally popped right back up! I had no idea how or why at the time, but I know why today. The harbormaster said that was unheard of, as the current is too strong for someone to survive. He said I could easily have swung under the docks and been swept away. He told me I was one lucky person. I was terrified, as I am not a good swimmer, and I am petrified of the water. My biggest fear was drowning all alone.

The Divine protected me that night, but it was the last straw for Joel. He just couldn't stand watching me slowly kill myself. He told me that I needed to stop. He told me to see a counselor, to see anyone, but I had to get help. I pretended I didn't hear him and shrugged off all my accidents as bad luck.

The universe was with me. The seeds of my pearls were accumulating and lying dormant, waiting for the universe to unfold the moment I shifted into my center. We are never alone.

My drinking was definitely progressing. I knew it, but I couldn't stop. I was afraid, but I didn't know what I feared. I got up every morning, looked myself in the eyes in the mirror, and said, "Not tonight." Every day I went to the gym to lift weights for an hour and run eight miles. I was trying to run off my guilt and shame. I was filling a void and punishing myself by working my body as hard as I could.

The void never got filled in those days. *We fill our void by bringing the center of our force to life.*

What I did to my daughter was heart wrenching. It was easy for me to drink, because Joel traveled a lot. My daughter knew when I'd been drinking, and she would call him on his cell phone and tattle on me every night. When I wasn't looking, she dumped my drinks down the sink. She was mimicking Joel. At least that's what I thought then.

"Mom, you're a drunk!" she screamed. "You have a serious problem! Why would you do this to your kid?"

I calmly replied, "Cassie, I am the adult, not you. Don't dump my wine down the sink or you will be grounded." She did it anyway. She had no respect for me.

She knew all of my hiding places—behind photos, inside canisters in the kitchen, inside cabinets. My drinking had progressed to the point that I woke up with terrible shakes every morning. At first I didn't know what it was. Then I learned that after I had two or three drinks, the shaking would disappear. Five o'clock couldn't come quickly enough for me to medicate myself and relieve the shakes.

My problem had started as an attempt to relieve the pain of my mind and emotions, and it had evolved into a need beyond my control. Even my ego was losing control. Alcohol was taking over.

One day early in September of 2007, I started drinking right before it was time to pick up my daughter from school. Carrie could smell it. Joel demanded that I make an appointment with a therapist. I agreed to go, and I did.

It didn't do a bit of good. I paid her so that I could lie to her. It was worth the money for me because it bought me extra time to get away with drinking for any reason. The universe had my days numbered. One night after a couple of weeks of shmooozing the therapist, I decided that my "I don't give a shit" approach was no longer working for me. Joel came home, and I was drunk again. He said we weren't married anymore because booze was my best friend.

My best friend, which helped me for so long, had stopped working. The illusion that booze was my best friend was just that, an illusion. I now accept all the problems and the mud that booze dragged me through during my journey to get where I am.

The lotus is the most beautiful flower, whose petals open one by one. But it will only grow in the mud. In order to grow and gain wisdom, first you must have the mud —the obstacles of life and its suffering. —The mud speaks of the common ground that humans share, no matter what our stations in life. —Whether we have it all or we have nothing, we are all faced with the same obstacles: sadness, loss, illness, dying and death. If we are to strive as human beings to gain more wisdom, more kindness and more compassion, we must have the intention to grow as a lotus and open each petal one by one. (Goldie Hawn)

I sat on the porch after our fight with a glass of red wine in one hand and a cigarette in the other. The tears that rolled down my face came from a place that had been waiting for release. As I sobbed, I looked up at the stars, and I asked for help. I said, "Please help me. God, Dad, Grandma, Grandpa, Nan—please help me! There is something seriously wrong with me. I'm begging you all. Please, please help me."

I was completely defeated. I had been brought to my knees by a very powerful disease. It is a disease that can be conquered with the intention and desire to surrender our will and have faith in ourselves, trusting with an open mind. The essence of self-realization unfolds. The rest comes in the form of love, acceptance, patience, courage, forgiveness, joy, and peace.

Chapter Thirteen

Growing Pains and Born Again

AMAZING GRACE

~ John Newton (1725-1807) ~
Stanza 6 anon.

Amazing grace, how sweet the sound
that saved a wretch like me.
I once was lost but now am found,
was blind, but now I see.
T'was grace that taught my heart to fear
and grace, my fears relieved.
How precious did that grace appear
the hour I first believed.
Through many dangers, toils and snares
I have already come;
'tis grace that brought me safe thus far
and grace will lead me home.
The Lord has promised good to me.
His word my hope secures.
He will my shield and portion be,
as long as life endures.
Yea, when this flesh and heart shall fail
and mortal life shall cease,
I shall possess within the veil,
a life of joy and peace.
When we've been here ten thousand years
bright shining as the sun.
We've no less days to sing God's praise
than when we've first begun.
(In Honor of the Late Clyde Allen Adams)

September 11, 2007, was the sixth anniversary of the terrorist attacks on the twin towers in New York. It was also the day when the structures that I had spent my entire life building to protect myself came crashing down around me. Joel had reached the end of his patience, and I was ready to meet my destiny.

When Joel had told me a few days earlier that he planned to accompany me to my next therapy session, I hoped he wouldn't remember. Not only did he remember, but he did all of the talking when we arrived. I was angry and hurt. I felt like a child who had misbehaved and was sitting in the principal's office pouting while my parents and the principle decided on my punishment.

I shut down completely and wouldn't answer any questions from either one of them. My ego was trying to answer, but my heart had cracked open the night before, and the nectar of my soul was beginning to strengthen my strand. When they asked me if I thought I had an addiction problem, I didn't answer. I also didn't deny it. My typical response would have been a defensive and immediate no, but I just sat there.

The therapist gingerly pulled out a brochure for a place called Bournewood in Brookline, Massachusetts. That's when I found my voice. I made a firm statement. "I am not going for treatment. I am not some drunk who lives in a tent in an underpass." While my voice was strong, inside I was shaking with fear. I knew I had a problem, but my idea of what an alcoholic was didn't match the way I saw myself.

Joel pulled back on his forceful tone because he saw that a vulnerable side of me had been revealed. However, he took the brochure on the way out.

Joel headed to work, and I cried as I drove myself home. My husband and my therapist had ganged up on me, and I felt threatened, exposed, and intensely weak. I was completely defenseless. I knew deep inside that I was all done, but I didn't have any idea what was going to happen to me next.

When I got home, my cleaning people were there. I ignored them and walked straight to the cabinet where I kept my potato vodka. I poured a huge glass, splashing it with pink lemonade. I needed to soothe my fears in a way that felt familiar.

I took a big gulp and called my friend Tara. Very emotionally, I told her that I was in big trouble, and I didn't know what to do. She asked me, "Do you think you can cut down on drinking by yourself?"

"No!" I said. "I don't want to. I don't have a problem." Even as I said it, I knew it wasn't true.

I stayed on the phone with Tara for an hour-long brainstorming session. While we talked, I drank one vodka and pink lemonade after another. By the time Cassie and her friend arrived home from school, I was bombed. Cassie called Joel, and he told her to hide the vodka bottle when I wasn't looking. He was on his way home.

Joel then called his sister and sent her to our house to pack me a bag. I didn't like having my privacy invaded, but I didn't fight it. My fight and resistance had been exhausted.

We have all fought against ourselves and have experienced varying degrees of pain from outer experiences during our journey through life. The quest to surrender strengthens our infinite soul's strand, and shiny pearls of growth become available to string on that strand.

Joel told me he was taking me to the ER. I was so drunk that I was laughing and crying at the same time. I didn't want to go to the hospital or to detox because that meant admitting I had a flaw. My father had preached to me that perfection was the only acceptable option. He would not be proud of me in that moment, and neither was I.

My daughter and her friend went to dinner with my sister-in-law while Joel drove me to the ER. We waited for hours. They don't rush things when someone arrives in an intoxicated state. The alcohol needs to wear off before they are legally allowed to discuss your options with you. As we waited, I must have stepped outside two dozen times to smoke cigarettes in an attempt to relax my fears and anxiety about the unknown.

Darkness is an illusion that disappears with the Light. Fear is an illusion that disappears with the Love. Ego is an illusion that disappears into the Oneness.

~ Author Unknown ~

I was making friends with anyone at the ER who would listen to my jokes. Humor is what kept me sane that night. Joel repeatedly asked me how much I'd had to drink; he said I was acting perfectly fine. I told him I didn't know. They finally called my name after 11:00 p.m.

They made me put on a Johnny. I hated that. Those things are butt ugly (no pun intended), and your butt literally hangs out of it. It was freezing cold in there, and I felt like a science experiment. They drew some blood, and the test came back with a blood alcohol reading of .0278. That is extremely high for the amount of time that had passed after Cassie took the bottle away from me. The doctor said most people would have been slurring their words and unable to walk. I had the tolerance level of an elephant. The technician explained that it takes one hour for the liver to process .25% of the alcohol, so I was going to be there for a while.

After a consult with the doctor, Joel was even more convinced that I had a drinking problem. The on-staff psychologist who dealt with addiction explained to me that we had to wait until my alcohol level cleared. Then we would discuss where I could be sent. He told Joel to go home. I didn't want to stay in that cold ER by myself. I was starting to get a hangover, and I was tired. I just wanted to go home, climb into my own bed, and go to sleep. Joel left me there alone.

I was dozing off very early in the morning when the psychologist finally came back and woke me up to talk. As he started to ask me questions, his approach was very cold. I had made up my mind that he was not the type of person I would allow to help me. He made me uncomfortable. I answered his questions, and that was it.

He asked me how often and how much I drank. Of course, my initial reaction was to sugarcoat my answer. I'm sure he was used to that, and he moved right into discussing my options for detox. When he told me that I had to be transported by ambulance, I said, "No frigging way! I'm not going to that place! I'm going home!" He rolled his eyes and called Joel.

I sighed with relief and quickly got dressed. I'd gotten my way, and I was going home. I didn't stay in the ER. I sprung myself and waited for Joel outside. When he pulled into the parking lot, he looked like he wanted to kill me. He was pissed. I was uncomfortable getting into the car, but I figured if I kept my mouth shut, he wouldn't yell at me. I felt like a teenage girl in trouble instead of the wife of the man driving the car. His voice carried an angry edge when he asked, "Why didn't you go to the detox, Deb?"

I didn't answer. I just gave him the silent treatment all the way home. I got into bed and felt an immediate sense of safety. I had beaten the system. I slept like a baby until I was awakened by the telephone. It was almost 10:00 a.m., and Joel was calling from work. He told me that he had made an appointment at Bournewood for noon, and he was on his way to pick me up. He instructed me to get up and get ready. "It's not up for debate," he said sternly.

My stomach sunk to my feet. I thought to myself, *What is happening to me?* There was a little whisper telling me I would be okay and that I needed to stop resisting. I had resisted my entire life. I was scared, but it was time to let go. I felt great despair, sadness, shame, and powerlessness. I was completely overcome and overwhelmed by fear. I felt embarrassed and didn't want anyone to know how weak I was.

Accepting and experiencing fear, pain, and every other emotion that comes up when surrendering shifts us into a spiritual destiny of freedom.

When Joel came into the house to get me, I cried. I surrendered. I didn't put up a fight like the Debbie he knew. It was time to begin my healing process. I knew the most difficult part would be the beginning, and nobody could do it for me. I was filled with so many emotions that they fought each other to see which would come out first. The only one I would allow out in that moment was grief for myself and my weakness. I had a disease, but I didn't really know it.

Weakness can make us feel like it's the end of the world, but having trust in ourselves allows us to channel our weaknesses into love and integrity. Awareness of weakness is a sign of strength.

Tears made tracks down my face all the way to Brookline. When we pulled into the pretty campus, my nerves got the best of me, and all I could do was chain smoke. As I looked around, I thought, *How bad could it be?* The campus was lavishly landscaped, and the main office building had a Victorian décor. I thought it might be like the Betty Ford Center, and I began to look forward to some pampering.

Bournewood was definitely not a place for pampering! After I was admitted, a staff member escorted Joel and me to the building where I would be staying. I lost control when I saw the condition of the other patients and the environment I would be living in for the next four days. The other patients looked like zombies. There were bars on the windows, and all of the doors were locked.

I was going to be locked in. I started to panic. What if I had an anxiety attack and needed to get outside to breathe? I bawled my eyes out and pleaded with Joel not to leave me there. "Pleeeease, pleeease, don't leave me!" I begged. "I don't belong in here! I don't belong with these people!"

He looked at me with tears in his eyes. "I'm sorry. I love you." He left me there, and they locked the door behind him.

I hated him for leaving me there. I could have left, but I didn't. Even though I was scared, I knew I was in trouble and needed help. I experienced every minute of the hell I was putting myself through.

They searched my suitcase, which made me feel like they were invading my privacy. They confiscated my pocketbook, cigarettes, hair dryer, and razor. I accused them of treating me like a convict. I stormed into my room, which had four beds in it, and I began to lash out by throwing my stuff.

A woman came in to comfort me. I knew she was trying to help me, but my ego jumped in. I growled at her to leave me the hell alone. She rolled her eyes and sauntered out. I felt bad that I might have hurt her feelings, but my feelings of pain, despair, and sorrow seemed more important.

Whatever your cross, whatever your pain,
there will always be sunshine after the rain.
Perhaps you may stumble, perhaps even fall,
But God's always ready to answer your call.
He knows every heartache, sees every tear.
A word from His lips can calm every fear.
Your sorrows may linger throughout the night,
But suddenly vanish in dawn's early light.
The Savior is waiting somewhere above,
To give you His grace and send you His love.
Whatever your cross, whatever your pain,
God always sends rainbows.
after the rain.
~ Shalabh Gupta ~

Once I calmed down and realized that I wasn't doing myself any good by acting like a child, I put my clothes in my designated drawer. When it was time for dinner, I was still in such a state that I couldn't eat. I just sat there and cried, feeling sorry for myself. I was sick to my stomach. I managed to eat a little bit of yogurt while sitting at a table alone. After dinner, we were let out of our cage to go outside for a cigarette

I must have been living under a rock, because I couldn't believe how many people were trying to detox from heroin. I made friends quickly during our smoking break, and most of them were there for heroin. After my cigarette, I went over to the woman who had tried to befriend me earlier. I apologized to her for being mean. She accepted and said she understood. It was her fourth time there. She said she had one day left in her stay, and that time she was going to stay clean for her kids. My heart felt her pain.

When we went back inside, it was meds time. I didn't understand the procedure at first, but I caught on quickly. The staff took everyone's blood pressure and heart rate. They needed to monitor us physically while we detoxed on medication. If our vitals were okay, they distributed the appropriate medications necessary for detox four times a day. They gave me a drug called Ativan. It tricks the brain into thinking that it is still receiving alcohol.

I was shocked when I heard they give methadone to heroin addicts. I thought it was just as bad. I certainly got an education in that place. They asked me if I wanted a sleeping pill, and I said no. They all told me I should, but I refused. About an hour after meds time, everyone was wasted. I simply couldn't believe it. "What the hell kind of place is this?" I asked. No one paid any attention to me. They knew I was lashing out.

I was content and maybe even a little buzzed after taking that pill, but I was also a bit scared. About 90% of the people in there were detoxing from heroin and their methadone made them so wasted they couldn't speak. Their eyes were red and rolled back in their heads. I retreated to my room.

When I went to bed that night, I fell asleep immediately. In the dead of the night, they admitted another heroin addict and put her in the empty bed next to mine. She moaned all night long! I was bugging out. I took the sleeping pill the next night, for sure! She still woke me up with her moaning, but at least I was able to fall back to sleep again.

On the third day, I had a major panic attack out of the blue. I was hyperventilating. There was no air, and I thought I was dying. My heart was beating so fast it hurt. I was positive I was having a heart attack. I tried to communicate with my eyes to let them know something was very wrong. They told me I would be fine and explained that they were gradually decreasing my Ativan intake, and that was why I was feeling strange.

When they checked my vitals, they were off the chart. They immediately gave me a pill because they were afraid I would have a seizure and die. I learned that detoxing from alcohol is more dangerous, but that detoxing from heroin is more painful physically. That explained the moaner. Hearing that blew my mind. I had no idea that detoxing from alcohol was dangerous. It terrified me.

Fear is energy from ego. Love is pure energy from the heart.

I spoke to Joel every night and begged him to visit me that Saturday. I waited all day, and he didn't show. I was heartbroken. Because I was in there over a weekend, I had to stay for five days. Joel came to pick me up on Monday afternoon.

I had entered Bournewood on September 12, 2007. It was the first of my growing pains. I had to endure 10 months of growing pains before the universe guided me to a path that will always hold a special place in my heart, a path where I discovered the pure joy of being born again. Before I was led to that path, I had to live through the most intense and painful time of my entire life. The process allowed me to gain the faith and trust in myself that was necessary for me to approach my healing with willingness and an open mind.

The last task I had to complete before leaving Bournewood was a meeting with Joel and a counselor. I was concerned because I was experiencing continued panic and anxiety attacks that literally hurt. They gave me an Ativan to take that night and explained that my insurance program was sending me to Bay Ridge, an outpatient program in Lynn, Massachusetts, for further therapy.

I got up the next morning and drove myself to Bay Ridge, and I was scared shitless. While I was waiting for someone to help me at the check-in counter, another major panic attack came over me. Someone gave me a paper bag to breathe into, and the doctor on staff gave me an Ativan. I felt better in about half an hour.

I started thinking that drinking had been a lot easier, but a whisper said that part of my life was over. It was time to strengthen my strand. My pearls were being cultivated.

The program at Bay Ridge was pretty comprehensive. We were in rotating classrooms, similar to high school, all day. I definitely learned a lot. I found out that alcohol attacks random sections in the brain, and it can attack the part of the brain that allows us to breathe. If that happens, we stop breathing and die. That fact alone was enough to keep me away from alcohol forever.

The other half of the program involved meeting with a pair of psychiatrists. Between the two of them, they had me convinced that I was bipolar. They put me on a cocktail of drugs that made me look and feel like the poor people at Bournewood that I had judged so harshly. I was so out of it that I shouldn't have been driving. I wrecked my car three times. They kept extending my stay there because I wasn't getting better. I wasn't getting better because they had me pumped full of pills that I didn't need. I ended up going there for a total of five months instead of five weeks.

Near the end of my time at Bay Ridge, Joel needed to go away on business. The doctors didn't want me staying with my daughter by myself, so they admitted me into their detox facility, where I was drugged up like a zombie for another four days. The procedure of misdiagnosing me and medicating me felt terribly wrong. I couldn't feel what I was supposed to feel because my mind was dramatically and unnecessarily altered. Finally, my little self beneath all of that medication came alive and put its foot down. I asked them point blank, "If I'm bipolar like you say I am, shouldn't your stinking meds make me feel normal?"

The psychiatrists gave me their stupid smirks, and one of them said, "Yes, of course you should. Don't you feel wonderful?"

I felt my blood boil as I replied, "No, I don't! I don't want to take your pills any more. Do you understand me? I want you to start weaning me off this stuff immediately." They agreed, and little by little I began to feel like myself again. My inner self and the universe came to light for me.

During that time, I was also attending AA meetings. I haven't been to one of those in three years. I'm not knocking the validity of AA meetings, as they work for many people. It just wasn't what worked for me. I would leave every meeting feeling extremely upset. The stories the people told about how miserable they felt were upsetting. I experienced such extreme highs and lows that there were several times when I felt like driving my car into a tree on the way home.

I refused to have my life dictated by what happened in that one hour. At AA, they told me not to go places where there was booze. I tried that, and I ended up living like a hermit, which made me dreadfully unhappy. I used my own will power to stay away from alcohol and filled the void by working out constantly. I was an utterly lost soul. I wasn't treating the root problem, but I was being prepared to do just that.

The universe had a plan. The plan was for me to endure as long as it took for me to find and accept my own soul. So I sat with my pain and my emotions. I felt them as I had never felt them before. It was not a time for me to feel content, at ease, or at peace. That block of time had been created to teach me many lessons all at once. It was a vital and necessary part of the plan for me to discover my hidden treasures in this life and begin to repair the strand of pearls.

Many pearls were waiting to be placed on my strand. Brian Weiss has said, "Forgive the past. It is over. Learn from it and let it go. People are constantly changing and growing. Do not cling to a limited, disconnected negative image of any person in the past. See that person now. Your relationships are always alive and changing."

I couldn't agree more. In fact, I wrote a poem after that revelation—Evolve to Resolve and Resolve to Evolve. *I was ready for the next synchronicity....*

One Tuesday night, I came across a group of people that had an attitude completely opposite that of the AA group I had been attending. They were shining bright! They smiled, told jokes, seemed happy, and spoke positively. They weren't moping and feeling sorry for themselves. They told me that with some hard work, an open mind, and complete willingness, I could be living life the way they did, at peace. They said I would be able to go anywhere in the world I wanted to go, because I would be cured. I wanted whatever it was that they had.

I befriended a woman named Janice and, in June, 10 months after going to detox, I finally got the nerve to ask her what the secret was. She told me it was a retreat in Plymouth, New Hampshire, called The Plymouth House. Plymouth, where Joel had attended college, was about to reveal a very special jewel to me.

I called the very next morning to find out what I had to do to get in. Greg interviewed me and asked me to get a note from my doctor stating I was in good health, because The Plymouth House was not a medical facility. When he told me I had to be four days sober, I laughed and said I had 10 months of sobriety. He then asked why I wanted to go there. I told him I was thoroughly impressed by the people I'd met that Tuesday night and that they had recommended The Plymouth House for me. I told Greg I wanted the peace and the life they had.

I explained to him that mentally I just didn't feel good. He said I didn't feel good because I hadn't treated the disease. The consumption of alcohol was just a symptom. The disease was one of mind and body, and treating it would be very emotional and spiritual. So far I had only treated the body. It was a disease I would learn all about when I checked into The Plymouth House on the first Friday in July.

Alcoholism is a symptom of the disease, not the cause. The cure was discovering my soul and letting it out. My gut told me that place was going to change my life forever. I could feel it!

For the first time, I had great hope and faith. Knowing that others had come out walking a path of love, happiness, and health gave me confidence. I trusted that the program would guide me into accomplishing the same. I had a willingness to let go of resistance, resentment, and anger, but I didn't know how. I wasn't going to allow a negative state of mind to exist and have power over me any longer. It was time to evolve. I was ready to let go of ego and bathe in the waters of heart and soul.

Plymouth was a two-hour drive from my home. Little did I know I was driving there to find my true home. I had the highest of expectations and intention. I arrived on a gorgeous, sunny, warm afternoon. The Plymouth House grounds had a rural atmosphere. A small chapel served as the focal point, and the housing was designed around a barnyard theme. It was inviting, and I felt extremely comfortable the second I got out of my car. The grounds were lush with green grass and seasonal lilies.

I parked, grabbed my suitcase, and went into the office. I was a bit nervous but cautiously optimistic. I had nothing to lose. I met with a couple of staff members to check in and have my luggage inspected. They gave me a tour and showed me to my room.

The accommodations were fairly new and in great shape. The common area, which was originally a barn, was very homey. The kitchen and dining area were clearly an addition to the barn, and they were also very pleasant. In the upstairs of the barn were a small yoga room, a small library, and a couple of additional rooms for staff. The other guests who would be part of my group arrived while I was getting my tour. Guests who were already there were abundantly welcoming. Everything about The Plymouth House made me feel terrific. I knew with my entire being that I was in the right place.

Later that evening, after dinner and a lot of sitting around, I learned about the mandatory wrap-up meeting they held every night. One by one, all the guests introduce themselves and then tell how their day went. They also announce whether they accomplished a goal they set during the mandatory morning goals meeting. It was awesome. Everyone made me feel welcome, and I made friends that I will have forever. I could really feel the love in the room.

The program was set up so that when guests arrive at the same time, they attend classes together in small groups until they reach a certain point in their progression. The next step is to join the larger group, where the progress becomes individual. That's when the real hard work begins.

Open your mind. Allow your feelings to be experienced, to be pushed out. Your heart will not break but will open, allowing free-flowing light and life energy from the core of your soul to come through.

A typical day at The Plymouth House started with coffee and breakfast. For me, it also started with a happy face and the belief that I was on a healing path. Goals group was great because it got everyone revved up for the day. The energy of all of us together was enough nourishment for me. After goals group, the men and women were separated for reflection group. That was usually very emotional for most of us. One of the staff members chose a reading from a spiritual book and based a reflection on the reading. Once we'd heard the staff member's reflection, we went around the room and listened to everyone else reflect on the reading. Most days we left for our next class feeling lighter after a wonderful, releasing, emotional cry.

My first day was very poignant, because I was asked what I wanted to accomplish. I said I wanted to feel happy and stop obsessing about what I should be doing next while I was doing something else. I didn't want to be grocery shopping and think about the laundry or my appointment three days away. I wanted to be able to do my shopping and enjoy that and only that. I needed to slow my mind and stay in the present moment. The thought of that goal remaining just out of reach without my knowing how to get there made me sob. I couldn't stop.

We took a break after reflections and then had our small-group class in the *Big Book*. After lunch, workshops were available for guests who had joined the large group. Then came free time, where we learned to sit with ourselves and become aware of the importance of patience. After dinner, we had more free time, followed by additional workshops and classes. We ended each day with wrap-up. That was my daily schedule until I progressed enough to start the hard work of looking inside.

Inside all of us is the peace we were born with. A common and lovely theme among all the staff members was the beautiful peace within them. I could feel it. It made my experience one of the best of my life.

There were six people in my group, four women and two men. I became close with Diane, Betty, Stanley, and my roommate, Amy. Stanley called Betty, Diane, and me his angels, Charlie style. He was the comedian of the group.

We were educated from Bill Wilson's eloquently written spiritual masterpiece, the *Big Book of AA*. An education about my sickness was exactly what my mind needed. The cure was the discovery of my soul and the power of my source within.

A disease of the mind and body affects the spirit, as well. In basic terms, the part of the disease that affects the body is like an allergy, and it creates the phenomenon of craving. To fix that, all you have to do is remove the alcohol. It sounds easy enough, but abstinence won't last unless the part of the disease that affects the mind is treated. That's where the brunt of the disease lies. It is the state of mind that is the primary problem. The mind houses obsession, resentment, selfishness, self-centeredness, anger, and RID. RID stands for restlessness, irritability and discontent. All of that made sense to me.

The solution is spiritual wellness. It relieves and cures the symptoms of both the mind and body. It cannot be done through will power. I understood that because I had lived it. Achieving spiritual wellness is a miraculous occurrence that comes from a complete psychic change and transcendence as a result of having a paramount life-changing spiritual experience. It produces a completely new emotional arrangement. Old ideas and concepts become irrelevant. It is a transformation that occurs by getting completely truthful with ourselves. The mind rewires itself, enabling us to think with compassion and altruism rather than ego.

They explained that it was going to be up to us. We had to be willing and absolutely and completely honest, or it would not work. Most importantly, we needed be open-minded and begin to pray to God or another power greater than us.

I understood the concept, but I couldn't yet grasp the process. However, I had an inviting sense of ease come over me. I started praying every night, and I still pray daily. The energy we put out does come back to us.

By the second week, our cozy little group of six had joined the others in the bigger group. It was time for the real work to begin. They introduced us to *The Solution*. *The Solution* was the 12 steps, and we would do up to 10 there. We had accomplished Step 1 by admitting we were powerless over alcohol and Step 2 by believing in a power greater than ourselves. I approached that part seriously, truthfully, and with an open mind. My life depended on it.

The evening before we were released to the bigger group, the six of us knelt in the chapel and recited the third-step prayer together.

God, I offer myself to Thee, to build with me and to do with me as Thou wilt. Relieve me of the bondage of self, that I may better do Thy will. Take away my difficulties, that victory over them may bear witness to those I would help of Thy Power, Thy Love and Thy way of life. May I do Thy will always!

That moment moved me tremendously. I felt the weight of everything I had carried for years begin to lift. It was a very special experience when the six of us made eye contact with each other after we were done. I felt the presence of the Oneness around us and in me.

One morning during week two, I woke up and realized my physical pain had vanished. My joints were no longer hurting me, and I was no longer a nervous wreck. The chatter in my head was gone. I was even walking more slowly. My miracle had begun! The intention energy that I had put out into the universe was returning to me with power.

The fourth step involved the hard work. We had to take a complete and honest inventory of ourselves. We started by making a numbered list of every person, place, or thing that we had felt resentment toward in our entire life. We then had to list every resentment we'd had, placing them under each number on the list. I listed more than 100 names, places, or things. For each of those, I wrote down 5 to 45 resentments. We also had to answer a series of four questions about each and every resentment on the list.

I had faith in the process, because the pen was moving so fast that it was as if I had help from a power I couldn't see but could feel. I had never been a believer before, but I felt one with the power that created me.

The questions were all about finding the blame, dishonesty, fear, selfishness, self-seeking, and mistakes in ourselves and our thinking. It was entirely eye-opening and definitely life-changing for me. I became sick of learning about my old self. I was disgusted with my old patterns and behavior. I had been utterly horrible, selfish, and mean. I didn't like that person.

It took place gradually and slowly, but it reached the deepest burial grounds of everything I had endured in my life. It was working. I wanted to scream it to the world. My heart had broken open, and my soul was nourishing me. Pearls were flying at me left and right, waiting for their turn to be strung.

The most profound moment during my stay at The Plymouth House was when I had my very first emotional/spiritual experience. It was in the large group during *Big Book* class. We were focusing on page 67. Aaron was at the podium sharing his experiences after reading some of that page.

I will never forget it as long as I live. It was an ah-ha moment that is as alive in me now as when it happened. It was at that exact moment that the Divine gave me the power for my consciousness to make a tremendous shift and expansion for growth.

Page 67 was about our list of people. If we had done our inventory with abundant honesty, we should have been able to feel for them and want to help them. We would have pity, compassion, patience, and tolerance for them, for they might be more spiritually sick than we were. We should not feel anger.

I felt an immediate revelation overcome my entire body, along with a humility I can't put into words. My essence was budding and ready to bloom and exuberate the fragrance of love. The rewards that I had no idea existed would surpass any happy moments I had ever experienced in my life. My body trembled with every emotion. A release of tears that carried fear, sadness, and anger washed down my face. Then they turned into joy, love, and happiness, just as the dark of the night turns into a golden sunrise of light.

The emotion of those tears was like the hurricane of a lifetime, releasing pent-up anger and fear as they flowed down my face like a waterfall. Before I knew it, they changed their color because the sun of transformation shone on them, turning them into a rainbow of peaceful bliss. I felt the release from every cell in my body and mind as they opened my spirit so that it could finally shine. Pure delight encompassed my being, but the ride had just begun.

My jewels were slowly washing to the surface, and I allowed myself to suffer and experience the pain that I had been burying for years. Tears are a magnifying glass into the truths of your heart.

I was on a very important mission, which had been waiting for my arrival for years. I was at The Plymouth House for a life-shifting purpose. I had been working on my inventory for two weeks straight, writing at every opportunity. It was a hot summer in New Hampshire, and there were amazing thunder and lightning storms every afternoon. The storms allowed me to simply focus on my hard work and discover the character defects that had allowed me to have so many resentments.

On the day I finished my complete inventory, with every rock overturned and nothing hidden, I breathed in calm and exhaled love. The next day was August 1, 2008. It was the day of my complete awakening, which allowed me to be born again. I read my inventory to God, the Divine, and the universe. Amy, my roommate, was my witness as I read aloud my entire life's inventory. It took me seven hours to proclaim my wrongs aloud that day. I asked for—and received—release from and forgiveness for all my character defects. I had completed the fifth and sixth steps.

It was then time to recite the seventh-step prayer and meditate for one hour. I sat for a moment and realized how different I felt. I was as light as a feather. I recited out loud and proudly to myself and the universe: *My Creator, I am now willing that you should have all of me, good and bad. I pray that you now remove from me every single defect of character which stands in the way of my usefulness to you and my fellows. Grant me strength, as I go out from here, to do your bidding. Amen.*

I did my one-hour meditation without a timepiece of any sort. It was a minor miracle that I emerged from the chapel exactly one hour after I had begun my meditation. My prayers had been heard and answered. I could feel it. When I emerged from the Chapel, I experienced a profound peace.

Peace. It does not mean to be in a place where there is no noise,
trouble or hard work. It means to be in the midst of those
things and still be calm in your heart.
~ Author Unknown ~

I had created so much space in my mind and body that there was not one single idea, concept, or thought. I had nothing on my mind. It felt as though I were using my senses for the first time. The grass, the color of the sky, and the flowers were all in brilliant colors, the like of which I had never seen. The sounds of the cars going by, the birds chirping their end-of-day chirps, and even the sound of quiet, all were miraculously lovely to me. The scents of the flowers and fresh-cut grass were candy to my nose.

Everything I touched, from my own skin to the food I ate, was all brand new to me. The air I was breathing (prana, the life force) felt like my first breath of air ever. It filled every corner of my lungs with energetic life. What an exhilarating feeling I had. I was aware at that moment that I was a part of the whole. All that I just described was me, and I was all of them. I had found a peace within me that is within us all.

I loved that moment of life, and I have loved every moment thereafter because I am finally aware and present in my life. The *Strand of Pearls* has been repaired, and each pearl has a significance of its own. My life has been transformed from the inside out. That day at The Plymouth House was just the beginning of a wonderful experience of this life.

The Divine gives itself to those who give themselves without
reserve and in all their parts to the Divine. For them, the calm,
the light, the power, the bliss, the freedom, the wideness, the
heights of knowledge, the seas of Ananda.

~ Sri Aurobindo ~

Chapter Fourteen

A Time to Reflect

I have arrived. I am home.
In the here. In the now.
I am solid. I am free.
In the ultimate I dwell

~ Thich Nhat Hanh ~

Glide your wings with an open heart,
And you shall soar to unattained heights

~ Deborah Livingston ~

When you experience spiritual transformation and discover the treasures in this life—and in you—it will be the first best moment you will ever experience. Your life from that point on will be filled with an abundance of miracles that follow one after the other. I promise!

If you have experienced this thrill in life, then you know there are no words that can fully and accurately describe it. If you simply want to deepen your consciousness and open up to a new passion for the zest of life, then seek spiritual transformation by taking a willing, open-minded, and completely truthful inventory of yourself. If you are exhausted from living as a victim of any life challenge, allow the evolution of your soul to carry you into survival.

The transformation that I was so honored to experience has enabled me to accept and view my life's synchronistic events from a nonjudgmental and completely nonresistant point of view. That viewpoint allows me to love what is and to know that everything transpires and unfolds as it is supposed to. I now view my life on earth as my school of growth.

The following quotation from *The Mother* (CWMCE, 6:349) demonstrates, in general terms, life's synchronistic events.

We must have the faith that always what is for the best happens. We may for the moment not consider it as the best because we are ignorant and also blind, because we do not see the consequences of the things and what will happen later. But we must keep the faith that if it is like that, if we rely on the Divine, if we give Him the full charge of ourselves, if we let Him decide everything for us, well, we must know that it is always what is best for us which happens. This is the absolute fact. To the extent to which you surrender, the best happens to you. This may not be in conformity with what you would like, your preference or desire, because these things are blind; it is the best from the spiritual point of view, the best for your progress, your development, your spiritual growth, your true life. It is always that.

And you must keep this faith, because faith is the expression of a trust in the Divine. And when you make it, it is something absolutely marvelous. That's a fact; these are not just words, you understand, it is a fact. When you look back, all kinds of things which you did not understand when they happened to you, you realize as just the thing which was necessary in order to compel you to make the needed progress. Always, without exception. It is our blindness which prevents us from seeing it.

It was no accident when I was a toddler that I broke the *Strand of Pearls*, as it was my Divine destiny to repair it and learn my many life lessons through extreme challenges. My first two and most important pearls of realization were the *Pearls of Acceptance and Forgiveness*. What I learned about acceptance is that I don't necessarily have to like someone's behavior. I don't have to like something as simple as a kind of flower or type of dessert. All I need to do is accept everyone and everything for whom and what it is. It's about accepting that it is enough just as it is.

The same goes for situations. I don't need to change or control situations that are out of my control, because there is no need to waste good energy on trying. Energy is better spent accepting. When you encounter a situation that is in your complete control and no one else's, it is yours to govern or manage within your means. The outcome will most likely be the result of destiny, in any event.

For example, my father abused me for the 13 years of my life, but the abuse stayed with me for years after I escaped. For 13 years, the situation was out of my control, so nothing I did could change it. Today I accept it. I don't like it, for obvious reasons, but I accept it. I also accept that my mother chose to be with my father and chose to do nothing to stop the abuse. Accepting brings me the *Pearl of Forgiveness*.

Forgiveness was quite effortless for me, as I know that my father was spiritually sick. I don't know how or why he became that way. I can only surmise, but that isn't the point. He played an important part in my life's lessons, and I forgive and love him for the man he was. He was my father, despite all of his hurtful flaws. He was the way he was because he had other lessons he was meant to learn during his life, and the abuse he inflicted was part of mine.

I also forgive my mother for her character defects, because she is who she is, and that is the way it is supposed to be. That is enough for me. We are part of something bigger and more powerful than us, and everything that happened was exactly the way it was supposed to be. In a sense, by gaining the treasures of acceptance and forgiveness, I have also restored a degree of the innocence that I lost all those years ago. Allowing acceptance for any situation or person, good or bad, is essential in forgiving.

I have forgiven everyone who hurt me in the past. They have their own shortcomings, as do I. I have forgiven myself for the accident and the loss of my friend Rob. We both made decisions that led us to a situation that produced tragic consequences. For years, I carried the full blame for those consequences and wished it had been me who died and not him. I now realize that I had been blind in the moments when we made our decisions and even more blind to the consequences. I now surrender and accept that it was and is part of the Divine whole and, as such, beyond my control.

Another pearl on my strand is the *Pearl of Patience*. Patience came much more easily once the chattering in my head had been kicked out for good. I can be at ease with most situations in my life now. I'm not saying that I am a saint; I am very human. However, there was a period in my life when I would quickly fly off the handle when patience would have been a much better choice.

Patience is the companion of wisdom.
~ St. Augustine ~

Patience is the ability to count down before you blast off.
~ Author Unknown ~

Experience has taught me this, that we undo ourselves by impatience. Misfortunes have their life and their limits, their sickness and their health.
~ Michel de Montaigne ~

Patience, for me, is the ability to relax instead of resisting, allowing moments to be as they are. Patience goes hand in hand with the ability to exercise tolerance. The *Pearl of Tolerance* is the appreciation of diversity and the ability to live and let others live. Tolerance is the essence of respecting another's way of interpreting life and expressing one's self. It is my blessing and treasure to be able to understand that there is no right or wrong way of being. Just be and observe others in their being, as well.

> *Tolerance and celebration of individual differences is the fire that fuels lasting love.*
> ~ Tom Hannah ~

I believe that tolerance comes from the source that fuels one's inner peace. Helen Keller believed that tolerance is a great gift of the mind. She should know. She had major obstacles to overcome, and tolerance was a necessity for her to grow. It enabled her to remain positive.

It was through achieving tolerance that I have been blessed with yet another pearl, the *Pearl of Positive Thinking*. Being positive encompasses the attitude of happiness and a willingness to find a positive outcome for the most unpleasant moments in life. Everything happens for a reason, no matter how difficult or easy it is to get through to the other side. The purpose is to come through with an understanding of the positive lesson the challenge presented. To be able to see the positive side of any consequences makes me thankful and grateful.

> *Nothing contributes so much to tranquilize the mind as a steady purpose, a point on which the soul may fix its intellectual eye.*
> ~ Mary Wollstonecraft Shelley, Frankenstein, 1818 ~

Two more pearls, the *Pearl of Thankfulness* and the *Pearl of Gratitude*, have been added to my strand. My heart holds hands with the sun even when it has been temporarily veiled by the clouds. No matter what life hands me—good, bad, or indifferent—I am thankful and grateful for everyone and everything that has crossed my path or walked parallel to it. I am grateful and thankful for the air I breathe, the ground I walk on, the sounds I hear, the rainbow of colors I am able to see, the nourishment I taste, the health of my loved ones, and the ability to love and share. For all of these gifts, I am thankful and grateful because they allow me to embrace life on the deepest, most passionate level of my soul's ability.

> *As each day comes to us refreshed and anew, so does my gratitude renew itself daily. The breaking of the sun over the horizon is my grateful heart dawning upon a blessed world.*
> ~ Terri Guillemets ~

Living in and for the present moment is the most wonderful feeling. It is one of the best treasures that the universe has offered, and it is the next pearl on my strand. Thich Naht Hanh believes that living in the moment is a practice of mindfulness. It is the essence of being completely aware, which requires achieving a certain level of consciousness. Awareness involves being sensitive to the now and becoming aware that the past and the future are variables of the now. It is the awareness of natural beauty and the serenity it holds. It is listening and extending empathy when needed.

It is the ability to take in every moment and be with that moment as that moment, feeling only that moment. The *Pearl of Present Awareness* is the gift of a serene mindfulness in the moment. Mindfulness requires that we abandon the clutter of focusing on "what if."

> *The secret of health for both mind and body is not to mourn for the past, worry about the future, or anticipate troubles, but to live in the present moment wisely and earnestly.*
> ~ Buddha ~

Mindfulness enables me to be in the present moments of life and fully embrace and experience them with my family, loved ones, and friends. I also enjoy the moments that I spend alone or in the company of my lovely animals. Animals are the best teachers of all when it comes to living in the moment and embracing it with the energy of love. Every present moment in my life on earth has become my school. Every person and every living thing is my teacher.

This journey of mine has been like that of the transformation of a butterfly. It is my spiritual evolution.

The butterfly counts not months, but moments,
and has time enough.
~ Rabindranath Tagore ~

Once I was a caterpillar, unnoticed and confined to exploring life from a single point of view. I was barely creeping along. Then I hid from the world and spun myself deeper and deeper into a protective cocoon. After a period of transformation, I resurfaced with a new ability to view the world from a completely different perspective. Because I have developed wings, my spirit can fly. Where I was once blind and saw no color, I now see the colors of brilliance. My wings enable me to experience the colors of the vibrant world and the beautiful colors of individuality as butterflies.

I now recognize all of you other butterflies not only as my teachers, but also as my role models. Everyone and everything that has come in contact with my life path has been and will be my role models for growth.

I am free and at peace. My freedom and peace are the fires that fuel my heart and soul to give and receive the brightest energy of love. I glow with joy and happiness.

I don't want to mislead anyone by claiming that I live my life in a bowl of cherries, because that is not true. Although I may smell good, all kidding aside, I am human. I have bad days just like everyone else. It's how we handle them that makes all the difference.

The blessing of emerging from my transformational journey wearing butterfly wings is having the ability to recognize and acknowledge the bad moments, accept them, own them, feel the emotions within them, embrace them, and let them go. The *Pearls of Freedom and Peace* should make the world go round. I wish freedom and peace for every living being here on earth and in the hereafter.

Encountering the absence of freedom and peace elicits extreme compassion from me for those in need. I am in a place that enables me to extend my hand to those in need and always say yes. We all possess tools for kindness.

There are wonderful people, places, and things that surround me in my life that the universe has placed on my path. Collectively, they help keep me balanced and grounded. They enable me to live life in harmony, accepting life on life's terms, not mine.

The practice of meditation has dramatically changed my life. It led me to move into a career that better aligns with my new body, mind, and spirit. The daily practice of yoga clears my mind, body, and soul, leaving space for me to claim my power from within and absorb the day with peace and an open mind.

The private study of metaphysics delivered to me by the universe has led me to the faith of Spiritualism. Spiritualism has completely opened me up to the gifts of healing. Whenever I feel myself becoming out of balance, I am able to recognize it immediately and turn to my truths for my answer. Honesty is what healed me, and I keep it close to my heart.

I live my life in freedom and peace, enjoying all it has to offer and experiencing it as it comes. I have been able to travel and see some of this beautiful world, and I enjoy the peak experiences and the simple joys equally.

I have no desire to change who I was or where I came from, as those formed the foundation of who I am today. All was and is as it should be. I am comfortable with my past, my present, and my future, because none of them define me. I live life from my heart.

You may wonder how my external life has changed since I discovered the gifts and treasures that the universe held for me until I was ready to receive them. I would like to share that part of my journey with you, just as I have shared the experiences that led me to my transformation.

Once the energy of my body, mind and spirit were flowing harmoniously, my intuition whispered that I was to begin helping others. After some soul searching and listening to my subtle guides, I was drawn to the study of Traditional Chinese Medicine (TCM). I am currently an AOBTA-certified Acupressure Therapist. I studied first at the New England School of Acupuncture and then continued my education at the Acupressure Therapy Institute, which is owned by Barbara Blanchard, one of my role models. I finished my studies in China, where I spent two weeks studying Tuina.

The study of TCM goes hand in hand with the beliefs I have long held that the mind, body, and spirit make the whole. When one flows out of balance or is blocked, it affects the harmony of the others. This can be treated by stimulating to either tonify or disperse the energetics of the appropriate points and meridians. This method of healing is profound, and it has been utilized for centuries. I am honored to have learned it and to now pass it along while treating the disharmonies in my clients.

In order to heal and help others, I must keep myself healed. I heal myself by maintaining harmony and balance within my own body, mind, and spirit. Daily meditation is a wonderful way for me to settle my mind and reach new levels of transcended consciousness. It allows me to stay in touch with my innermost self and helps me access my intuition on a spiritual level and contact my guides. Meditation is a great healer that has been proven to reduce stress and high blood pressure and enhance the immune system. It keeps me grounded and at peace, so that I am able to know exactly who I am and who I am not.

In addition, I practice hot power yoga every day at Empower Yoga in Beverly, Massachusetts. Yoga has the same beneficial effect for me as meditation. It is, in fact, a moving, breathing form of meditation, which focuses on prana.

Through yoga, I can achieve unity and harmony of the mind, body, and spirit. It detoxifies the body, as well strengthening and promoting flexibility over time. Yoga creates emotional balance through detachment and release. The ultimate goals are self-realization and enlightenment. The practice of yoga helps your heart and soul to open fully. Performing asanas with the proper prana heals the whole and produces an eternal bliss.

My spiritual transformation, the repair of my Strand of Pearls, ultimately shone a beam on my path, which guided me to study metaphysics. I had never heard of the term before then. I learned that metaphysics is a philosophy that encompasses the fundamental explanation of being and the world. It includes, but is not limited to, spirituality, religion, mind and matter, quantum physics, ethics, cosmology, space and time, identity, and change. I have read many books on the subject, and they have landed me in a faith that was waiting for me to discover it.

The faith of Spirituality has enhanced my life on a most profound level. I am a member of the Swampscott Church of Spirituality, and we welcome all people. The church has given me so many like-minded friends. They are kind, compassionate souls. I make it my mission to try to live by all of the principles to the best of my ability. I live my life with an open, loving, compassionate heart. I continue to grow and learn through the challenges life presents. Spirituality enables me to learn the positive lessons from each and every challenge. Positive energy is healing energy, while negative energy promotes sickness. Spirituality is an open-denomination faith, which is available to everyone here and in the hereafter. Spiritualism believes in infinite spirit, the existence of which has been scientifically proven through mediumship.

Today I practice unfolding my spirituality through psychic/mediumship unfoldment classes and circles. It enables me to heal and help people by contacting their loved ones and receiving loving, healing messages from them. It is my life's purpose to heal people through the gifts that I have been given. Traditional Chinese Medicine and mediumship are my gifts to heal people, and they are special pearls on my strand.

Today I love my husband and daughter, my extended family, NASCAR, boating, Buddhism, comedians, movies, sports cars, Omega, loving to laugh, and laughing to love. I am, and I love. I still love my jewels, which include my animals, nature, art, and running on the beach with my dogs.

My goal for sharing my personal journey with you is to demonstrate that healing from every life challenge is possible. You can be transformed from a victim of abuse, tragedy, loss, anxiety, depression, addiction, and despair to become a survivor. Pull up your big-girl/big-boy pants and rise to the occasion of spiritual transformation so that you can discover your own hidden talents and treasures. Open your heart and live from it instead of living from your ego.

I am your biggest fan, and I support you. Go for it. We have nothing to lose and every miracle to gain. Love and be loved. Peace and love to you!

Pearl of the Soul

By Deborah Livingston

Within us all lays a pearl of the soul
Each shape unique, eternal evolution and glow
Some small as a granule,
Others luminous in layers of divine growth
All possess an eternal beauty
Of varied manifestation of creativity
It is those times that dim the pilot light of our spirit
That our pearl grows its layers
Of wisdom, love, compassion and care
The illusions of life that create our reality
Are challenges of a graceful balance between polarities
The moments that obscure our body, mind and soul with pain
Shall be embraced ultimately
Making room for expansion through the balance of yin and
yang
Letting go of the dark and replacing with light
Revealing truths of the heart and shines our clarity bright
Each layer of white beauty and shine are the intelligence of our
lessons this time
Enabling our souls during our human experience to be of love,
peace and free
All are the elements of the wealthiest pearl and eternal
prosperity

(IN HONOR OF MY MOTHER,
GWENDOLYNN HART ADAMS BRUNET)

Resources

Sri Aurobindo Society
Pondicherry, India
www.sriaurobindosociety.org.in

The Plymouth House
446 Main Street, NH 03264
www.theplymouthhouse.com

The American Federation of Spiritualist Churches
Sagamore Beach, Ma 02562
www.afschurches.com

Amanda E. Edwards Photography:
Visit on FB page/978-223-8309

Spirituality Resources-A Woman's Journey-Spiritual Growth
www.awomansjourney.com

Arthur Findlay College
Stanstead Hall
Stanstead, CM248UD
England, UK
www.arthurfindlaycollege.com

Forgotton Beach Photography by Lisa Tulk Snow
www.byronbay-spirit.com

National Coalition against Domestic Violence
www.ncadv.org

National 1-800 Crisis Hotline-24 hr Alcohol & Drug Abuse
www.allaboutcounseling.com

Info on AA
www.aa.org

debliv@yahoo.com

on FB Deborah Adams Livingston

CPSIA information can be obtained at www.ICGtesting.com
Printed in the USA
LVOW040329270112

265824LV00001B/5/P